Acting Egyptian

Acting Egyptian

Theater, Identity, and Political Culture in Cairo, 1869–1930

CARMEN M. K. GITRE

University of Texas Press *Austin*

Printed in the United States of America
First edition, 2019
First paperback printing, 2025

♾ The paper used in this book meets the minimum requirements of ANSI/NISO Z39.48-1992 (R1997) (Permanence of Paper).

Library of Congress Cataloging Data

Names: Gitre, Carmen M. K., author.
Title: Acting Egyptian : theater, identity, and political culture in Cairo, 1869–1923 / Carmen M. K. Gitre.
Description: First edition. | Austin : University of Texas Press, 2019. | Includes bibliographical references and index.
Identifiers: LCCN 2018055237
ISBN 978-1-4773-3360-0 (cloth : alk. paper)
ISBN 978-1-4773-1919-2 (library e-book)
ISBN 978-1-4773-1920-8 (non-library e-book)
Subjects: LCSH: Theater—Egypt—Cairo—History—19th century. | Theater—Egypt—Cairo—History—20th century. | Cairo (Egypt)—Civilization—19th century. | Cairo (Egypt)—Civilization—20th century. | Theater and state—Egypt—Cairo—History—19th century. | Theater and state—Egypt—Cairo—History—20th century.
Classification: LCC PN2973 .G58 2019 | DDC 792.0962/16—dc23
LC record available at https://lccn.loc.gov/2018055237

doi:10.7560/319185

To Téta Josephine and Gidu Nessim, for inspiring me in life and in spirit.

Contents

Acknowledgments

I cannot imagine ever having written this book without the support of so many mentors and friends. It is a joy to finally have the opportunity to thank them in print.

Classes at Northwestern University ignited my love of history, particularly those with professors Tilde Sankovitch and Edward Muir, who inspired me in more ways than I can count. Professor Sankovitch in particular took me under her wing, and, over many meals and a book of Cavafy poetry, she encouraged me to pursue a PhD.

I did so at Rutgers University, where I was fortunate to learn from some of the most generous individuals a person could hope for. They modeled a standard of teaching and scholarship that inspires me to this day. Classes and conversations with Alastair Bellany, John Gillis, Al Howard, Jennifer Jones, Toby Jones, Temma Kaplan, Don Kelley, Jackson Lears, and Bonnie Smith nourished and challenged me to contemplate and interrogate more deeply the histories we read and the stories they tell. I learned much from the ways these dedicated individuals made scholarship come alive for students. Michael Adas, especially, guided and influenced me from the start. He encouraged me to read more broadly, to write more carefully, and to think more deeply. He also maintained that it is just as important to attend the opera as it is to write about it.

Institutional support funded the Arabic-language study, research trips, and writing that made this project possible. I am grateful for financial assistance from Rutgers University–New Brunswick for research travel and from Middlebury College for Arabic-language study. A Fulbright-Hays award supported archival work in Cairo and London. And the Rutgers Center for Historical Analysis and grants from the Virginia Tech College of Liberal

Arts and Human Sciences and the Virginia Tech Department of History provided funds to support writing time.

In Cairo, the staffs at Dar al-Watha'iq (Egyptian National Archives), the National Center for Theater, Music, and Folkloric Art, and Steve Urgola in the Rare Books Collection at American University in Cairo kindly assisted my work in their archives. Dr. Emad Hilal did his utmost to help me navigate Cairo's resources and welcomed me to the Egyptian Society of Historical Studies. And Lucie Ryzova invited me into her home to access her magnificent private collection of theater photographs and journals. In London, the helpful and efficient staffs at the British Library and British National Archives made research a pleasure. I am especially indebted to Amira Mitchell, who happily shared rare newspaper clippings and fresh-picked blackberries with me.

I have benefited greatly from various forms of mentoring since I completed graduate school. At Seattle University, Marc McLeod and Tom Taylor helped to ease my transition to the Pacific Northwest and always made time to discuss teaching, writing, and good places to eat. At Virginia Tech, Mark Barrow, Kathy Jones, Marian Mollin, Peter Potter, Helen Schneider, and Brett Shadle continue to offer insight and friendship on work and life issues. And informal writing partners and groups have made the writing process much more enjoyable. For their commitment and camaraderie, thank you to the ASSI group, Lissa Badri, LaDale Winling, Matt Wisnowski, and the Skype super-writers.

I am deeply indebted to all who have read portions of my manuscript over the years. It is impossible to overstate the magnitude of my gratitude to Danna Agmon, Zeynep Celik, Paul Clemens, Melanie Keichle, Hussein Omar, Robert Stephens, and participants in the Historians Writing Group at Virginia Tech. I offer a special thanks to Beth Baron, Israel Gershoni, Pamela Haag, Eve Troutt Powell, and Rachel Scott, all of whom read early drafts of the manuscript in its entirety, and the two anonymous readers whose suggestions were invaluable to its improvement. Their time and care, along with the patient and enthusiastic guidance of Jim Burr, Sarah McGavick, and many others at the University of Texas Press, have helped bring it to fruition.

I cannot imagine having navigated Cairo without the know-how and companionship of family and friends. I am especially grateful to my two indefatigable cousins, Emmanuel and Marie Therese, who, among countless other things, facilitated my research by teaching me how to cross Cairo's streets. They, along with their families, my cousin Ashraf, and my aunties, Samia and Isis, enveloped me with laughter, nourishment, and advice throughout my stay, and I thank them from the bottom of my heart. Sharing Cairo and its many inexplicable experiences with my dear and adventuresome friends Matthew Ellis, Jennifer Pruitt, and Shana Minkin made it even more memorable. Reading, writing, and translation partners, you have nourished me and this project in too many ways to count. Friendship forged in Cairo is eternal.

There are many people whose support fed this project, even as life and time may have separated us. At Rutgers, Tim Alves, Jessica Anderson-Hughes, Kristen Block, Lesley Doig, Justin Hart, Catherine Howey, Steve Jankiewicz, Danielle McGuire, Louisa Rice, Margaret Sumner, and Daniel Wherley were partners in work and play. Karen Routledge and Rebecca Scales, though miles separate us, chocolate and pastries keep us bonded. Teresa Delcorso and Lynn Shanko hired me for the best on-campus jobs imaginable. Longtime friends Elkie Griffin, Jennifer Mersereau, Catherine Delagrange, Christa Middleton, Kristin Nickels, Kefira and Murat Philippe, and Melissa and Pascal Saura have always cheered me on. In Charlottesville, Neslihan Cevik, Slava Jakelic, Lucia and Michael Regan, Cherry Stewart, Jason Varsoke, Abby Wilson, and Josh and Molly Yates shared thoughtful conversations, Turkish coffees, child care, and evidence that it indeed is possible to create some dynamic equilibrium between family and academic life. Seattle was sunnier because of Kyle and Bryce Donovan, Dayna Dealy, Soeren Eberhart, Heidi Iverson, George Laszlo, Jill Luoto, Kerani Mitchell, and Peter Pauzauskie, who appreciate oysters and good company as much as I do. Not least, to Jackson and Karen Lears I offer heartfelt gratitude for a precious and life-giving friendship and for the memory and promise of "Maybewood."

My deepest thanks go to all the members of my enormous, wonderful family. To the Gitres far and wide, Halakas, and Stiners, thank you for your unfailing love and support. Thank you, Uncle Samir Rizk, for insisting on sharing with me the pleasure of a good debate. Thank you, Nancy Halaka, for always listening and for always making me laugh. To Mom and the late Pops (Susan and Stephen) Gitre, thank you for your wholehearted embrace (literally) from the first moment I met you. You are models of humility, hard work, and sacrifice. To my mom and dad, Mary and Gamil Khair, there are no words sufficient to thank you for your limitless support and faith in me. You have traveled miles and provided warm meals, child care, Arabic-language deciphering, and bottomless emotional support. Your selflessness, strength, and faith have shaped my sense of how the world should be.

Ed Gitre deserves more thanks than I could possibly express. He has read everything I have ever written and shared in my sorrows and achievements.

For his patience, diligence, remarkable ability to prioritize things, delicious bread, and unwavering faith in me, I am eternally grateful.

Xavier and Madoc, my beautiful boys, I love your sense of wonder, your limitless affection, your love of puns, and the dramatic theatrics that undeniably make you Khairs and Gitres. Thank you for stretching me in ways I didn't know I could and for always reminding me of what matters most.

Note on Transliteration

I have used a simplified system of transliteration of Arabic words based on the *International Journal of Middle East Studies* (*IJMES*). Diacritical marks are used only to indicate the Arabic letters *hamza* (ʾ) and *ayn* (ʿ). The Arabic letter *jim* appears as j, except in Egyptian colloquial phrases or a few cases when Egyptian pronunciation is more common. All Arabic names are transliterated using the simplified *IJMES* system, unless a more commonly accepted version exists or when the person named has provided a transliteration.

Acting Egyptian

Introduction

In July 1906, the journal *al-Muqattam* posted an ad for a new play. *The Pigeon Hunt* would premiere in Cairo's main theater district the evening of August 9. A "historical, political, Egyptian story," the play was a reenactment of a traumatic clash between British officers and the villagers of Dinshaway that had occurred only one month before. The play, the ad assured, would allow audiences to "acquaint themselves with the calamitous effect [the incident] had on our souls."[1]

The confrontation had started simply. A group of five British occupation officers, bored and seeking distraction from the dry desert heat, decided to go pigeon hunting in Dinshaway. Peasants (*fellahin*) in this small delta village bred pigeons primarily for food. Angry at what had become a regular British pastime of shooting their property for recreation, the fellahin attempted to stop the officers by seizing their weapons. Fighting intensified, and in the melee, a threshing floor caught fire, the local imam's wife was shot, and a British army captain suffered head trauma and died.

It was the British response to the incident that galvanized Egyptian anti-British sentiment to an unprecedented degree.[2] The British had occupied Egypt since 1882, ostensibly stepping in to put down a mutinous army and staying to fix what the British consul general, Evelyn Baring (1st Earl of Cromer), described as an arbitrary government, a bankrupt treasury, and a total lack of order.[3] Colonial administrators in Egypt feared the Dinshaway incident would be a potential flashpoint for dangerous new trends in pan-Islamic rhetoric and anti-British activity.[4] To quash further violence, Baring called for a special tribunal to try fifty-two defendants, all peasants accused of murder. He believed the court proceedings would serve as a lesson and warning against seditious activity, regardless of what had actually motivated the villagers' actions.

On the day of the trial, a crowd of spectators gathered early in hopes of securing seats inside an already-packed courtroom.[5] A mix of British and Egyptian judges and advocates sat at the front on a raised dais. When the trial commenced, the four surviving British officers took the stand in turn to share their shock and confusion at what had happened that fateful day. The next day, the special tribunal called on all fifty-two accused to plead their cases at the same time. The accused denied culpability and tried to defend themselves with alibis and counteraccusations. An *Egyptian Gazette* correspondent complained that the fellahins' evidence "was almost impossible to follow and the interpretations given by the translator were almost equally incomprehensible."[6]

The following morning, Minister of Justice Butrus Ghali Pasha handed down the verdict: Hassan Mahfuz, Yusef Hassan Salim, Saʿid ʿIsa Salim, and Muhammad Darwish Zahran were all found guilty of premeditated murder. They would be publicly executed in Dinshaway the following day. ʿAbd al-Nabi Mahfuz, the imam whose wife was shot, was one of two men sentenced to penal servitude for life. Fifteen other defendants were sentenced to combinations of public flogging and penal servitude of up to fifteen years.[7] In total, the trial and sentencing took only three days.

Egypt's last khedive, Abbas Hilmi II (1892–1914), recalled in his memoirs that "the Dinshaway affair stained the history of the English occupation in Egypt with blood." Nationalists would seize upon Dinshaway as a unifying symbol to rally a broad group of Egyptians for more revolutionary activity.[8] Prominent nationalist leaders like Mustafa Kamil, along with journalists like Shaykh ʿAli Yusuf, demanded an inquiry into the case that had "allowed no more than thirty minutes for all the defendants, numbering over fifty individuals, to make their statements."[9] They blamed both the merciless British and inept Egyptian councilors for failing to enact justice.[10]

The Dinshaway play tells the story differently.[11] After a brief introduction, the drama focuses on the pious peasantry of the community. They are frustrated that their village leader (*ʿumda*) has been negligent in forwarding to the British army their complaints about the yearly village pigeon hunt. They agree that, from this point forward, they will maintain careful watch over their pigeons by keeping them closer to home, and they plead with God to continue their days in peace. Before long, British officers arrive in Dinshaway and begin their hunt. When one of the bullets accidentally hits a woman, the officers run away, callously shooting at pigeons as they attempt to escape. A group of angry fellahin stop them. One seizes an officer's rifle while others carry an injured captain to a neighboring village, where a devout fellah quietly attends to his injuries. When the captain dies, the fellah delivers a lengthy monologue extolling God as the sole source of power. A British officer suddenly appears and, mistakenly assuming the fellah has murdered the captain, kills the fellah.

In the courtroom scene that follows, the public prosecutor praises the British regime and heightens the tragedy by calling for total annihilation of the city of Dinshaway. The Egyptian defense lawyers are a most pathetic lot, one even forgetting that he is supposed to be defending the accused. After the judges' severe sentencing, a final act returns to Dinshaway, where the public executions are about to take place in the presence of victims' kin. One of the condemned publicly professes his Islamic faith and bids an emotional farewell to his family. The flagellations of the condemned are described in detail.

Though the first three acts of the play focused on dialogue and narrative, the last act reads more like an emotionally charged propaganda pamphlet. It concludes with the author's lyrical declamation to Dinshaway: "Your name will be whispered," he cries, "and you will be remembered with fear."[12] Wistfully he confesses that there is nothing he can do to console the village. He can offer only this verse as a testimony to pain, and he dedicates it to the executioner who has "gripped the lives of four of your sons, so gaily, with such a light heart."[13] The third verse reads:

> Denshawai, oh Denshawai, doubtless your name will be immortal, and what immortality!
> Do not forget to tell your daughters, in the coming centuries, of the blow that was brought down upon you
> So they know what the arrival of civilization in the twentieth-century was like under British domination.[14]

In this version of Dinshaway, the British were cold and vicious. The fellahin were brave but tragically, wrongfully accused. And women were victims, witnesses, mourners, and receptacles for historical memory. They would receive and impart the story of Dinshaway.

Five days after the ad for the play posted, *The Pigeon Hunt* was banned.[15]

Theater and politics in early twentieth-century Egypt engaged many of the same questions regarding identity, modernity, and authenticity. An examination of theater reveals much, however, that political action does not. Indeed, the physical space of the theater, the content of performances, and discussions surrounding them both mirrored and shaped the ways in which Egyptians understood themselves, their relationships to one another, and their roles and responsibilities in a modernizing society.[16] Often misperceived as solely elite activity, performance in a range of formats and spaces was an important medium of expression for all of Egyptian society.

The playwright Hassan Merʿi's title, "*effendi*," signified that he was part of an emerging class of urban male professionals with secular educations and nationalist leanings. Effendis wielded what was a new space—the proscenium theater—as a forum for both the education of urban audiences and for the formulation of their own particular notions of Egyptian identity. The theater was one public arena, bolstered and complimented by the Arabic press, where effendis contested the authority of their occupiers to frame history and to situate Egypt and Egyptians in the contemporary world. Many of the same effendis who had built up turn-of-the-century Egyptian theater and made theater an effective handmaiden of their anti-British nationalist cause continued to assert dominance after the colonizers had been removed. Indeed, it was their class-driven conception of nationalism—and with it of modernity, authenticity, gender, and history—that would become hegemonic, even by the 1920s, despite the heterogeneity of effendis themselves. For the same effendiyya that had mastered the stage also recorded the history of the nation, portraying the country and its people as a unified economic and political entity composed of a cohesive society. To be an effendi was to be a modern Egyptian, and vice versa. The urban male effendi came to represent more than one particular social class. It came to represent all Egyptians, regardless of socioeconomic background, education, regional identification, ideology, religious beliefs, or gender.

Merʿi's Dinshaway play contributed to this narrative. It wrested control over the meaning of Dinshaway from the British occupiers to Egyptians themselves. Merʿi wrote the play in a simple, colloquial Arabic that was full of religious expression and idiom, appealing to a broad, indigenous audience. He devoted significant time and space for the fellahin to "speak for themselves," a reclamation not only of testimony but also of the courtroom where fellahin had scarcely been allowed to speak. Though the actual trial was a spectacle of British colonial authority and power, the play seized control of the narrative to portray indifferent and violent British officers in contrast to pious and innocent Egyptian victims. It also castigated Egyptian elites—here represented by courtroom judges and defense lawyers—by portraying them as arrogant and complicit in British cruelty. It represented and upheld an effendi ideal of women as witnesses to injustice and bearers of memory. While the English-language press and colonial courtroom had eulogized and celebrated the heroism of its British officers, the play would leave no one to doubt who were the true heroes: the fellahin.

Merʿi transformed the courtroom characterization of the accused Egyptians from criminals to devout Muslims, from "savages" to martyrs.[17] In effect, the Dinshaway play restored moral agency to women and the peasantry, making them symbols of an exploited Egypt.

And yet, while the Dinshaway play was an attempt to rehabilitate the fellahin of Egypt, it was not in their own words or terms. Merʿi spoke back to the British, but he also spoke *for* women and peasants, casting them as an undifferentiated mass of pious, innocent victims. As a member himself of the effendiyya, Merʿi identified with a social group that imagined themselves as, in the words of one historian, "the embodiment of Egyptian modernity and the building blocks of Egypt itself."[18] The effendi, as the historians Lucie Ryzova and Wilson Chacko Jacob observe, "conjures an ideal type" that came to dominate in the early twentieth century as British rule became increasingly oppressive and as events moved Egyptians toward direct political action.[19] There was no female version of an effendi; the effendi was gendered male. A performative and proselytizing figure, the effendi repeatedly demonstrated his modernity and masculinity through behaviors and practices that embraced nationalism, fashion, competitive sports, and self-discipline.[20] He proselytized this ideal via schools, newspapers, and theater.

Effective as the hegemonic portrayal of Egyptian nationalism may have been, Egyptian society was anything but a single and harmonious social class. It teemed with diverse voices and perspectives. To better understand the turn of the last century, historians have made excellent use of elites' texts. Yet little has been written about those who typically did not record their own thoughts in writing but were nonetheless vocal participants in society. Women and men, working classes and elites, people up, down, and across society lived out divergent notions of Egyptianness. Varying perspectives, sometimes tolerated or ignored, other times co-opted or censored by those in power, all contributed to shaping the anti-British sentiment that would culminate in demands for British expulsion from Egypt in 1919. To hear the full range of voices, not just the urban male intellectuals who dominate Egypt's nationalist histories, one must seek them out in other, less obvious sources. In its examination of theater and performance, this book does just that.

Acting Egyptian contends that, at the turn of the twentieth century, theater and performance sites—spaces of imagination, role-play, satire, and mockery—were vital and matchless venues for imagining, mirroring, debating, and shaping competing conceptions of modern Egyptian identity. Theater was a space of play, where norms were more easily tested, transmitted, and transgressed. In an era of changing economic and political parameters, efforts to forge a unified national identity could not erase identities shaped by class, religious, regional, gendered, colonial, and other influences and building blocks. Even the effendiyya who led the way in crafting a unifying theme of modern Egyptianness were never homogenous and lockstep in their commitment to a single ideal. Nowhere was this more visible than on the dramatic stage.

Over the course of the nineteenth century, modernity itself was taking shape in the West as a new conception of and relationship to time and space that celebrated rational science and technological progress as evidence of civilization. Colonial projects enhanced this view, as Europeans encountered peoples whom they considered to be steps behind on the path to development and in need of reform even as, paradoxically, these same populations were deemed timeless and incapable of advancement. Effendis were vocal in their responses to these conceptions. Many of them concurred that Egypt needed greater scientific and technological knowledge. But they also pushed back, bemoaning the dangers of rapid social change and the alienation that derived from mechanization and the efficiencies of clock-time.[21]

At the turn of the twentieth century, a diverse Egyptian populace engaged with these rapidly changing political, economic, and social forces, as evidenced in a variety of performances and spaces. And as one might expect, they did not arrive at the same interpretation of what these changes meant. Indeed, performers and audiences played with competing conceptions of modern Egyptian identity rather than tacitly accepting the dominant effendi version of modern Egyptianness. This book focuses on four social groups that vividly illuminate the possibilities: elites, effendis, the urban working class, and performing women.

Nineteenth-century Egyptian elites who controlled Egypt in the period just before bankruptcy and British colonization emulated elements of European and Ottoman cultures, but they did not consider themselves subservient to them. Instead, they saw themselves as modern, on par with European rivals. A rising strata of effendis critiqued elites whose greed, they believed, created an opportunity for British colonial intervention. As a new cultural class, they constantly struggled to situate themselves in a colonial context that saw them as not modern enough while they, too, branded other Egyptians as "behind" and in need of reform. Particularly effective targets of reform were a growing number of urban workers, many of whom became wage laborers in new industrial enterprises and the transportation sector.

The work lives of this burgeoning population demanded acclimatization to elements of standard clock-time and work discipline. But in their personal lives, urban workers cultivated an increasingly shared social identity that reappropriated the power of the state and of the effendi and asserted their own vision of their place in the world. Performance was an essential space to enact what Hanan Hammad calls "the rich drama of ordinary and everyday life."[22]

The everyday lives of women performers tell a different story. Pragmatically engaging with nationalist and feminist discourse, and presented with new possibilities for commercialization and stardom, working women took effendi and feminist aspirations in unexpected directions. They provided a glamorous alternative to the effendi and elite feminist ideal of the patriotic wife and mother, and they modeled a very different type of liberation.

Together, these stories challenge assumptions that an effendi model of modern Egyptianness was a unified and universally held ideal. Theater and performance spaces were places for Egyptians—even those considered "voiceless"—to challenge those in power, make sense of their place in society, and play with modern identities. As the scholar Nandi Bhatia eloquently contends, "theater's visual focus, emphasis on collective participation and representation of shared histories, mobility, potential for public disruption, and spatial maneuverability" allows for a nontextual historical recuperation, not just of the subaltern, but of all segments of society.[23] Indeed, the significance of theater as a space for shaping national identities, allowing subaltern speech, and critiquing political and social conditions appears in theater throughout the global South.[24]

Theater was not the sole preserve of elites and middle classes. Most Egyptians witnessed performances in streets, private homes, and coffeehouses, and every performance space provided opportunities for very different people to gather, interface, and cross social boundaries, even if only fleetingly. Arabic stage theater may have emphasized the mores of an emergent effendi class, but it was not reserved solely for effendis. It attracted elites as well as foreign visitors. Egyptian theaters, more broadly, were permeable and porous spaces that appealed to a mixture of people. Cabarets, filled with dancing and singing women, drew foreign troops stationed in Cairo, landowners from the provinces who visited cities, indigenous middle-class men, and top Egyptian politicians. And all theatrical spaces—exempting, perhaps, private performances—faced degrees of surveillance and censorship from both colonial and Egyptian authorities.

In each performance context, societal expectations for degrees of interaction and behavior varied. New commercial performance spaces called for different, modern listening and viewing practices, demanding a type of self-regulation that theater owners and chief patrons—effendis—were at the same time cultivating among and within themselves. Whereas street performance included the audience in the spectacle, encouraging vocal and active engagement, the middle-class stage was to be a source of moral education. The food and drink offered in *salas*, or cabarets, created a more convivial (and potentially provocative) atmosphere than that of the more formal Arabic stage theater. In the latter, the audience was expected to sit quietly, listen, and ingest the ideals of those who would become Egypt's political leaders. Multiple, sometimes contradictory, discourses regarding identity and modernity emerged from these varied experiences.

Exploring a range of performance spaces illustrates that hegemonic effendi culture was not imposed from the top down. Instead, as the historian Jackson Lears observes, hegemonic culture is persuasive, it "preserves a certain indeterminacy and open-endedness. As a result . . . even the most successful hegemonic culture creates a situation where the dominant mode of discourse . . . becomes a field of contention, where many-sided struggles over meaning are constantly fought out."[25] Yet even as *shaʿbi* (popular and working class) and women's cabaret performances challenged effendi cultural norms, they also validated those norms by naming, representing, and critiquing or upholding them. Performers and playwrights could be as explicit as they wanted, but in the end one could never account for the unintended consequences of theatrical performances. What audiences experienced, how they interpreted what they saw and heard, depended on a multitude of factors, including their past experiences, expectations, moods, and desires. I do not examine here plays that overtly sought to overthrow the cultural and political order, but the playfulness and liminality of theatrical events and their unexpected consequences meant that the threat was always there.

Scholarship that explores the effendi hegemonic project and its contradictions have laid the groundwork for many of the concerns of this book.[26] *Acting Egyptian* contributes to a lively discussion on the place of elites, effendis, the shaʿb, and performing women in Egyptian nationalism and modernity. It does not claim that marginal voices were equals in debates over modern Egyptianness. Rather, I argue that performance themes, spaces, actors, and audiences not only generated pluralistic ideas about nationalism, modernity, and Egyptianness but also helped to foment and consolidate effendi articulations.

Acting Egyptian surveys the significant ways individual performers played with and represented themselves on stage. It does so to restore agency to the many who contributed to the construction of what were complex modern Egyptian identities. And it takes seriously the influence of ideas and people at the margins, interrogating how, where, and to what end hegemony is challenged. In essence, the book addresses the historian Nancy Reynolds's concern that "erasing the ambivalences of pre-1952 Egyptian life has strengthened nationalism's self-justificatory, and at times quite coercive, claims to represent an authentic and eternal society."[27] This book demonstrates how a focus on theater and performance revivifies those ambivalences.

Questions about identity were pressing concerns in what was a turbulent era. The late nineteenth and early twentieth centuries were periods of especially intense social and political disruption in a waning Ottoman Empire that was continually challenged by European incursions into a Middle East while verging on economic collapse. In the course of a mere forty years, Egypt would go from being an Ottoman province to a British protectorate (1882–1922) to an independent nation-state (1922). Egypt's leaders grappled with European critiques of an Egyptian society they claimed needed guidance to become a modern nation. In response, a flourishing periodical press debated the status of women in society, Muslim clerics proffered reinterpretations of Islam, reformers pushed for an end to slavery, and engineers called for the adoption of transportation and communication technologies. Together, these intellectuals, journalists, clerics, reformers, lawyers, and other professionals saw themselves as arbiters of Egyptian modernity, nationalism, and civilization.

Rather than fixing identity as something intact and irreducible, this book draws from the cultural historian Stuart Hall, who sees identity formation as "conditional, lodged in contingency," a fluid "process never completed."[28] There is no apotheosis in this understanding, even though an individual or group may strive for some sort of ideal. As such, examining process is more useful than assessing its satisfactory achievement. Theater and performance served as crucial sites of identity formation in the ways envisioned by Hall because these venues provide spaces for individuals to play, knowingly and self-consciously, with personal and group narratives.[29] History, language, culture, and ambition were raw materials out of which to shape and represent the self and larger communal assemblages.[30] Elites, effendis, the shaʿb, and women imagined their place in the nation. At the same time, they were sorting out their own social positions within it.

Most evident in studies of turn-of-the-twentieth-century Egypt is that nationalists were actively forging a conception of national culture that unified Egyptians against occupiers. Yet as Hall explains, national cultures are never fully unified; rather, "we should think of them as constituting a *discursive device* which represents difference as unity or identity. They are cross-cut by deep internal divisions and differences, and 'unified' only through the exercise of different forms of cultural power."[31] Individuals disseminate this notion of national culture through stories, literature, and popular culture that navigate through and across these divisions and differences. Performance spaces were and are therefore crucial for enacting, debating, and spreading ideals of modern Egyptianness and national identity.

The divergences that threaten the cultural narrative do not disappear, however, in the telling of national stories. To the contrary, the effendis' deliberate forging of a single national identity highlighted power differentials, crosscutting allegiances, and internal incongruities more than ever.[32] Invoking euphemism, language play, and improvisation, performers of all social backgrounds could disseminate messages that challenged top-down definitions of modern Egyptian identity. Performance could in fact magnify differences within and among social groups. But highlighting difference did not spell the demise of a unified Egyptian identity. Nationalists incorporated aspects of nonelite culture to demonstrate the flexibility and scope of modern Egyptian identity. And performances that challenged effendi hegemony reinforced effendi ideals simply by representing them as uniform targets of critique.

In many ways, theater seems innocuous and removed from the real world. Theater is, after all, a form of play, which the theorist Roger Caillos characterizes as "not obligatory . . . circumscribed in time and space, undetermined, materially unproductive, rule-bound, and concerned with an alternate reality."[33] As a spectacle and social experience, theater offers access to the familiar and the unfamiliar, to parallel realities and fantasies, and it does so within a social context that recognizes the value of these borderline practices. Its emotive power lies in its attention to local issues at the same time that it can transcend local specificity. Theater highlights tragedy, the ridiculous, the oddities of how we live and the assumptions we make, providing an opportunity to rethink the familiar in new ways. It calls for a suspension of disbelief. It is an event outside of normal time.

Theater's remove from routinized, everyday reality is precisely its source of potency. The theorist Victor Turner's discussion of the "liminoid" is useful in this regard. Turner applied the concept of liminality to modern experiences of leisure, referring to them as "liminoid spaces." When individuals step away from conventional structures of life and into circumscribed leisure spaces, he explains, they are more susceptible, more open to chance and change, than they are in everyday life.[34] The ambivalence of these possibilities, along with the sheer pleasure of attending and/or participating in entertaining events, made theatrical spaces ideal not only for invigorating anticolonial sentiment but also for encouraging a reassessment of dominant ideologies and challenging them in what is always a social context.[35] Audiences are expected to interpret what happened on stage, and they do so in numerous, idiosyncratic ways. Even a recurring performance differs from one staging to the next, not least because the composition of each audience varies. The spectators' reactions affect what is happening on the stage. Every performance contains elements of contingency and unpredictability.[36]

Despite each audience member's unique interpretation of events, all who are involved in a performance become part of it. Erika Fischer-Lichte elaborates: "Whatever the reactions of those who prefer to watch, they are perceived by all other participants—sensed, heard, or seen. Such responses in turn influence the further course of the performance. . . . [A]ll participants act as co-creators of the performance which, in many respects, remains unpredictable and spontaneous."[37] While it is true that theater might function to strengthen an audience's cultural assumptions, in many cases it could be also disruptive. This was especially the case for street performance in Cairo, which resembled Mikhail Bakhtin's description of *carnival*. During carnival, as Bakhtin describes, "the laws, prohibitions, and restrictions that determine the structure and order of ordinary, that is noncarnival, life are suspended," making carnival "the place for working out, in a concretely sensuous, half-real and half-play-acted form, *a new mode of interrelationship between individuals*, counterpoised to the all-powerful socio-hierarchical relationships of noncarnival life."[38]

In 1900, a play critical of the Egyptian nationalist hero Ahmad ʿUrabi (1841–1911), an army officer who helped orchestrate a failed uprising against the Ottoman-Egyptian government, angered audiences so much that one newspaper reported that members of the audience "took some chairs and threw them at each other and the stage."[39] Whether audiences sat in assigned seats inside a theater building or gathered closely together in a circle surrounding performers in a public space, the liminality of their experience, the degree to which they suspended disbelief as they witnessed and/or engaged in theatrical play, made it impossible to anticipate the effects of theater. Audiences were supposed to sit quietly during performances in the new Arabic theater buildings, so violence at the ʿUrabi play—perhaps a logical extreme of a vocally and physically engaged audience—was met with police force. Street theater, in contrast, demanded that audiences assert their thoughts and feelings throughout, and storylines changed based on audience demands. Their engagement empowered all of its participants to help shape the narratives in keeping with their desires.

Social experiences like being part of an audience have the potential to build what Victor Turner described as *communitas*, "a modality of human interrelatedness" that "can play across structural systems [liminal, liminoid, or otherwise] in a way too difficult for us at present to predict its motions."[40] The unpredictable consequences of communitas were a source of concern for effendis, as evident in voluminous journal articles debating proper theatrical content and audience behavior. Even as experiences and expectations of performance and audience behavior varied in different performance settings, the experience of communitas was possible across the board. There was always the prospect that the communitas forged within the liminoid performance experience might spill out of the theatrical arena and into the real world to challenge structures of everyday life. These concerns were well founded. After all, the shared experience of Egyptianness in opposition to British colonial power made possible the mass uprising of 1919.

In the years after Dinshaway, the Egyptian government would pass several laws regulating ownership, seating, stage content, and public security of theaters.[41] Though the Fine Arts section of the Ministry of Education typically vetted issues related to theater, playwrights also had to submit copies of their plays to the Ministry of the Interior to obtain permission for production. The government claimed it was concerned with avoiding offenses to morals or to "Egyptian or foreign susceptibilities."[42]

Unsurprisingly, the government's decision to censor Merʿi's own play expanded its audience. The press updated its readers on events surrounding the ban and published Merʿi's letter of complaint to the censor.[43] Merʿi published and sold copies of the play for five piasters apiece, creating a wider reading audience than the number who would have been able to fill the theater had the performance gone on for more than a few nights as originally planned.[44] The existence of these documents is a happy outcome, so far as historians are concerned, but it points to one of many methodological challenges to completing a study of Egyptian theater history.

Even if a play makes it to the stage without being censored, the scholar must contend with the reality that the experience of theater is ephemeral. Each performance differs from the last due to the shifting relationships among actor, stage, audience, and the broader context. To ameliorate such challenges, this book draws from a broad range of sources. Personal journals, photographs, play scripts, advertisements, sound recordings, and reviews provide a sense of who attended performances, the spaces they occupied, the broader context, and the reactions of audience members. Advertisements, for example, pitched special evenings like "ladies' matinees" to encourage women's attendance, and ticket prices indicate who may have been able to afford a seat in a show. Individuals' personal journals offer rich detail about performances, including what theatrical spaces looked like and who was in the audience. Together, the combination of sources reveals broad swaths of a society keen to debate and define modern Egyptianness.

Acting Egyptian opens with the urban renewal of Cairo and the inauguration of the Khedivial Opera House in 1869. It closes with Egyptian demands for independence from Britain and with the burgeoning of women's cabarets in the 1930s. The book moves chronologically, and most chapters focus on a specific case study of a playwright, performance, or performer. Situating each case in its larger social, spatial, and political milieu, *Acting Egyptian* illuminates the ways Egyptians of many stripes reckoned with what it meant to be modern and Egyptian.

Chapter 1 ("*Aida* in Egypt") focuses on the opening of the new Khedivial Opera House and the Cairo premier of the opera *Aida*. A blend of Ottoman and European design, the opera house opened in tandem with the inauguration of the Suez Canal in 1869. Egyptian court elites, including Khedive Isma'il (Ottoman governor)—who commissioned the opera *Aida*—provided Giuseppe Verdi with an invented storyline, one that enhanced the image of a modern Egypt commensurate with European powers and in opposition to a "backward" sub-Saharan Africa. The opera house's architecture provided Egyptian court elites a visibility that solidified being part of a unique social class.

Such visibility would make elites targets of an emerging effendiyya. While elites cultivated what they saw as good taste and exemplary modernity, effendis viewed elites as decadents, capitulating to Europeans, and bringing ruin to Egypt. Rather than elevating the nation, the elites' patronage of opera and culture imperiled the creation of a modern Egyptian identity in the eyes of critical effendis. Still, in this period before the preeminence of effendi-as-arbiter of Egyptian identity, chapter 1 demonstrates that elites forged their own version of a modern identity, one that borrowed from but did not bow to European power. After all, Egyptian civilization could claim to have preceded European civilization by millennia, as *Aida* celebrated.

Isma'il's impressive projects, which extended well beyond the construction of the Khedivial Opera House, led to Egyptian bankruptcy and greater vulnerability to European creditors. Chapter 2 ("How to Be an *Effendi*") moves forward in time to the era of British occupation (1882–1922) that followed Isma'il's urban renewal. The focus is 'Imad al-Din Street, the heart of a growing middle-class, Arabic-language theater district that drew primarily from an emerging professional and intellectual social strata of effendis. Theater buildings in the district included raised stages and assigned seating, similar to the opera house, but on a smaller and less elaborate scale. As effendis sought to secure their position in Egyptian society, they endeavored to create a myth of consensus and unity around shared aspirations and interests, and they did so on the Arabic stage.

Such values were evident in Syrian playwright Farah Antun's 1913 play, *Misr al-jadida wa Misr al-Qadima* (New Egypt and Old Egypt). The modern Egyptian identity that actors negotiated and promulgated on stage was one that reflected the "civilized" identity they were forging for themselves, one that was defined in contrast to European cultural and colonial impositions. It was also defined internally against elites, peasants, and the *shaʿb* (urban workers). But effendis were never as unified as the narrative they created, and, ironically, individuals like Antun—a Syrian Christian who participated in creating an Egyptian effendi identity—ultimately wrote themselves out of its increasingly narrowing definition.

Chapter 3 ("The Case of Ahmad the Rat") turns to improvisation and street performance to illuminate the importance of performance among Egypt's urban workers, people collectively referred to as the "shaʿb." While the street performance that proliferated among the shaʿb encompasses an array of entertainments and players (e.g., mimics, shadow-play artists) in a range of spaces (public streets, private homes, coffeehouses), chapter 3 focuses on a particular form of satire called *fasl mudhik*. In the early twentieth century, fasl mudhik was typically performed in street celebrations or private parties. But it also began to appear in Arabic-language proscenium theaters during intermissions or at the end of tragic dramas. This appearance has left scholars with a trace historical record of a particularly ephemeral cultural practice.

Though street performers appealed to broad swaths of people, chapter 3 focuses on the urban workers who were some of their most ardent fans. The coalescing social group was simultaneously, and increasingly, becoming accustomed to industrial labor and to routinized clock-time. The chapter focuses on what one improvisational performer, Ahmad al-Far, and his skit, "Riwayat al-Saʿidi" (The Upper Egyptian's Story), reveal about urban workers' concerns and identity. Intriguingly, two written versions of the play exist, with each version offering bafflingly contradictory messages about urban workers' shared values. I ask what it means for the same play to mock effendi identity explicitly, as one iteration champions workers as arbiters of Egyptian identity, whereas the other contradictorily praises effendi and foreign values.

At the end of World War I, Egyptians moved en masse into the streets to demand independence from Britain. Chapter 4 ("Munira al-Mahdiyya and the Revolutionary Stage") delves into the era of 1919 and the subsequent rise of women-led troupes and cabarets. Following the career of the popular female singer-actress and manager Mahdiyya, along with some of her peers, chapter 4 examines the ways performing women infused theater and the public sphere with nationalist and feminist language to create new public roles for themselves.

Just as the effendi claimed to speak for the shaʿb, an Egyptian women's reform movement claimed to speak for nonelite women. But their concerns often did not address the realities of working women's lives, particularly in an era of increasing consumption and commercialization. Even as elite women asserted a particular form of modern Egyptian womanhood, there were women who deviated from the ideal, both engaging and challenging it, as chapter 4 observes. Unwittingly, female performers offered an alternative vision of independence, a different sort of feminist ideal. The combination of celebrity and modern media technologies pushed the limits of acceptable visibility. And yet their desire to appeal broadly led them to uphold and even celebrate the norms that they simultaneously challenged.

Ultimately, *Acting Egyptian* demonstrates that metanarratives are not born complete but instead evolve in the context of competing ideas. Despite the ways hegemonic thought and culture appeared to erase alternatives, disparate conceptions of modern Egyptian identity persisted and new ones arose, sometimes in conflict with, occasionally complementing, and other times contributing to the construction of dominant ideals.

The Pigeon Hunt was a story threatening enough for the British to suppress. Its significance and danger lay in its seizure of interpretive control of the Dinshaway affair. This was true of theater more broadly. Theater could mirror, provoke, comfort, mock; it offered, as the theater historian Marvin Carlson observes, "cultural and social metacommentary, the exploration of self and other, of the world as experienced, and of alternative possibilities."[45] The ambivalence of these possibilities, along with theater's engagement with audiences, made performance spaces ideal for challenging both British and Egyptian elite definitions of modernity, entertaining feminist and regional identities, and invigorating anticolonial sentiment. The juxtaposition of theater, performers, and audiences makes visible the continuous process of making, contesting, and creating meaning out of modern Egyptian identity.

CHAPTER 1

Aida in Egypt

Cairo's Khedivial Opera House was filled to capacity long before curtain time on the evening of December 24, 1871. The bedecked, eager audience had assembled to witness the world premiere of Giuseppe Verdi's highly anticipated opus, *Aida*.[1] Over the next few hours, spectators witnessed a tragic love story between Aida, an Ethiopian slave, and Radames, an Egyptian military commander, set sometime during the "reign of the Pharaohs," a vague, 3,000-year period.[2] Boundaries between fact and fiction, reality and spectacle, blurred as the production unfolded. The actress and society writer Mabel Caillard described European actors mingling with "genuine Ethiopians and real slaves . . . [who carried] statues and figures of the ancient gods" from Cairo's Museum of Antiquities.[3] By the end of the opera, some claimed that spectators had witnessed 3,000 actors—and nonactors—cross the stage.[4]

By all accounts, the production was a smashing success. One spectator raved that it was a production of "superlative magnificence . . . this premier performance of *Aida* was simply perfect."[5] Critics from a host of foreign journals sang Verdi's praises. The Italian journalist Filippo Filippi reported "prolonged applause, warm ovations, unanimous cries of enthusiasm" so disruptive that an impatient audience member cried out, "It's not finished!"[6] In total, he reported a surprising—perhaps hyperbolic—thirty-two curtain calls at the end of the show. Immediately after the performance, Superintendent of Khedivial Theaters Paul Draneht sent a telegram to Verdi commending him for the "triumphant success" of the opera.[7] "Not one number passed over in silence," Draneht wrote; "total fanaticism. Enthusiastic audience applauded absent Maestro. Congratulations, thanks."[8]

The Ottoman governor of Egypt, Khedive Isma'il (r. 1863–1879), had invited Verdi to compose an original opera worthy of Cairo's new opera house.[9]

Under Isma'il's patronage the opera house was constructed in 1869, on the eve of completion of the Suez Canal. Isma'il asked the French Egyptologist and director of the Museum of Antiquities, Auguste Mariette, to propose a storyline to Verdi—a story that would be, in Isma'il's words, "purely ancient and Egyptian."[10] Blending scientific Egyptology and popular Egyptomania, Mariette drew the plot of his story from the reign of the pharaoh Ramses III, even patterning costumes after scenes from his tomb and insisting that all actors be clean-shaven, as the ancients appeared not to sport facial hair.[11] The storyline captured Verdi's imagination, and, together with the librettist Antonio Ghizlanzoni, he composed the opera that would become a global success and a staple of operatic repertoires in both Egypt and abroad.[12]

Most scholars and fans see *Aida* as a European opera about Egypt. What complicates this is the fact that Egypt's khedive—a hereditary title granted by the Ottoman sultan to the leader of Egypt—initiated the project and fully funded its creation. Isma'il's request that the opera be "purely ancient and Egyptian" raises a host of questions, not least because opera did not resemble any indigenous forms of musical performance.[13] As the historian Donald Reid asks: "What does authenticity mean in a European musical extravaganza that no ancient Egyptian and few Egyptians of his own day could have understood?"[14] Isma'il's choice to make a "purely ancient" Egypt the subject of the opera is also intriguing in light of his efforts to modernize the state and its inhabitants. Why did Isma'il select ancient Egyptians as the subject of the opera as opposed to modern Egyptians? Was this, as scholar Edward Said asks, simply one more Orientalist opera, or was it something more?[15]

Aida's premier was part of a larger program of urban renewal that had peaked with the Suez Canal's inauguration on November 17, 1869 (figure 1.1). Isma'il considered celebrations surrounding the inauguration as an opportunity to showcase a new Cairo to his visitors and to match the impressive European exhibitions of the nineteenth century. To this end, he instituted a massive public works program to modernize the sections of Cairo and Alexandria that visitors would most likely see—or be directed to see.[16] Wide boulevards, landscaped gardens, and luxury hotels built of the iron, steel, and improved glass of the nineteenth century spread across what had once been a swampy floodplain. The jewel in the crown was the construction of a new Khedivial Opera House.

The grand, four-act opera *Aida* opens in the royal palace in Memphis. Radames, a captain of the Egyptian Guards, learns that the Ethiopian army is planning to attack Egypt. The audience quickly recognizes that this poses

Figure I.1. Suez Canal Inauguration, November 17, 1867. Hulton Archive/Getty Images.

a personal conflict for him, for he is in love with Aida, an Ethiopian slave in the king's court. By the second act, Radames has defeated the Ethiopians. Before he returns home, however, the king's daughter, the jealous Amneris, who is also in love with Radames, tricks Aida into believing Radames died in conflict. Aida's distress reveals that she, too, is in love with Radames, and Amneris threatens her in anger.

Aida's fortunes worsen when the victorious Radames returns to Thebes with her father, Amonasro, as a captive. In the third act, as Aida sings longingly for her homeland, her father appears and asks her to gather information about the Egyptian army from Radames. He quickly hides when Radames appears, and soon Radames promises to marry Aida, willingly revealing the Egyptian army's plans at her request. Having caught Radames revealing the army's secrets, Amneris appears, and she accuses him of treason. In the final act, Radames is condemned to be buried alive, and he refuses Amneris's promise to save him if he would leave Aida. Before the vault is sealed, Radames discovers that Aida has placed herself in the crypt to die with him.

When Isma'il first broached the idea of an opera with Verdi, Egypt was part of the Ottoman Empire. The opera, however, showcased an ancient and civilized Egypt, one with an empire of its own. Its presentation not only served to entertain but also was very much tied to power and control over the depiction of history and imperial identity. A European opera about ancient Egypt, *Aida* was nevertheless Isma'il's view of modern Egypt. At the same time that Egyptians were Ottoman subjects, Isma'il was fulfilling some of his own imperial ambitions, extending Egypt's reach into the Sudan and eyeing further expansion. The modern Egypt he and fellow elites imagined was an imperial and cultural force on par with European powers and distinct from sub-Saharan Africa.

The Khedivial Opera House, *Aida*, and the larger project of urban renewal were not merely Western interventions or meaningless foreign imports. Instead, patronage of all three was a testament to Egyptian cultural achievement and evidence of commensurability with European civilization. Urban design was shaped to fit local needs and architectural patterns.[17] Opera house construction asserted the primacy of Ottoman court culture and power, and the production of *Aida* presented Egypt as a powerful, imperial force grounded in and legitimated by its ancient history. In effect, the Ottoman-Egyptian court harvested Egypt's ancient history to claim its own modern authority.

Just as urban design functioned to organize Cairo, making it attractive and navigable both for Egyptians and Egypt's visitors, so too the opera *Aida* packaged and presented ancient Egypt in an intelligible and pleasurable manner to its viewers. While the redesign of Cairo involved the implementation of a certain understanding of modernity, the opera *Aida* delivered that message to viewing audiences.[18] A show of imperialism and power, *Aida* brought a particular vision of Egypt to life on stage. Everyone and everything—from the building, to the show, to its audience—was part of the spectacle.

Taken together, *Aida*, the opera house, and the new Cairo facilitated the forging of a modern Egyptian elite and asserted a privileged view of Egyptian identity. In the era preceding Egyptian bankruptcy and British colonial control, Ottoman-Egyptian elites selectively borrowed elements of European and Ottoman culture, fashioning themselves as inheritors of ancient Egyptian imperial greatness. Modernity was imposed from the top down, and renovated streets and the theatrical stage made that modernity visible.

In the nineteenth century, members of the Egyptian elite, including both *aʿyan* (notability) and *dhawat* (urban notables), forged a distinct group identity by cultivating a network of social relations in discrete social spaces and by creating markers of difference between themselves and others. Though much of their status derived from wealth and descent, elites, in a place like the new opera house, cultivated "good taste" and fostered bonds of community as they saw and visited one another in their private boxes. Seating arrangements offered a visibility that solidified a sense of being part of a distinct Egyptian social class. This did not require uniformity of thought. Indeed, some pashas (senior civil officials and military officers) complained about being forced to purchase season tickets to opera house performances and personally host and pay for visiting European dancers at their own expense. Nevertheless, the communal experience of attending the theater contributed to cementing a group identity that excluded those who could not or were not interested in participating.

Elite efforts to modernize Egypt would be judged harshly in later decades. A new middle strata—the *effendiyya*—saw elites as self-indulgent decadents unfit to lead an Egypt that was transitioning to independent nationhood. *Effendi* writings in the early twentieth century would critique what they saw as elites' Ottoman loyalties, capitulations to Europe, and indebtedness to European banks that demonstrated total disregard for the Egyptian people. The Khedive's representation of a "pure" Egypt in opera form was, for them, the antithesis of what a modern Egypt should be.

By the early twentieth century, elites who found themselves in an increasingly nationalistic age found it imperative to shed their more Ottoman orientations to Egyptianize themselves. But in the preceding period, before Egyptian bankruptcy, British colonial control, and the rise of the effendi, elites navigated a world in which European power was on the rise and modernity was taking shape in the context of empire. They viewed themselves as equal players on the global stage.

South of the Azbakiyya Garden stood the Khedivial Opera House, a focal point for the new center of Cairo. The Italian company Fasciotti and Rossi designed it in the eclectic Italian neo-Renaissance style of La Scala in Milan, and corvée labor of Egyptian *fellahin* (peasants) completed it in a mere four or five months (figure 1.2).[19] Inside, sumptuous burgundy and gold brocade hangings lined the white, four-story structure, and gilt-scrolled private boxes for pashas and the khedive made up the second floor (figure 1.3). The entire house seated approximately 800 people.[20] Despite its attractive appearance and luxurious décor, most of the building had been constructed of wood and plaster. Before gas lighting, candles lit the interior, making it necessary for a fire brigade to stand ready for emergencies behind the scenes at every performance.[21]

Opera house construction was but one facet of massive mid-nineteenth-century transformations. Legal reforms such as new Mixed and National Courts based in French law shifted emphasis away from shariʿa law. To support a European-educated Egyptian elite, Isma'il expanded the budget for

Figure I.2. Khedivial Opera House. Bibliotheca Alexandrina's Memory of Modern Egypt Digital Archive.

education more than tenfold. He promoted the growth of primary and secondary school systems, specialized technical schools, female education, and educational missions to Europe. Al-Azhar, the venerable site for religious training in Cairo, became one choice among many, as these modern, secular state schools attracted a new generation of Egyptians. The most important technical schools included Dar al-ʿUlum (1872), a school for training Arabic-language teachers in the new state system, and the School of Languages (1868), later the Cairo School of Law, which offered a highly desirable French-based legal education.

Construction of the Khedivial Opera House must be traced back to earlier events. The second half of the nineteenth century was marked by tremendous transformation in the map of the world. It was a period of European rivalry for global material resources that propelled the expansion of empire. Social Darwinist principles underwrote anthropologists' efforts to organize the world into national and racial hierarchies. The fact that some people were more advanced than others, they claimed, was scientifically valid. Such conceptions were visible in the European exhibitions of the nineteenth century.

In 1867, Egypt participated in the Universal Exhibition held in Paris. The practice of hosting exhibitions or world's fairs started in England with the Great Exhibition of 1851. These were visual showcases of Western industrial power and innovation, but they were also architectural representations of

Figure I.3. Interior of the Khedivial Opera House, *al-Musawwar*, February 4, 1927. Courtesy of the Rare Books and Special Collections Library, The American University in Cairo.

empire. Visitors to the nineteenth-century world's fairs moving through exhibits virtually journeyed through their country's empire. Thus exhibitions did a number of things. The placement of pavilions on exhibition grounds revealed a world order mapped by Western powers. And the architecture of the pavilions emphasized colonizers' impressions and conceptions of Islamic culture.

In some cases, commissions composed of people from the countries represented created their own exhibits and provided written materials to accompany them. As people in the Islamic world were navigating European encroachment, this provided a means and forum to present their regions as integral to the larger narrative of modernization. Coping with European technological and scientific advancement was one thing, but sorting out how to deal with European culture—and Europeans' assumptions about Islamic/Arab culture—was another.

The same Auguste Mariette who created *Aida* was responsible for the 1867 Egyptian exhibit in Paris. The exhibit was an amalgam of temporary structures that included a temple to represent "antiquity," an "Arab-style" pavilion to represent the Middle Ages, and a caravanserai with a *mashrabiya* (lattice screen) to represent the modern period.[22] What was vaguely described as an antique temple served, ironically, as the "Egypt of the future," within which the chief French engineer of the Suez Canal, Ferdinand de Lesseps, gave lectures on the canal's construction.[23]

Isma'il was enthralled by the entire scene. He greeted visitors in the *salamlik* (a greeting area for men) of the temple, further fusing fiction and reality, past and present.[24] Outside the boundaries of the exhibition, Isma'il strolled down Parisian boulevards that had been redesigned under the direction of Baron Georges-Eugene Haussmann in time for the 1867 exhibition.

Egypt's soon-to-be minister of public works, ʿAli Mubarak, also visited the Universal Exhibition that year. For several weeks he studied new Parisian buildings, streets, and sewage systems, and his fictional novel *ʿAlam al-Din* channeled this experience. The book's protagonists registered "astonishment at how well it is organized . . . the breadth of its streets and their order, the vigour of its commerce and the elegance and tidiness of its commercial establishments."[25] To them, it was the order, cleanliness, and calmness of life that made material and social progress possible.

Isma'il's visit to the exhibition would profoundly affect his vision of what Cairo could be.[26] Though he had already begun to build on his grandfather's educational and military reforms, Isma'il's experience in Paris is widely acknowledged to have renewed his call for public works projects that would physically alter the landscape of sections of the city.[27] Indeed, most literature on the nineteenth-century modernization of western Cairo emphasizes the influence of Baron Haussmann and his redesign of central Paris on Cairene urban renewal.[28] Haussmann's concern lay in the unity of urban space; circulation of people, air, and water within that space; straight lines and attractive facades; and a pleasant, convenient urban environment. These themes influenced decisions that were made in Cairo as well.[29]

But those who claim that Cairene urban renewal in the 1860s and 1870s blindly followed a French model miss the complexities of change in Cairo at the time.[30] Without denying the influence of French, Italian, Austrian, and British design, all of which have been well documented, a closer look at architectural developments in nineteenth-century Cairo challenges the notion that European—particularly Haussmann-style—innovations were imported blindly and forced onto the Cairene urban fabric.[31] Rather, changes in Cairo incorporated local needs and architectural patterns. Moreover, a number of design elements attributed to Haussmann predated his work in Paris and reflected earlier shifts in Ottoman design in Egypt.

The Cairo that Isma'il inherited was a city divided into ten quarters separated by gates that closed at night.[32] Between the twelfth and eighteenth centuries, elite residential areas existed close to the Citadel, the fortified center of political power. Those sections now are considered the eastern and southernmost parts of Cairo. As those areas became crowded and overpopulated, middle-class and elite families began moving westward to an area called Azbakiyya that had previously been swampland.[33] Mehmed ʿAli drained the area in the mid-1830s by way of a canal that raised it above the Nile's flood level. It was then filled with a lake and surrounding garden. By the 1840s, Azbakiyya played host to numerous public ceremonies and housed some of Cairo's best hotels. The neighborhood became a locus of entertainment and residences for upwardly mobile local families, tourists, and, as the century progressed, foreign residents.

Upon Isma'il's return from the Universal Exhibition, efforts to modernize portions of Cairo began in earnest. Taxation and forced peasant labor were critical to the success of the building projects, but principal financial support came from two other sources: cotton and European bank loans.[34] When the outbreak of the American Civil War effectively halted American cotton exports to Britain, Egypt and India became its chief cotton suppliers. Consequently, the price of Egyptian cotton increased fourfold between 1861 and 1863, and income from cotton exports increased from 918,000 pounds sterling in the early 1850s to 10 million pounds sterling in the late 1800s.[35]

This boom alone, however, was not enough to finance all of Isma'il's schemes and extravagant spending. He increasingly turned to European financial institutions to contract loans. Isma'il had been encouraging the growth of financial societies in Egypt to promote foreign investment and gain what appeared to be the benefit of long-term credit.[36] Increasingly, he turned to the Anglo-Egyptian Bank and Crédit Lyonnais to cover not only public works projects but also theatrical production.[37]

Isma'il charged his minister of public works, ʿAli Pasha Mubarak, with designing a master plan that focused on modernizing western sections of Cairo but also encompassed the older southern and eastern sections.[38] This involved the construction of straight, wide streets that extended out from central squares (*midans*) throughout the city and the construction of a road lined with sphinxes, sycamores, and acacias built to connect Cairo with the Pyramids at Giza. Isma'il hired the French landscaper for the city of Paris, Monsieur Barillet-Duchamp, to create a lake surrounded by a garden with shrubbery, shady parks, cafés, and grottoes to replace Mehmed ʿAli's canal.[39]

To the west of Azbakiyya sat the venerable Shepherd's Hotel, the premier home away from home for European guests in Egypt.[40] To the north and east were European shops and private houses fronted with shady arcades. And to the south stood the new Khedivial Opera House and Comédie Française. Other cultural institutions included the Khedivial Library and a Geographical Society, and additional display halls were added to the Bulaq Museum of Egyptian antiquities.[41] Karl Baedeker's and Thomas Cook's travel guides included detailed maps of the area and assured visitors of the district's many pleasures.[42]

But staging the modernity of the city did not involve a mere overlay of new design over old, nor did it mean total Europeanization. Local architecture, histories, and needs shaped the city's new form. In the first half of the nineteenth century, for example, Mehmed ʿAli's court welcomed a variety of mostly Greek architects who built in Rumi, Greek, Balkan, or Albanian styles.[43] Rumi design in particular was a carryover from Greece and the area surrounding Mehmed ʿAli's hometown of Kavala. Two-story buildings with decorative wooden friezes separating the stories epitomized the style. They boasted irregular internal ground plans; plain, geometrical facades; and "vertically elongated" windows. The last two elements—large windows and geometrical facades—typically attributed to Haussmann's style, predated Haussmann in their appearance in Rumi architecture. Furthermore, Rumi construction, typically wood or wood covered in plaster, was the framework for Isma'il's "European-style" opera house.[44] Rita Abrahamsen suggests that the hybridity of Cairo—its blend of Europeanization and local design (and people)—signaled a creative adaptation, interpretation, and transformation of Western cultural symbols and practices.[45] In effect, the incorporation of European architectural design, even by the Francophile Isma'il, was subject to local conditions and preferences.

The arrangement of new boulevards and squares in nineteenth-century central Cairo was not simply about urban reconstruction. As the scholar Timothy Mitchell explains, the new layout represented a "principle of order" that it "inscribed in the life of its inhabitants."[46] The layout rendered the city knowable and navigable to its visitors by overlaying it with a type of ordered plan, one that was intended to turn Egypt into a modern state.[47] Mitchell argues that the western city's streets and facades appeared to be organized specifically for the observer as a picture or stage set that represented "some reality beyond."[48] Visitors' observations testified to the fact that the new, open streets of central Cairo introduced a "principle of visibility and observation, the principle of exhibition."[49]

In some ways, renovations that included wide thoroughfares and public monuments were more about appearances than deep infrastructural change. Isma'il did not, for example, invest in a sewage network to help reduce disease and improve drinking water, as had been the case in the redesign of Paris.[50] But wide streets and glass storefronts did signal economic change beneath the surface. The modernity on offer correlated with the circulation of capital and the increasing promotion and visibility of consumption. As was also the case in Paris, heightened visibility of people and products made the "act of buying into something performative where the consumers become part of the spectacle."[51] Modern subjects were both an audience for and actors in this embodied experience.

Making Cairo legible, or comprehensible, to visitors and occupants materially and socially affected Egyptians' lives. Economic, social, and state factors encouraged urban development in the area including and surrounding Azbakiyya, what has been termed the "core area" of Cairo.[52] The historian Nelly Hanna argues that the western area from Azbakiyya to Isma'iliyya has been misguidedly termed "the European quarter" when, in fact, only certain pockets of the area hosted a majority European population. Instead, Egyptians chiefly populated these quarters. Its privileged position in the city was not due solely to European interests but "because it represented the interests of a class of people who were involved with a growing new economy, linked to European capitalism."[53] The core was where the institutions necessary to sustain this economy—the Post Office, Telegraph Office, Mixed Courts, tourist companies, and hotels—were situated.

As Cairo's so-called core developed, it witnessed an influx of poor migrants. Between Mehmed 'Ali's census of 1845 and the census of 1907 the population of Cairo increased two and a half times.[54] Concern with delimiting boundaries between city quarters and keeping impoverished people from entering and contaminating a modern clean and orderly core meant that circulation and visibility—two hallmarks of Haussman-style renewal—meshed with indigenous, local Egyptian concerns and social hierarchies as well. This is illustrated by the implementation of several laws that affected only this section of the city, such as an 1891 law that instituted payment of an entrance fee and "appropriate" dress to enter the Azbakiyya gardens.[55] The law was meant not only to keep European visitors in the neighborhood shielded from the poorer members of local society; it also addressed middle- and upper-class Egyptian concerns with drugs, crime, and prostitution. Undoubtedly, urban renovations benefited the interests of some segments of the indigenous population who lived in the area over others.

European responses to Isma'il's modernization of Cairo ranged from pleasure to suspicion. Baron de Kusel wrote favorably about the Suez Canal festivities in his recollections. As he described it, "large marquees had been erected in which tables beautifully decorated awaited those who wished to eat or drink" imported delicacies and much wine. The day after the inauguration, some guests went to Cairo "where some remained two or three weeks, sight-seeing, and enjoying themselves at the expense of the Khedive, even the carriages hired by them. . . . The expense . . . must have been enormous."[56] Azbakiyya, in the words of an enthusiastic visitor, "forms a handsome European town, intersected by broad, well-paved, and gas-lit boulevards, flanked by shops and villas worthy of the Riviera, owned for the most part by pashas, beys, and wealthy foreigners to whom the Khedive has granted free building sites on the sole condition of the houses erected being of a certain architectural merit."[57]

Others were not convinced that progress and modernity penetrated far beneath the surface. The actress Mabel Caillard, for example, saw the new construction as "cardboard monuments": flimsy, superficial, and somewhat "unreal."[58] Another guest stated: "The civilization of the place, so far as it has any, leaves nothing to be desired. . . . But in spite of all these things is scarcely a veneer of modern progress. . . . [I]t is very easy, when walking about the European quarter, to mislead one's self into an over-estimate of the extent to which modern progress has established itself."[59]

European accounts even raised questions about the degree to which Egyptians themselves internalized the changes. A visitor commenting on people in the streets saw individuals as a spectacle, even comparing them to fictional characters: "In Cairo only are now to be found in the scene and most of the *dramatis personae* of the *Thousand and One Nights* within stone's throw of nineteenth-century civilisation in many of its latest results."[60] For the English court tutor Alfred Butler, "real" indigenous voices only disrupted reveries about the civilized ancients. As was common at the time, Butler, along with several servants, had climbed to the top of a pyramid for a better city view before recording his musings. As he lay down after enjoying a filling meal, he described his time "pondering . . . surveying . . . thinking . . . recalling, perhaps, quaint Herodotean gossip about the building and builders of the pyramid" before his thoughts were interrupted by the "harsh and jarring" Arab voice of one of his servants. "Such chatter," he writes, "soon put an end to our would-be sublime imaginings."[61] The pleasure of his fantasies, in contrast to his dismissal of real Egyptian voices, exemplified how imagining the ancient past was preferable to engaging with Egypt's contemporary realities. A sense of superiority permeated such writings and implied that Egyptian modernity was partial or incomplete.

While Egypt's leaders shared a general interest in reforming Egypt, they differed considerably in what changes to implement. As the historian James McDougall argues in the context of colonial Algeria, the main issue was not "a perpetual conflict between 'tradition' or 'authenticity'—or 'Islam'—vs. 'modernity,' but about an ongoing struggle over what *kind* of modernity, and what kind of modern politics and culture, should be assumed."[62] Generally, elites seemed to agree on a notion of progress that meant incorporation of European technologies and know-how. But the selection of what to incorporate, the speed of implementation, and the limits of change were subject to much debate. This is evident from the aspects of Cairo that Isma'il highlighted as authentically Egyptian. While he supported modernization projects in the western half of Cairo, he also supported what some term the "medievalization" of eastern sections of Cairo that were renovated to highlight Ottoman design and obliterate the preceding Mamluk and Arabic periods of Egyptian history.[63] All of this complicates nationalist and royalist histories of the twentieth century that ignore the persistence of any Ottoman past.

Isma'il's decision to build a road leading visitors directly to the pyramids highlighted the "pure" Egypt he sought to showcase: Egypt's ancient past. European fascination with ancient Egypt has been well documented, but less has been said about how Egyptians understood their own ancient history. As nineteenth-century archaeologists unearthed more historical sources of Pharaonic Egypt, leading scholars began to formulate a concept of modern Egyptian identity that was tied not to history but to land. The Egyptian scholar Rifa'a Rafi' al-Tahtawi described antiquities or monuments as "a history awakening . . . to the past ages, and a witness to the books of revelation."[64] Antiquities were part of both Islamic and Egyptological history. Though Isma'il's Francophile leanings influenced the shape and scope of modernization in Egypt, elements of Ottoman and ancient Egyptian culture and history persisted and were, in some cases, reinterpreted in a modern context.

Paul Draneht, superintendent of State Theaters and director of the Khedivial Opera House, traveled to Italy and France yearly to assemble troupes for both the new Comédie Française and the opera house. His letters to Isma'il's ministers detail his travels and meetings with artists. Draneht made a point of attracting top talent, noting that the performers he met were "distinguished subjects who have proven themselves in Europe's grand theaters."[65] Concern with attracting top stars meant considerable budget expenditures, an issue Draneht raised frequently in letters to the head of the Council of Ministers, Riaz Pasha.[66] He argued, for example, that to "do the thing properly" *Aida*'s premiere would surpass the allotted budget by 70,000 francs.[67] Top stars translated into large audiences—a desire shared by theater directors, Isma'il, and local journalists.[68]

Isma'il's generous opera house budgets came from European bank loans and the government's coffers.[69] To supplement these, he ordered pashas to rent loges (boxes) each season and charged them with the responsibility to cover ballerinas' expenses for the duration of their stay in Cairo. Opera house budgets paid for building maintenance, stage sets, performers' salaries and passages to Egypt, and special seats set aside for guests of the khedive. The best seats were reserved for visiting diplomats and the police prefect; others were reserved for municipal and Egyptian police, European-language journals, directors of other theaters including the Cairo Circus, and major foreign bank officers.[70]

Elite patronage of religious and secular entertainments had a long history in the Arab world. In nineteenth-century Egypt, for example, ruling elites hosted events in public spaces (particularly around Azbakiyya), in private homes, and at the khedivial court.[71] Alfred Butler, court tutor to Isma'il's grandsons, gave several accounts of such experiences. On the occasion of *'Id al-Fitr*, a feast day to mark the end of Ramadan, Butler observed court servants, 4,000 troops, ministers, bodyguards, and merchants praying on a rug that had been laid in front of the palace steps. When the khedive arrived, their prayer was interrupted by "four bands of music [that] clashed out the khedivial hymn, and the troops presented arms."[72] Royal weddings raised the bar, as was the case in 1873 when Isma'il held a forty-day celebration in honor of his three sons' and daughter's weddings. The celebration included stunning public illuminations and music in the Azbakiyya Garden.[73] An Ottoman theater troupe, Turkish comedians, Egyptian singers, musicians, acrobats, and dancers performed at the Qasr al-Nil palace.[74] Isma'il's favored singers, people who synthesized Turkish music with local Egyptian folk music like 'Abd al-Hamuli, Muhammad al-Aqqad, Mahmud 'Uthman, and Almaz, appeared regularly in the palace.

Descriptions of the opera house mirrored some of how the Egyptian eyewitness and chronicler of the French occupation, 'Abd al-Rahman al-Jabarti (1754–1824), described French theater. Jabarti was intrigued by theaters built in Cairo to entertain members of the Napoleonic expedition. He described one "of what in their tongue is called La Comédie. It is a place where Frenchmen assemble once every 10 nights for some four hours to see plays performed by a French troupe, in French, for pleasure and entertainment. To enter, one has to have an admission ticket and suitable garb."[75]

When the Khedivial Opera House opened in 1869, it provided a new venue for performance marked by elements that distinguished it from other theatrical spaces and practices. Unlike more traditional performances that were connected to larger events and celebrations, this venue offered entertainment for its own sake. Attendees traveled to a building designed specifically for performance rather than watching performance in public spaces or, in the case of wealthier patrons, having the performance come to them. Spectators purchased seats that were theirs for the duration of the performance. And performances, which took place on a proscenium stage, were primarily European in language and style, demanding different listening and viewing practices than the interactive and vocal audience engagement to which Egyptians were accustomed. Indeed, throughout the nineteenth and early twentieth centuries, the opera house remained a venue for predominantly European performances. While some Egyptian actors and singers sought permission to appear on the opera house stage (and occasionally succeeded), most did not appear there and sought alternative venues for their performances.[76] Arabic theater was given space only when there was no other European attraction.[77]

What happened under the proscenium was not all that mattered, however. Inside the opera house, loges offered not only a better view of the stage but also the opportunity to observe the occupants within. As in European theater, this was significant, since what happened offstage was often of equal, if not greater, importance than what happened on it.[78] Indeed, the physical design of the opera house made hierarchy visible (and contestable) in new ways.[79] It allowed spectators to note who was in attendance and facilitated visits between audience members in their loges, illuminating increasingly complex and stratified hierarchies in Egyptian and European societies that were undergoing rapid political, economic, and technological transformations.[80] An article in the *Egyptian Gazette* was quite critical of this, complaining that "it is notorious that a goodly proportion of the habitual opera-goers of Cairo confine themselves during the entr'actes and overtures to a survey of the frocks and faces—doubtless charming—which they see around them, and subside, on the lifting of the curtain, into a comatose lethargy."[81]

A clear example of the importance of what happened offstage occurred one night in 1893 upon the new Khedive ʿAbbas II's first visit to the opera house after his accession. The rumor of his intended visit had stirred much gossip and anticipation, which the khedive had tried to thwart by sending out a counter-rumor that he had decided not to go. He eventually arrived, quietly (though not without a welcome by the head and some members of the Council of Ministers), while the first act was in progress. When he appeared in his loge, the performance, which happened to be *Aida*, stopped, and the orchestra played the khedivial hymn four times as the audience cheered.[82] The fact that attendees that evening included the British agent Lord Cromer, the diplomatic corps, and, according to the *Egyptian Gazette*, "the most distinguished and brilliant of Cairo society," illuminates the political significance of the event.[83]

The epitome of the colonial administrator, Cromer had first come to Egypt in 1877 as the British commissioner to the Public Debt Administration, which had been set up to protect the interests of European creditors after Isma'il plunged the nation into debt. He later returned in 1883 to administer the British occupation of Egypt, fiercely protecting British economic interests by promoting the Egyptian cotton trade and promoting agriculture over industrialization and limiting Egyptian access to higher education. His self-righteousness bordered on what the Cromer biographer Roger Owen described as "megalomania."[84] Thus, the visual and vocal support of 'Abbas II in a space of ostensibly benign entertainment made possible a veiled critique of Lord Cromer even while it was enacted in front of him.

Egypt's elites exercised both political and cultural power and were defined by a mix of economic, educational, familial, and cultural markers. Those who attained the most distinguished positions in the viceregal household and state bureaucracy were members of the dhawat (upper class/aristocracy/persons of high state rank). In the early part of the century, they typically had a military background and were given the titles "pasha" and "bey" to reflect rank and status. For much of the nineteenth century, the dhawat differed from a'yan (rural, Egyptian-born notables) in terms of ethnicity, wealth, seniority of public office, and residence (urban versus rural). By the last quarter of the century, however, the lines between dhawat and a'yan blurred as Turks and rural notables intermarried, and a'yan—enriched by increased involvement in global markets and cotton cultivation—moved to cities to pursue political interests, enjoy urban life, and offer their children a better education.[85] Isma'il promoted a good number of these indigenous Egyptians to high posts in the state bureaucracy. The *Majlis al-Nawwab*, a privy council composed of landowning and merchant families, for example, consisted entirely of Egyptian notables.[86] Whereas under Mehmed 'Ali the great majority of members of the ruling class were Turks, midcentury changes in recruitment incorporated technicians, Egyptian provincial officials, and Europeans who challenged Turkish control and changed elite culture.[87]

The acquisition of personal wealth in the form of cash and land became a measure of status and influence for high-ranking officials. Tastes and consumption patterns changed with this greater wealth. Generally, by the 1860s, officials were less concerned with smoking *narghila* pipes and riding horses and more interested in steam engines, European cigarettes, and carriages. Men wore frock coats instead of robes and sported mustaches. Women dressed in Parisian fashions.[88] And most urban elites spent evenings at the opera house.

But the cultural orientation of elites was not only westward: even as Isma'il worked to distance Egypt politically from Ottoman control, he and the elites who surrounded him looked to Istanbul as a cultural touchstone. Men who wore frock coats also wore fezzes instead of turbans, while their wives wore gossamer veils, an imported style. They vacationed in both Paris and Istanbul.[89] And while the opera house offered mostly European performances, Isma'il's court hosted a variety of Egyptian and Ottoman singers and musicians. A midcentury style of household architecture termed "Constantinopolitan," a mix of European and Turkish influences, modeled this blending.[90] As the historian Ehud Toledano explains, "in *social* and *cultural* terms, Egypt remained very much within the Ottoman orbit" even as the Mehmed 'Ali family dynasty worked to separate itself from Ottoman political rule.[91]

Just as people spent time looking at each other in the opera house, they knew that they were being watched as well. Attendees included members of the police force, adding another dimension to the spectacle of the opera house. They also included journalists and critics. Press critiques of performances commented on productions but also on spectators—their dress, chatter, orderliness, or disorderliness. On the opening night of *Aida*, for example, audience members attracted so much attention from critics that it was difficult to determine if the spectacle was the audience or the performance onstage.[92] The noted Milanese critic Filippo Filippi's review of the opera focused more on the exoticism of the theater, the dress of the Jewish and Coptic merchants, and his glimpses of the harem ladies than on the performance itself.[93] After commenting on the beauty and elegance of the European women, he went on to note: "I ought to also say, from love of truth, that by the side of the handsomest and the best dressed were to be seen every evening the faces of Copts and Jews, with strange headgear, impossible costumes, colours which clashed so violently that nothing worse could be imagined."[94]

Some elements of the opera house, however, thwarted visibility, to the frustration of many. Despite its Italian design, the opera house's physical interior highlighted what was the epitome of Eastern "otherness." On the second floor, adjacent to the stage and opposite the khedive's loge, the women of the royal harem attended performances in harem boxes. These were specially designed loges with private staircases guarded by eunuchs. And, as Ellen Chennelle, the English governess to Isma'il's court, described: "They were a novelty to be seen in no other country.... [T]he whole front of these boxes was covered with a fine network of iron, painted white, and covered with flowers in gold. It had the effect of lacework, but it was all iron, and the elaborate pattern of the flowers made it more difficult to distinguish any person or thing within the boxes so covered."[95]

For many European audience members, the harem boxes seemed, oddly, to publicly assert private or segregated space. The fact that harem boxes were loges—elevated sections that ordinarily allowed for heightened visibility for those within and without—created dissonance by being covered and inaccessible. They effectively provided a "hidden visibility" that captivated visitors' imaginations. The Oriental secretary to Lord Cromer, Ronald Storrs, voiced this fascination in his account of how it was possible to catch "flashes of magnificent jewels and even more magnificent eyes from behind the harem boxes."[96]

This apparently contradictory juxtaposition of public and private was in many ways an extension of Ottoman court culture. As the historian Leslie Pierce observes, the "public display of splendid isolation" was an old practice inherited by the Ottomans from Islamic and Christian Byzantine monarchies.[97] The Ottoman sultan, for example, might be visible to his subjects as he moved through the palace or city but was cordoned off by the physical and human boundary of his entourage. In the case of the opera house, the harem boxes effectively and appropriately functioned to display the women in their isolation. Confounding clear divisions of public and private space, these boxes physically and metaphorically domesticated the opera house by forcing its structure, and guests, to comply with Ottoman court culture.

Viewing the opera house as an extension of the royal court cautions against easy labeling of the venue's interior as paradoxically divided between private and public spaces.[98] Rather, it introduces alternative spatial designations more relevant to Ottoman culture, namely, privileged/common, sacred/profane, and interior/exterior.[99] The interior/exterior binary was inscribed in the physical structure of Topkapi, the sultan's palace in Istanbul until the nineteenth century. As the art and architectural historian Gulru Necipoglu writes, Topkapi "once served as a vast stage for the enactment of a ceremonial, codified down to the smallest detail, whose symbolic language emphasized the elevated status of the sultan vis-à-vis his subjects, his dignitaries, and the representatives of foreign powers who came to his court."[100] As the sultan was considered sacred, the palace's architecture made visible imperial seclusion and the sultan's aloof relationship to the outside world. Topkapi's design was a series of circles within circles. This created distinctions in which interior spaces were places where people with familiar connections to the ruler mingled and dwelled. The interior was, by extension, of greater political significance than exterior sections of the court. This complicated a public/private dichotomy that situates politics solely in the public realm.

Hierarchy in Ottoman court culture was, thus, metaphorically and physically conceived not as vertical but as horizontal, and a critical index of power was one's degree of access to the center or interior of the physical palace. As the royal harem was situated at the center of the palace, this meant that women had the greatest access to the physical body of the sultan.[101] By extension, this meant that women who lived in the harem had considerable power. Indeed, court women in Egypt and Istanbul participated in the exercise of sovereignty through cultural, architectural, educational, and religious patronage; through marriage and motherhood; and through public participation in imperial ceremonies.[102] Isma'il's mother, for example, was a formidable figure whose actions were regularly reported in the press. She had her own palace; founded the Rafa'i Mosque (the main mausoleum for the royal family); supported the Egyptian nationalist Ahmad ʿUrabi; and exercised significant influence over her son.[103]

It was in the context of reinventing Cairo that Khedive Isma'il approached Giuseppe Verdi with repeated requests to compose an original opera that was "purely ancient and Egyptian."[104] Speaking through various agents, he made clear that he would accept any of Verdi's conditions should he agree to compose the opera. "*This is serious*!!" Camille Du Locle wrote to Verdi, "I receive letter after letter from Egypt. The Viceroy cannot resign himself to the thought of not having one of your works."[105] As Verdi was reputed to be selective with his commissions, it is possible that word that his rival, Wagner, was Isma'il's second choice may well have encouraged Verdi's acceptance of the charge.[106] And Auguste Mariette sent assurances to Verdi: "Everything will be arranged according to your wishes. . . . Nothing will be neglected here for the *mise-en-scène*, which the Viceroy wants to be as splendid and magnificent as possible."[107]

The scholar Edward Said observed that an individual like Mariette was made possible by Napoleon's *Description de l'Égypte* and Jean-François Champollion's deciphering of hieroglyphics—in other words, a legacy of imperial Egyptology that produced an individual and an opera—that embodied "the authority of Europe's version of Egypt at a moment in its nineteenth-century history."[108] Isma'il's preference for an opera about the grandeur of ancient Egyptians echoed the esteem that Europeans accorded to ancient versus modern Egyptians. Perhaps the Anglo-Egyptian resident E. L. Butcher summed this up best when she stated: "Like everyone else, I was too much absorbed in the Egypt of the Pharaohs to care much about their degenerate descendants." Ancient Egypt, for many, had attained heights of civilization that the moderns simply did not inherit.[109]

Such notions predated but were considerably enhanced by waves of Egyptomania that accompanied the unearthing of ancient tombs, temples, and other antiquities. Before Napoleon's *Description de l'Égypte*, European architectural design, Mozart's opera *The Magic Flute*, and interest in Freemasonry reflected a general fascination with ancient Egypt.[110] Nineteenth-century archaeological discoveries only fed the interest. Egypt was commonly imagined as an antique, exotic land of pharaohs, the bible, Herodotus, and *Arabian Nights*.[111] Archaeologists contributed to the blending of Egyptology and Egyptomania by writing chapters for travel guides, organizing exhibits at European exhibitions, and writing fictional histories of the ancients.[112] The opera *Aida* contributed to this cultural production, offering a framework for presenting ancient Egypt to European spectators.

But Egyptians were in attendance too. *Aida* was intelligible to most Egyptians in attendance by virtue of 300 Arabic translations of the libretto in circulation during the performance. Correspondence between the opera house superintendent Draneht and Isma'il's secretary, Khairi Pasha, for example, included discussion of details regarding *Wadi al-Nil* editor Abdullah Abu al-Suud Effendi's (1820–1878) offer to translate the libretto of *Aida* into Arabic and Turkish. He earned 1,270 francs for the job.[113] A letter from Draneht to Khairi Pasha noted that five days before the première "four hundred copies of *Aida* were printed in Turkish, and three hundred in Arabic at the *Wadi al-Nil* press."[114]

Al-Suud's offer to translate was not incidental to his career as a journalist, as he was a professional translator for the School of Languages, Egypt's first institution of professional translators.[115] Under its first (and returning) director, Rifa'a al-Tahtawi (1835–1849, 1864–1868, 1868–1871), the bureau translated various texts in topics ranging from engineering and medicine to politics and literature. In the 1860s, it added opera libretti to its repertoire, starting with Jacques Offenbach's operetta *La Belle Hélène* in January 1869.

Newspapers that promoted attendance at European theatricals—such as *al-Ahram*, *al-Mahrusa*, *al-Waqt*, and more—encouraged readers to buy opera translations, manuscripts that patrons could pass from hand to hand while watching performances to make plays more accessible and, more important, more useful educational tools (figure 1.4).[116] Based on the writings of a correspondent for the journal *al-Jawa'ib*, the translations were indeed put to use. Observing Turkish and Egyptian notables, Indians, and foreigners, he noted that "each of them had in his hand an Arabic text [containing] a translation of these plays. I saw a black slave in a white turban, and in his hand was a translation of *Don Juan*." The correspondent went on to quote the theater director as saying: "'Nothing delights me more than to see the people of Egypt pleased with these theatres. Now they have entered through all the doors of civilization, with the theatre providing its relaxing side.'"[117]

Viewing their own ancient history on stage must have resonated in different ways with Egyptians than it did with Europeans. In the few decades before *Aida*'s premiere, Egyptian intellectuals like Shaykh Rifa'a al-Tahtawi had just begun to write about Egypt in a new way—as a living legacy of its ancient past. Previously, historical texts explicitly divided Egyptian history into two parts: pre- and post-Islamic. The pre-Islamic era was characterized moralistically as an age of ignorance. Tahtawi, however, was influenced by the work of Ibn Khaldun (d. 1406), who interpreted history as a process of advancement, decline, and renewal. Tahtawi used this reasoning to reinterpret Egypt's pharaonic past as an era of scientific, political, and military strength, whereas its more recent history was one of foreign rule and decline. Unlike colonial discourse, which presented a similar argument about the moderns, Tahtawi saw decline as not requiring external salvation but rather as providing an opportunity to renew past greatness.[118]

Tahtawi's experience leading student missions to Paris and his examination of French thought and culture profoundly influenced him. In France he first witnessed the combined effects of Egyptology and Egyptomania. He returned to Egypt determined to promote the pharaonic legacy among modern Egyptians. In his lengthy and influential career as educator, translator, and journalist, al-Tahtawi published numerous translated and original works on ancient Egyptian history that carefully elucidated the ancients' accomplishments. For al-Tahtawi, such heights were not merely historical; they could, once again, be regained.

The desire to recall an age of Egyptian greatness must be understood in the context of Egypt's relationship to the rest of the Ottoman Empire and Africa in the mid-nineteenth century. While Mehmed 'Ali's earlier reforms allowed Egypt some degree of disengagement with the sultan, Isma'il managed to wrest so much control from Istanbul that Egypt's provincial status was merely nominal during the course of his reign. Primarily by way of gifts and bribes, Isma'il had forced Sultan Abdulaziz to elevate his title from

ايده

اسميله مسمى اوپرانك ترجمه سيدر

باارادهٔ حضرت خديوانهمى

غزلنسونى طرفندن انشا و تنظيم و ويردى

نام موسيقى شناس معرفتيله موزيقه نوطه‌سنه وضع و توقيع

اولنه‌رق

اشبو تياترو موسملرنده مصر تياترو خانه‌سنده بالفعل

اوينادلمشدر

اشبو اوپرا اوقايعده راسم و چلبى افنديلر معرفتيله تركجه‌يه

ترجمه و تحويل

و دفعهٔ اولى وادى النيل مطبعه‌سنده

طبع و تمثيـــــل اولنمشدر

سنه ١٢٨٨

Figure I.4. Flyer announcing the availability of Turkish translations of *Aida* published by *Wadi al-Nil* (1288 AH/1871 CE). The opening lines read: "A Translation of the opera called *Aida*. At the behest of His Excellency the Khedive, produced and arranged by Ghislanzoni, and with music composed by the distinguished musician Verdi—it is, in fact, being put on this theater season at the Egypt Theater (*Misir Tiyatrohanesi*)." Courtesy of Israel Gershoni, private collection. (Translation courtesy of Matthew Ellis.)

viceroy to khedive and had earned rights to expand his army, issue his own currency, and contract foreign loans without the sultan's approval.

At the same time that Isma'il was claiming greater independence from Istanbul, he was working to expand his own empire in Africa. He hired British and former Confederate American soldiers to lead the Egyptian army into the Sudan, Ethiopia, Uganda, and beyond, ultimately claiming control over most of the Nile Basin, a territory that was approximately half the size of the continental United States.[119] Soldier-explorers like Sir Samuel Baker and General Charles Gordon established outposts for Isma'il in the outermost reaches of the Nile.[120] But two major factors would bring an end to Isma'il's imperial ambitions: strained budgets and the rise of a young Sudanese religious leader named Muhammad Ahmad. Ahmad, known as the Mahdi, led a Sudanese uprising that took back most of the Sudan by 1884.

Egypt's relationship to the Sudan in the nineteenth century was ambivalent and fraught. The Sudan was considered to be both a fearful place of exile and a target for an Egyptian civilizing mission, and elites imagined it as deeply connected to developing notions of Egyptian identity.[121] As Isma'il expanded his empire into the Sudan and beyond, his expressed aim to British critics was a desire to civilize eastern Africa. Notwithstanding the material and political benefits derived from empire-building, Isma'il and the dhawat who surrounded him articulated their own civilizing mission for sub-Saharan Africa—one that included banning slavery. For Isma'il and ruling elites, Egypt was an imperial civilizer, separate from and superior to sub-Saharan Africa.

Reflecting this, the opera *Aida* clearly demarcates Pharaonic Egypt from Africa. The separation between a "militaristic Egypt" and a "suffering Ethiopia" is inscribed deeply—not in the lyrics but in the music. As the historian Paul Robinson observed: "Egypt is characterized by music that is regular, diatonic, and brassy . . . distinctly European."[122] The more "exotic" music in the opera is reserved for Egypt's victims—Moors and Ethiopians—and women. This is achieved through the use of the oboe and an Eastern *maqam*, which include unequal and microtonal intervals and special pitches as opposed to Western scales.[123] Thus exoticism in *Aida* is both gendered and racial, separating women and sub-Saharan Africa from a Europeanized Egypt.[124]

As Egypt was vulnerable to European expansion but also fulfilling its own imperial aims in tension with European expansionist aims, it becomes increasingly apparent that the opera *Aida* was not merely a tribute to a bygone age of Egyptian greatness. It was an assertion of modern Egypt's power in the face of increasingly menacing European states. Hearkening back to a civilized Egyptian past in operatic format was not nostalgic. For Isma'il, it was evidence of Egypt's distinction from the rest of Africa and proximity—culturally and politically—to Europe.[125] "My country," Isma'il once famously stated, "is no longer part of Africa. It is a part of Europe."

At the heart of both *Aida* and Cairene urban renewal were efforts to reframe both contemporary and ancient Egypt, presenting it as a tenacious and formidable force to European and elite Egyptian audiences. The physical space of the opera house, with its Italianate décor, visible loges, and harem boxes, enforced hierarchies of power that reflected a mixture of elite European and Ottoman court culture. For European audiences, the opera's depiction of a triumphant and powerful ancient Egypt tapped into a wealth of Orientalist knowledge and assumptions about its pharaonic history.[126] The opera made Cairo legible by representing exoticism at an observable distance, but also somewhat familiar, as it represented Egypt as similarly European and within a recognizable musical format. For Egyptian and Ottoman audience members, the message differed: it represented a version of ancient Egypt that reflected the glory of a past that might be regained. And, to Isma'il's satisfaction, *Aida* represented Egypt as a modern imperial power. Taken together, Aida, the opera house, and Cairo's streets were new spaces for elites to cultivate a top-down vision of a prosperous, and politically potent, Egyptian identity.

How audiences interpreted each of these messages was, of course, a different story. For some, the opera *Aida*'s representation of ancient Egyptian power and the opera house's design tapped into a source of cultural pride. For others, opera was dull and elicited only indifference. Through the 1870s, elites and the local press worriedly discussed limited Egyptian interest in the opera house. Despite the fact that Egyptians' toil and taxes paid for the opera house's construction, as was also true of the urban redesign, most urban dwellers were financially unable, unwilling, or simply uninterested in enjoying it. Despite Isma'il's promotion and support of libretti translations in the service of civilizing the Egyptian people, there was a vast separation between civilizing rhetoric and reality. Educational reforms and the expansion of European mission schools increased the number of Egyptians who could understand European theater, but the numbers of attendees remained small.[127] One journalist complained of audience members "who have no ear for European music," who talk during overtures, and "are obviously bored by all except the ballet, and scenes that represent duels, executions, or conspiracies."[128]

It is not safe to assume that elites were enamored with opera either. Pashas who were ordered by the khedive to purchase private boxes at the opera house did not seem very interested in performances. Though attendance at the opera house became central to elite lifestyles, reports indicated that pashas purchased the boxes but often left them empty "rather than submit to the tediousness of listening to fine music."[129] According to one European observer, Muslim women of the harem, similarly, were "about as enthusiastic as their husbands as they listened, half asleep, to Offenbach's opéra-bouffe."[130] By contrast, the governess of Isma'il's harem noted that a eunuch who had accompanied her to the opera house "apparently follow[ed] the performance with great interest."[131]

Urban developments in western Cairo and the introduction of opera to elites and some of the middle classes were changes foisted upon the broader population and induced everything from indifference to outright contestation. Despite Isma'il's lofty aims, civilizing the populace by way of new sanitary regulations or opera house performances could only go so far if most Egyptians were unable or uninterested in participating in them. Despite that, new spaces for the production of these cultural forms created opportunities and visible frameworks within which an elite populace could begin to imagine themselves as a coherent whole.

Shortly after *Aida*'s memorable premier, the cotton boom that had first financed Isma'il's projects came to an end, and the high interest rates, brokerage commissions, and other charges connected to Isma'il's massive bank loans sent Egypt into a downward spiral of debt. Egyptian debt before Isma'il's governance had been 3 million pounds sterling; by the end of his reign it was more than 100 million. The khedive's desperate attempts to sell everything—from his palaces to the family silver—in efforts to stay afloat failed. By 1875, the threat of bankruptcy forced Isma'il to sell all Egyptian shares of the Suez Canal to Britain, and one year later, fearing Egypt's potential insolvency, Egypt's European creditor nations set up the Public Debt Administration in Cairo, effectively turning over financial control of Egypt to Britain and France. Isma'il's attempts to resist loss of economic control led French and British consuls to force the Ottoman sultan to remove him; the sultan, weakened by the Ottoman Empire's own fiscal problems and debts to those same creditors, complied. Isma'il was forced to abdicate in 1879.

It had been only a few years before that Isma'il proudly declared Egypt no longer a part of Africa but a part of Europe. It is unlikely that he could have foreseen how devastatingly true this would be. Within ten years of *Aida*'s premiere, Egypt came to be subsumed, economically and then politically, by Britain.

All of this would feed into effendi critiques at the turn of the twentieth century. As the new middle class sought to define their own history, they created a narrative of modern Egyptian history that would demonize elite greed and blame it for creating the opportunity for British colonial intervention in the 1880s. The effendiyya, by their account, were the only ones capable of representing the people, steering Egypt out of colonial and elite domination and leading the way to an independent nationhood that was Egypt's irrefutable destiny.

Elites continued to wield power in the post–World War I period, but the strength of effendi nationalism necessitated a cultural reorientation that encouraged a more fulsome embrace of Egyptian identity. Despite attempts to adopt that orientation, ideological differences among elites turned them and their political alliances against one another, eventually splintering their hold on power.

CHAPTER 2

How to Be an *Effendi*

The Syrian-Egyptian journalist and playwright Farah Antun (1874–1922) regularly visited Cairo's Coffeehouse of Joys and Pleasures—but not for enjoyment. At the popular destination, patrons smoked, drank, gambled, and flirted with women as the café's Greek owner enriched himself at their expense. Antun, however, went to the notorious café to stoke his disapproval. As he put it, he wanted to "get to know the nonsense that took place beyond those walls."[1]

Though coffeehouses had been part of Cairo's urban fabric for centuries, European-style cafés of this sort were relatively new.[2] Antun, like other cultural critics of his time, felt the activity he witnessed was profligacy, sapping individuals and broader Egyptian society of its hope and vigor. There was not an ounce of social benefit to be gained in this sort of overindulgent and exploitative leisure, and he found it deeply upsetting.[3]

Nonetheless, his fascination with the problem spurred several more visits, inspiring him to channel the experiences into a new play: *Misr al-Jadida wa Misr al-Qadima* (New Egypt and Old Egypt). Drawing from characters he met at the real Cairo coffeehouse, Antun's play wove together four subnarratives that intersected in their relationship to a crooked Greek cabaret owner named Christo.

Misr al-Jadida opens with five passengers on a boat approaching the Alexandrian harbor. As conversations between them unfold, the audience learns how each one is connected to Christo. Among the passengers is Muhafhaf Pasha, a member of the wealthy, old, self-serving Egyptian elite. A French couple, Etienne and Pauline, are on board with plans to set up their own business in Cairo. The young, poor French girl with them believes she will work as their secretary, though in truth, Etienne intends to sell her to perform in Christo's coffeehouse.

The play's protagonist is Fu'ad Bey, cousin of Muhafhaf Pasha, and an *effendi*, a title that connects him to a rising Egyptian middle class. Christo's establishment seduces the married "handsome youth," Fu'ad, who falls in love with one of its singers. But the cousins' fates diverge as Muhafhaf's overindulgences eventually lead to bankruptcy and ruin. Fu'ad, instead, recognizes his shameful moral weakness, makes amends, and transcends the vice surrounding him. By the end of the play, it is clear: the foreign Christo and "stagnant" elite Muhafhaf Pasha are Antun's Old Egypt. The hardworking effendi, Fu'ad Bey, is his beacon for the New Egypt.

Antun wrote *Misr al-Jadida* out of concern for the trajectory of Egyptian society. He shared, with other young men of his generation, similar questions and anxieties about his place in the modern world. These were a diverse and growing middle stratum of society that included government bureaucrats, intellectuals, and members of the so-called new professions such as medicine, law, and journalism. As individuals, effendis negotiated between a secular education that stressed individual moral autonomy, social mobility, and universal citizenship with older, established hierarchies and communitarian or collective notions of identity.[4]

In Antun's time, effendi identity and narratives about Egyptian history were stories in the making. Though scholars have illuminated ways the *effendiyya* tested and shaped their ideas in journals and newspapers, little is written about how they enacted those ideas on the new Arabic-language theater's proscenium stage.[5] Theatrical performance spaces were instrumental in developing and disseminating consensus on effendi identity and helping give shape to a modern citizenry. Those stories took shape in the context of a growing nationalist movement, one that effendis would lead in the early twentieth century. As their influence amplified, their own narrative about Egyptian history would emerge as the hegemonic national history of the country, and effendis would hold themselves up as models for how to thoughtfully incorporate elements of Western thought into Egyptian life.[6]

Up and down the dynamic ʿImad al-Din Street of central Cairo, middle-class, Arabic-language theaters flourished in the 1910s and onward. Not just spaces for leisure, theaters acquainted the greater population with the merits of work and other effendi values that were being cast as modern and Egyptian. This modernity was not blind imitation (*taqleed*). Indeed, many wrote with great concern about the problems of over-Europeanization—obsession with food, feminization, and consumerism—in modern Cairo's new social spaces.

Instead, effendis constructed modern spaces and identities by blending elements of Western culture and technology with local practices and ways of life that they deemed authentic. From those spaces, effendis demanded political independence as a crucial step in demonstrating progress and attaining modernity. Antun took full advantage of these new possibilities in his journalism and playwriting. His play *Misr al-Jadida* was one example. It was a secular morality play that instructed audiences in how to participate in an economically viable and independent Egypt by virtue of individual action and self-improvement.[7] For viewers, the message was clear: discipline, hard work, and self-reliance were crucial to overcoming the subversions and deceptions of Western, modern, urban life. For the effendiyya, such notions were central to their conception of modern Egyptian identity.

Reviews describing the play as "patriotic," portraying the "traditions of the country," and "an accurate reflection" of what was happening in the country suggest that the message was effective.[8] As a critic for *al-Jarida* wrote, the play was significant because it was not an adaptation of a European play but rather "the first play that comes out of our culture and is performed on our stage." This was not entirely accurate, as original stage plays in Egypt appeared at least as far back as Yaʿqub Sannuʿ, in the mid-nineteenth century, and even longer if one includes street theater. But the statement indicates that *Misr al-Jadida* resonated with its effendi supporters. It told a story they wanted to claim as original and true.

As but one representation of Egyptian society and its ailments, *Misr al-Jadida* epitomized the concerns and prescriptions emanating from those who identified themselves as modern Egypt's most able leaders. But the effendiyya were never entirely of one mind, nor were they of one unified background. Antun himself was a Syrian Orthodox Christian with socialist sympathies and—at least initially—promoted pan-Arab over national identity. As an individual, Antun points to the limitation in both scholarly literature and effendi narratives that assume uniform identities concomitant with a territorial Egyptian nationalism.

Ironically, Antun's writings bolstered an evolving Egyptian nationalist project that wrote out differences to create a myth of consensus and shared culture. As identity came to be inscribed legally and discursively, nationalist writings gradually delineated who could be counted as an Egyptian, and Syrians like Antun were increasingly marginalized in the country.[9] By promoting an effendi vision of a unified Egyptian identity, Antun furthered trends that narrowed categories of identity to favor nationality above all, making otherness more visible. In effect, Antun's work contributed to making himself a foreigner in Egypt.

When Antun started playwriting, *ahli* (indigenous) theater in early twentieth-century Egypt was on the brink of tremendous growth. Most histories of theater in the region attribute the beginnings of Arabic stage performance to Marun al-Naqqash, a Maronite Christian from Sidon, Syria, who wrote and produced the play *al-Bakhil* in Beirut in 1848.[10] The play's success encouraged him to build a theater where his musical farces were performed until his death. Not long after, in 1876, Marun's nephew, Salim al-Naqqash, along with his friend Adib Ishaq and a troupe of actors led by Yusuf al-Khayyat, traveled to perform for a season at the Zizinia Theater in Alexandria. Though their adaptations of *Charlemagne*, *Phedre*, *Andromache*, and other plays did not attract as much attention as they had hoped, al-Khayyat won favor with the Ottoman Egyptian governor of Egypt, Khedive Isma'il. This would not last, however. His staging of *al-Zalum* (The Tyrant) offended Isma'il enough to banish al-Khayyat from the country.[11]

Nevertheless, Syrians continued to participate in theatrical activities in Egypt. Syrian journalists and acting troupes that arrived in increasing numbers in the mid-1870s contributed much to the expansion of Arabic theater. Syrian-edited journals like *al-Hilal*, *al-Ahram*, and *al-Mahrusa* advertised performance dates, announced the sale of theater scripts, and encouraged audiences to attend theatrical productions. By the late nineteenth century, they printed reviews of stage performances and educated readers in theatrical terminology, much of which was imported from French and Italian and sometimes Arabicized or Egyptianized.[12] An article from *al-Muqtataf* in 1899 encouraged talented individuals to join the "ambitious project" of writing "useful plays" to promote "discipline and civilizing."[13] Indeed, a good number of journal editors, such as Jurji Zaydan and Muhammad Taymur, were playwrights as well.[14]

The first theater buildings to open in Cairo were the Khedivial Opera House and Comédie Française, but these appealed primarily to a select group of elites that included foreigners, the khedivial family, and governmental ministers. In 1882, the new khedive, Tewfiq, allowed Sulayman al-Qirdahi's troupe to perform some plays in the Khedivial Opera House. The Qirdahi troupe included former members of al-Khayyat's troupe, Qirdahi's wife, a female singer, and the popular Egyptian singer and actor Salama Hijazi. The troupe toured the provinces and regularly performed in a wooden theater in Cairo. Other Syrian troupes followed, including ones led by Abu Khalil al-Qabbani, who also performed in a wooden theater in al-ʿAtaba al-Khadra, and Iskandar Farah, whose company dominated the Egyptian theatrical scene for eighteen years.[15]

Most of the early plays performed for the stage were adaptations of French comedies and dramas. Molière's *Tartuffe* was a favorite, as were plays by Victor Hugo and Alexandre Dumas.[16] Translators like the prolific ʿUthman Jalal altered plots, names, and places to fit local contexts, so that, for example, a character like Tartuffe, a hypocritical Christian devotee, became Shaykh Matluf, a hypocritical pious Muslim.[17] Often, plays incorporated music, as singing and musical comedies attracted the largest audiences.[18] Iskandar Farah's troupe paid translators and writers, including Farah Antun and other Syrians, between twenty and sixty guineas per piece. They were well paid, considering the highest salary in Farah's company was thirty guineas per month.[19]

A playwright's choice of language was critical for the successful dissemination of particular messages to an audience, and the decision of whether to use *fusha* (formal Arabic based on the language of the Qur'an), colloquial dialect, or some combination of both was the subject of much debate. Underlying the decision was the question of whether or not colloquial Arabic was suitable to express profound emotion or to portray tragic situations. Those who favored fusha saw it as the only way to express deep emotion and voices of authority. For others, the colloquial was preferable, as it offered a more realistic form of speech with which audiences were more likely to identify. Earlier playwrights like Yaʿqub Sannuʿ laid the foundations for professional colloquial theater, communicating much through the accents, dialects, and vocabulary of their characters. Organized colloquial Egyptian theater, however, was not the norm until World War I.[20] Antun chose to write most of *Misr al-Jadida* in what he termed an "elevated colloquial" or "diminished fusha," a decision that marked a new path.[21] In this way, he made linguistically distinct the voice of the effendi—a decision that accentuated other efforts to distinguish the effendiyya as a unique social group.

In the first decade of the twentieth century, playwrights, actors, and singers began performing in, and later opened, their own Arabic theaters in the district west of the Azbakiyya Gardens, in the region of ʿImad al-Din Street (see map 2.1).[22] Though entertainments existed in various sections of early twentieth-century Cairo, ʿImad al-Din Street emerged as a center for the growing number of tiatros (theaters), cafés, cinemas, and salas that offered various forms of Arabic performance.[23]

A stroll down the street presented individuals with numerous options for an evening out.[24] At its northernmost point sat the venerable Printania Theater that hosted such esteemed performers as the actress and singer Munira al-Mahdiyya, the comedian Najib al-Rihani, and the king of melodrama, Yusuf Wahbi, in addition to English-language performances.[25] Next door was the Metropole Café, a popular gathering spot for local artists. A few paces south, on the corner of al-Alfi Street, sat the Italian-run Kursaal Theater, the largest in Cairo, in which international performers like the ballet dancer Pavlova, the Egyptian singer Umm Kalthum, and comedians like

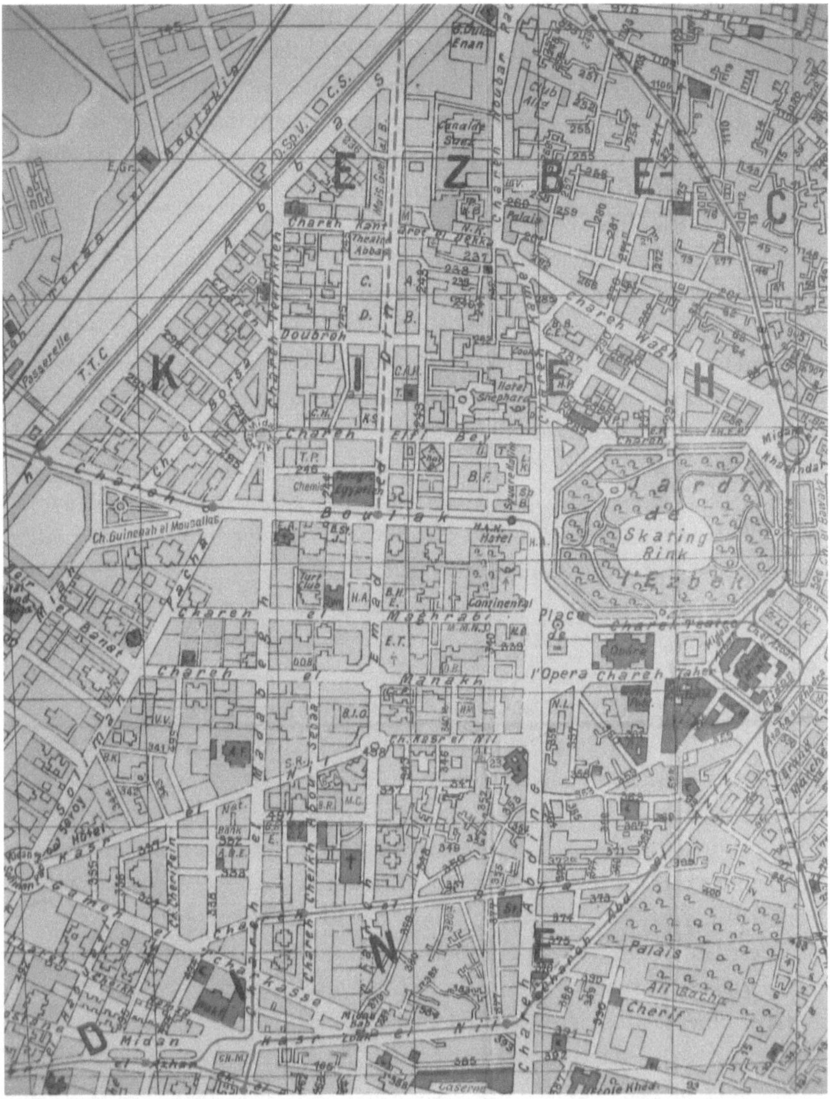

Map 2.1. Central Cairo, 1914. ʿImad al-Din St. runs north-south down the center. MFQ1 1379 59, 1914, The British National Archive.

al-Rihani graced the stage.[26] Down al-Alfi Street was the Abbé de Rose cabaret, where al-Rihani first unveiled his comic character, Kish-Kish Bey.[27] Farther east, on the north side of the Azbakiyya Garden, sat *Dar al-Tamthil al-ʿArabi*, where "The Nightingale of the East," Salama Hijazi, sang. South of al-Alfi, back on ʿImad al-Din Street, was the Muhammad Farid Theater.

Makhzin Marʿi, a store that sold clothes for the theater, sat between it and the Majestique Theater, home to al-Rihani's chief competitor, the beloved comedian ʿAli al-Kassar. Nearby, the Restaurant Santi and Champs-Elysées coffee shops offered evening motion picture screenings, starting in 1906.[28] At the south end of the street sat Casino de Bari and the tented Egyptianna Theater, both hosting al-Rihani, among others.

The ʿImad al-Din Street theaters appealed most to a gradually coalescing middle-class Egyptian audience. Social and economic changes in Egypt—including large-scale industrial production, the development of a national economy, and shifts in systems of communication and education—all contributed to the building of this class.[29] Whereas in the 1890s "effendi" was an honorific title conferred on bureaucrats and khedivial school graduates who pursued advanced education in Europe, by the late 1920s "effendi" was a title that, as the historian Yoav di-Capua explains, "reflected a particular social and economic class that had shifted their urban alliances from al-Azhar, the family business, and the neighborhood to modern avenues of participation in education and professional specialization."[30]

Effendis were young men from disparate social, geographic, and economic backgrounds who increasingly fashioned themselves, according to the historian Lucie Ryzova, as "members . . . of a new social elite . . . based on knowledge, individual merit, and commitment to the national cause."[31] The title did not necessarily imply wealth. It included individuals of many income levels, though new concepts of social mobility meant that all could hope to be part of a rising middle class over time.[32] Their secular educations produced a growing number of youths who stood in a cultural and intellectual middle ground between rural and urban experience. Effendis turned this to their advantage, using their distinct perspective to bridge between European and indigenous cultures, between local elites and the broader population.[33] As teachers, physicians, students, lawyers, bureaucrats, engineers, managers, and journalists, effendis were "functionally and conceptually . . . linked to modernity" and made tremendous contributions to all sorts of intellectual enterprises, including socialism and Egyptian nationalism.[34]

Ryzova's work on the effendiyya illuminates ways in which effendi autobiographical narratives outlined journeys from rural to urban life and from the traditional to the modern. They cast their self-fashioning as a struggle against great odds to educate themselves and ultimately break from the past. "At the core," she writes, "was a claim on modernity, institutionally codified through (modern) education and (modern) employment, and expressed by (modern) dress. . . . [T]he boundaries were disputed and included people

. . . dressing up as effendis . . . or adopting specific fields of social practice . . . writing certain types of texts, or becoming social reformers or political activists."[35]

Effendi self-fashioning was also a claim on a particular gender identity. In response to a colonial discourse that claimed "Europe is active and virile, the East degenerate and feminine," the effendi cultivated what the historian Wilson Chacko Jacob termed "effendi masculinity."[36] The nationalist Mustafa Kamil personified the self-discipline central to effendi masculinity. His published daily schedule included time for prayer, exercise, socializing, work, rest, and reading, and it was published and shared as a pedagogical tool for others.[37] Effendi masculinity was manifest through a range of activities and discourses including scouting, competitive sports, sex talk, and fashion. And its ideals appeared on the proscenium stage. Nationalism and manhood were mutually constitutive. The performance of effendi masculinity on stage and in real life had to be repeated to become normalized and to seem stable, yet each repetition could lead to unintended consequences.[38]

New sites of urban sociability were crucial for the coalescence of an effendi identity. These included sports clubs, literary salons, legal and bureaucratic institutions, capitalist print media, and voluntary associations and theaters.[39] Organizations such as mutual aid societies promoted leisurely pursuits such as attending choral music performances and lectures and writing poetry, all for the cultivation of a particular effendi culture.[40] Café Riche, for example, was a coffeehouse and tiatro in central Cairo that became a popular gathering space for intellectuals. It promoted "authentic voices" of famous Egyptian female performers such as Ruz al-Yusuf, Umm Kalthum, and Munira al-Mahdiyya.[41]

Effendis sought to secure their position in Egyptian society by creating a myth of "societal consensus and unity" around shared aspirations and interests.[42] Theater offered an ideal conduit for the cultivation and dissemination of such ideas. It presented effendi culture not only to the effendiyya but also to anyone willing and able to purchase a ticket. The theater was unmediated space in which effendis could cultivate, transmit, and promote their own mores as those of the emblematic modern Egyptian. Transformation—framed as an individual awakening to a moral, ethical, and cultural imperative—was intended as a model for a broader Egyptian population living under colonial influence.

The process of transformation was deeply personal. The modern Egyptian identity negotiated and promulgated onstage was one that reflected the civilized and respectable identity effendis were forging for themselves. It stood apart from and contrasted European cultural and colonial impositions. It was also defined internally against *ibn al-dhawat* (local elites), *fellahin* (peasants), and the *sha'b* (broader urban Egyptian population). Perhaps it was the instability of effendis' social position that made movement and mobility central to their way of life. Their shared interest in exploring political and social modernity led them to value political action and social engagement, and they used the technologies of a nascent public sphere, such as newspapers, journals, and theater, to spread those ideas. Political and social action in the public sphere was central to effendi identity.

Yet effendis were not as monolithic as such a description implies. Generational, religious, social, ideological, and ethnic diversity within the effendiyya necessarily meant that definitions of "modern" and "civilized," as well as methods for transmitting ideas, would differ within the group. This was apparent in debates over the purpose of theater. Should plays draw from European or indigenous sources? Should they promote nationalism, Islam, or socialism? Should they offer historical lessons, political analyses, and/or contemporary social critiques? The possibilities explored in those debates attest to a shared sense of the potency of theater, even if specific answers to the questions raised depended on a playwright's aims, resources, and disposition. Despite this, even as differences among effendis persisted, the narrative of consensus dominated.

A closer look at the lives of individuals who identified as effendis demonstrates the range of effendi experiences. As the historian Hussein Omar put it, not all were "triumphantly replacing their shaykhly turbans with the tarbushes of modernity."[43] The story of Fathallah Barakat, nephew and cousin of the renowned Sa'd Zaghlul in the era of 1882 to 1910, for example, strays from dominant effendi narratives of progress and self-fashioning. Rather, Barakat experienced modernity largely as personal and political loss rather than an unalloyed goal. Barakat's own writings, Omar suggests, "reveal something of the discomfort that he felt with 'the infrastructure of historical practice' that was designed to forge a monolithic national (and more deeply, monarchical) identity." Rather, Omar continues, "his autobiographical project opposed the push for group cohesion that was necessary at the expense of accuracy and nuance."[44]

Muhammad Wahid, president of the Egyptian Liberal Party (ELP), also pointed to disagreements among Egyptian intellectuals and leadership in a letter to the British foreign secretary, Sir Edward Grey, that expressed concern about Egyptian representation abroad. Unlike members of Kamil's Nationalist Party, the ELP was concerned with maintaining good social relations with the British government, and its supporters included Copts and Syrians in Egypt:[45]

> Inasmuch as there are three persons, named Mustafa Kamil, ʿAli Yussef and Hafez Awad, going about Europe delivering speeches, and getting certain European newspapers to publish what they wish . . . pretending that they represent the Egyptian people and voice their wants and aspirations, we feel it our duty to declare that these three persons do not by any means represent the Egyptian people, but are three journalists, of a certain class, whose object is self-advertisement . . . whose ambitions are incompatible with justice and with the welfare of the Egyptian people.[46]

Wahid went on to detail the damage the self-declared representatives of Egypt have inflicted on Egyptians through their respective journals. He accused them of "arousing racial and religious animosities" and "agitating and inciting the Egyptians" against anyone who did not share their pan-Islamic, anti-British convictions.[47]

Farah Antun's story offers another example of the complex backgrounds, personalities, and concerns of individuals tied up in the effendi narrative of national identity. Antun was born in Tripoli in 1874 to an Orthodox Syrian family.[48] Unlike Maronites, who were powerfully concentrated in the mountains of northern Lebanon and supported by French patrons, the Orthodox Christians were scattered throughout Syria and lived side-by-side, without foreign protections, with Muslim neighbors.[49] Whereas many Maronites hoped for eventual independence in the form of a French-protected Lebanese state, most Arabic-speaking Orthodox lay intellectuals, like Antun, sought ways to break out of their *millet*, or confessional community—which, in his case, was dominated by Greek clergy—and participate in a secular Ottoman state as equals to Muslims. Such aspirations colored Antun's articles and plays in later years.

As prestigious bureaucratic and military careers in the Ottoman Empire were closed to non-Muslims, Antun might easily have followed the path of his father—and many other members of the Syrian Ottoman community—to become a merchant or artisan. His education in an Orthodox school, however, exposed him to an array of subjects, such as the natural sciences, mathematics, history, and, most important, French. Antun's liberal education inspired him to pursue a very different career from his father, but it was not an uncommon one for young intellectuals of his era. For several years, Antun worked as a schoolteacher in Syria before abandoning his job and home to pursue journalism in Egypt.

Antun's interest in the sciences and passion for anticlerical French authors did much to shape his intellectual leanings and secular proclivities.

Though he practiced Orthodox Christianity, he promoted the separation of religion from science and governance. His concern with equality and full citizenship for all Christians attracted him to the secular ideals of the French Revolution and French Romantic writers. It also drew him to sympathize with secular Ottoman nationalism, a feminism that promoted women's education inside the home, and forms of socialism that emphasized more egalitarian distribution of wealth, without class struggle. All of these positions evolved over time, most notably his shift from Ottomanism to Egyptian nationalism in the early twentieth century.

When Antun arrived in Alexandria in 1897, the Syrian Christian community was in the midst of rapid growth that began in 1860 and peaked by 1930. While the Syrian population in Egypt in the 1830s numbered 5,000, by 1907 it was 34,000.[50] People fled Syria to escape religious tensions, local economic pressures, and the censorship and creative restrictions placed on them by Sultan Abdulhamid II. Many had been educated in the new professions, and Syria could not support them all. In Egypt, Syrian merchants found success in various commercial activities. Syrian professionals found an Egyptian population in need of doctors, teachers, and lawyers; others found a growing bureaucracy in need of multilingual bureaucrats.

Still, the influx of Syrians into Egypt's bureaucratic positions was not without repercussions. Though Napoleon, Mehmed ʿAli, and Isma'il all employed Syrian Christians in government over the previous century, Syrian bureaucrats' numbers were greatest during British occupation when Lord Cromer placed them, along with Armenians, in 30 percent of higher government posts. This was in comparison to 28 percent of Egyptians who held such offices.[51] Those most threatened by Syrian Christians were Copts, the indigenous Christian minority in Egypt, who were the ones most often displaced by the better-educated and multilingual Syrians. Thus, though affinities existed between the coreligionists, many Copts resented the influx of Syrians and, in the late nineteenth century, pushed for educational reforms to make themselves more competitive employees.[52]

While Egyptian nationalists like Mustafa Kamil and Ahmad Lutfi al-Sayyid publicly called for acceptance of migrants, particularly Syrians, loyal to Egypt, they also considered Syrians to be "intruders." The historians Israel Gershoni and James Jankowski note that native Egyptians expressed a "sense of distinctiveness, of superiority, and sometimes hostility . . . toward other Arabs in the late nineteenth and early twentieth centuries."[53] As many Syrian immigrants were well-educated and ambitious individuals who prospered in British-occupied Egypt, Egyptians who competed with them for work resented their overrepresentation in government, business, and a cultural arena that included journalism, acting, and playwriting. This points to a central tension in Antun's work. As a Syrian émigré promoting modern Egyptian nationalism, to what extent was he included in this vision? The scholar Marilyn Booth's observation that "not only is nationalism not homogenous; elite nationalisms are not uniform" is instructive in Antun's case.[54]

Antun started the journal *al-Jamiʿa* in Alexandria in 1899. It ran for five years before financial difficulties and a public debate with Shaykh Muhammad ʿAbdu encouraged him to attempt something new.[55] He decided to try his hand in New York City and moved there in 1905. For all Antun's apparent radicalism, his faith in Western models of modernity was shaken when he came face-to-face with the West that, until then, he had only read about in books and magazines. Having already failed to run a paper successfully in Egypt, Antun confronted in the United States what he considered an excessive materialism, an exaggerated quest for money and power, and an absence of moral and spiritual grounding—all of which dampened Antun's ardor for a Western model of progress. He returned to Egypt and published a few more issues of *al-Jamiʿa* but realized he would have to seek financial support in other ways. Thus, he turned to writing articles for various nationalist journals, such as Mustafa Kamil's *al-Liwaʾ*, and, increasingly, to playwriting, which offered him a direct means by which to express his views on the proscenium stage.[56]

Thus Antun's political loyalties and sense of identity evolved over his lifetime. The historian Donald Reid's extensive work on Antun's life illuminates these transitions. As a Syrian, Christian, and Ottoman, his espousal of a secular Ottoman identity above all for most of his life seems logical. For much of his life, he was publicly neutral on Egypt-Britain relations, but around 1909 Antun seems to have more purposefully embraced Egyptian nationalism. Antun's shift in loyalties mirrored the nationalist Saʿd Zaghlul's shift from moderate reformism to anti-British nationalism after 1908, but it is not clear whether or not that made the difference for Antun.[57] The shift was, however, indicative of a decline in his faith in the viability of Ottomanism. His embrace of Egyptian nationalism correlated with a period in which his journal, *al-Jamiʿa*, collapsed, and he returned to Egypt from New York. His decision to write articles for other journals in support of Egyptian nationalism seemed like a logical way to buoy his career without compromising his support for secular governance.

An illustration of Antun's fraught position as both inside and outside of Egyptian nationalism is made vivid in Reid's study of Antun's funeral in 1922. Of the approximately 1,000 multifaith attendees, Wafdists from the journal *al-Ahali* praised Antun's contribution to the nationalist cause, as did the Coptic judge Butros Ghali. The nationalist leader Sa'd Zaghlul sent condolences to Antun's sister.[58] But the ceremony was held at the American University in Cairo instead of an Egyptian university, underscoring Antun's persistent marginality, even in death.[59]

Though no professional school for theater education existed at the turn of the century, work related to theater slowly developed among the new professions. Many playwrights also engaged in other careers, particularly in the early years when lines between professions were hazy.[60] Antun benefited from this career fluidity. Over time, he translated and wrote several plays and operettas for performers like the esteemed dramatic actor Jurj Abyad and the Egyptian singer and actress Munira al-Mahdiyya. Few playwrights and journalists, in the early years, were of Egyptian origin. Most, in fact, were Syrians who dominated the theatrical scene in Cairo from 1876 through the end of the century. The Egyptian climate of arts promotion, particularly under Isma'il, encouraged Syrian playwrights like Adib Ishaq and Salim al-Naqqash to come to Egypt in hopes of securing patronage and escaping Sultan Abdulhamid II's harsh censorship.[61]

Antun felt that he could most efficiently reach the larger population by way of the theater.[62] Perhaps the realities of limited regional literacy bolstered his position. Census data indicates that, in 1897, only 4.1 percent of the Egyptian population was literate; in 1917 it was 6.8 percent. Of those who were literate, fewer than 5 percent are thought to have purchased newspapers in 1914.[63] But the historian Hoda Yousef stresses that the type of literacy measured by the census was a narrow interpretation of reading and writing. Her argument, that "literacies—in the plural—exist along a continuum of practices and contexts that often include multiple valences of orality and textuality," implies that the written press and the theater worked in tandem to promote new ideas.[64] This was evident in Egypt. Journalists recognized that, much like the nascent press offered new spaces to debate aspects of Egyptian life, theaters also offered spaces for translation, interpretation, and deliberation. Accordingly, a number of those journalists, like Antun, edited papers and also translated, adapted, and wrote original plays.[65]

The proscenium stage offered a respectable space for the representation of national sentiment and effendi values. Indeed, respectability was intertwined with effendi self-definition and nationalism. Antun's description of Christo's cabaret as "a casino built on the bondage of the innocent, tempting daughters with immorality, depravity, drunkenness ... eating away at the common wealth" tapped into a larger argument that critiqued certain forms of immoral, undisciplined entertainment and promoted others.[66] Whereas public and private moralities were considered by many to be lost in the coffeehouse, they were inculcated in the theater. While Egyptian capital and potential labor were wasted in the former, they were channeled toward the well-being of Egyptian society in the latter. The theater did not deprive people of entertainment; it simply offered more edifying leisure time.

Theater could even rehabilitate criminals. An article written by a Nazmi Effendi argues that, on stage, "sin reveals itself in the worst light . . . a guilty person sees the horrible deeds of his criminal life on stage . . . he is moved and his conscience makes him feel guilt." He continues: "As children get educated in school with professors and shaykhs, adults get educated in the theater . . . when our teachers' lessons are good for our psyches, they will correct our condition."[67] In essence, stage performance was more than a school for teaching morality. Representing sin on stage forced adults—criminals beyond their school years—to see their own shameful behavior and its devastating effects before their very eyes. The effect, it was assumed, would be both personal and societal. Theater would change each viewer's psyche, and through this dramatic catharsis it would heal the whole of society.

The concept of theater as a school was not new, however. It had been in circulation well before the early twentieth-century Egyptian theater boom. The influential Islamic reformer Jamal al-Din Al-Afghani, for example, encouraged the playwright Yaʿqub Sannuʿ, one of his many disciples, to "use the theater as 'an instrument of public education.'"[68] He considered writers to be "doctors of the spirit," who were to treat society's illnesses, alongside religious figures (the *ʿulama*), by informing people "of events around the world" and warning "of the dangers of neglecting society's afflictions."[69] Earlier in the century, Egyptian scholars like Rifaʾa Rafiʾ al-Tahtawi had championed French theater as similar to *adab*, an indigenous concept that referred both to classical literature and the valued dispositions and norms of behavior that the study of such literature could instill.[70]

Tahtawi first experienced French theater when he served as leading imam on a number of Egyptian educational missions to Paris. Though students traveled to Paris ostensibly to learn professional and technical skills in law, medicine, and engineering, the many months that students spent abroad exposed them to French culture as well. Such experiences included visits to the theater. Tahtawi observed, "In reality, these plays (*alʿab*) are serious matters in a humorous form (*hazl*): one is usually taught good lessons because one sees both good and evil deeds enacted; the former is praised while the latter is condemned." "One of the wonders," he continued, "is that in the performances they quote and go into profoundly extraordinary problems of science and other complicated matters, so you would think that they were savants (*ʿulama*)."[71] For him, theater was "a great public school" and source of morality, even through comedy.[72] Access to Tahtawi's views in Egypt was considerable, as his writings about Paris were read aloud in schools and given to all senior officials in the Mehmed ʿAli administration.[73]

The idea that theater might function as an educative and moral tool intersected with British colonial justification of their civilizing mission in Egypt. In 1882, for example, an M. Ernest Wilkinson requested the following year's opera house commission, a short-term position granting him the right to administer the opera house. His letter to the Ministry of Public Works reflected concerns with Egyptian modernization: "Egypt is progressively achieving its place among the civilized and free nations, opening to its population a new era of prosperity," M. Ernest Wilkinson wrote, "but it is dependent upon certain results that are difficult to achieve . . . amongst those are education of the masses; and from history, we see that the theater, as a moral element, has significantly contributed to bringing people . . . wisdom and morals."[74] It was rare, in his eyes, for one to witness "virtue oppressed by despotism and perversity" on the stage and leave the theater without feeling one's indifference "penetrated by sentiments of justice." If granted control of the opera house, he promised to "educate" Egyptians by incorporating Egyptian actors into his plays. He explained that he hoped to inspire other Egyptian stage talents and to overcome their "ignorance" of the art of acting.

As the Arabic theater became more popular, the question no longer merely centered on the benefits of the opera house but began to address more pressing political and social concerns. The discussion took on particular urgency in light of larger nineteenth- and twentieth-century debates on the limits, benefits, and dangers of foreign cultural influence. Was theater to be a realistic representation of events, an escape from reality, a moral tool?

Syrian and Egyptian journalists in Egypt, most of whom were effendis, attached importance to the moral and educative functions of the stage. However, the moral element they extolled came not from the art of acting but from the realism of theater, the emotions it evoked, and the lessons it drew from history. They promoted theater as a critical component to a modern society.[75] The Syrian journal *al-Jinan*, for example, included an article on the benefits of theater, claiming "it is known that plays (*al-riwayat al-tashkhisiyya*), called theatricals (*al-tiyatrat*), are amongst the most important indications of progress and one of the most important reasons for the reform of customs and implanting of historical wisdom in the minds of the people."[76] An article in the journal *Wadi al-Nil* concurred, stating that plays were an "excellent innovation and a way for general education [which is] commendable because it makes people see things in their true light. They depict the events of man before his eyes [to his perception] so that he acquires the virtues and avoids the vices, apart from [having] other worthy benefits and important advantages."[77] The translator ʿUthman Jalal attempted to explain the powerful modernizing force of theater: "We have witnessed it amongst the Europeans, who started plays [*tiyatrat*], and made them a powerful force to civilise their countries. For civilisation involves training and educating the soul to adopt good morals. This can only be done by acquainting 'souls' with information about the ancient people and the histories of advanced nations."[78]

Similarly, for Antun, the theater was a space in which most directly to address diverse audiences about contemporary social problems. To him, the "consequential plays of this age are societal plays."[79] Thus, notwithstanding Antun's idiosyncrasies, his plays reveal what he and other secular reformers considered to be some of society's most urgent problems and how to correct them. They also give an indication of what effendiyya, like Antun, were identifying themselves with and against.

It was not only the stage performance that could educate turn-of-the-century Egyptian audiences; audience behavior and rules within the theater were other outlets for the effendiyya to promote, and for audiences to practice, effendi culture. Whereas older forms of street performances varied depending on whether they were performed in nobles' homes or in the street, for men or for women, modern theaters brought everyone under the same roof. Though some degree of social stratification persisted in the range of seating options and associated ticket prices, the entire audience was presented with the same scripted content and expected to behave according to a particular code of conduct.[80]

New theatrical social spaces meant a different set of rules for audience engagement than had previously existed. Those rules differed considerably from the unspoken but widely understood practices for witnessing street theater or for listening to traditional musical performances. The ethnomusicologist ʿAli Racy's analysis of behavioral norms for listening to musical performances in Egypt offers a useful point of comparison. In traditional settings, the emphasis lay in the importance of a shared emotional state between performers and listeners—a public attuned to musicians' needs and feelings. False enjoyment of music, according to Racy, was anathema to the shared experience of *tarab* (ecstatic engagement) that the performer induces. Audience members who were attuned to the feelings of a performer were to "instill within him the right mood through affectionate words of approval" as the performance took place. In other words, audiences were to actively engage with performers, for "that is what gives the singer the sense of comfort and the right disposition to engender *tarab* within you."[81] The experience of tarab was emotionally charged, relatively uninhibited, and highly interactive.

Practices such as sitting quietly through a performance were not self-evident and were discordant with local conventions for relations between performers and viewers. Yaʿqub Sannuʿ wrote about the challenges that modern theaters posed to audiences, actors, and playwrights in his book *Masrahiyyat Mulyir Misr wa Ma Yiqasihi* (Quandaries of the Egyptian Molière: A Dialogue). The book is full of anecdotes recounting the difficulties of sustaining realism in performances due to actor and audience behavior. Actors in Sannuʿ's troupe repeatedly broke out of character to greet audience members they knew and to explain that the opinions they presented on stage were not really their own. Sometimes, audience members would jump on stage to interact with performers. And, in one case, an audience that was displeased with the conclusion of a performance refused to applaud until the playwright came on stage to be scolded for it.[82]

Such challenges were addressed by a prescriptive literature that instructed audiences in listening and viewing practices deemed appropriate for the modern theater. It was not unlike a similar literature that appeared in Paris nearly a century before.[83] One example instructed viewers: "We should not disturb others when we take our seats by talking with a loud voice, as we may bother them. . . . [W]hen the audience likes things from the actors, they should clap, not whistle. If the play is funny, it is not polite to 'ha, ha' loudly or stomp feet. And when clapping, they should not bang their sticks and feet on the ground."[84] The playwright Ibrahim Ramzi added:

> If you want to see a play, be there before it starts and sit before the curtain rises. . . . [I]f the theater attendant refuses to let you in if you're late, even though he'll upset you, he is doing his duty and is to be thanked heartily for doing his job. Don't ever talk or whisper during the play or during the music. . . . [R]egrettably, most people who attend performances do not stop talking and creating noise.[85]

Ramzi urged people not to leave the playhouse in the midst of a performance, as that would indicate "they are not well-bred."[86] With such instruction, effendi playwrights explicitly aimed to train audiences in appropriate, civilized (i.e., effendi) behavior through their active engagement.

Government regulations also enforced proper behavior. Though most theaters were in Alexandria and Cairo, Port Said, Isma'iliyya, Suez, Tanta, Mansura, and Zaqaziq also had theaters that fell under government directives.[87] Regulations were to impose order, assure safety, and monitor stage productions. A 1904 legislative act, for example, enumerated acceptable numbers and widths of doors (based on the number of visitors) and regulated lighting and availability of fire extinguishers. Amendments in 1911 further regulated theater interiors and set forth guidelines for safety inspections. Furthermore, they stipulated that space be made available for police to watch the performances. Names and information about actors, dates and hours of performances, and scripts or performance programs had to be presented to police in advance of shows, and "plays contradicting public order and morals" were forbidden.[88] Unless special permissions were granted, all theaters were to close by 1 A.M., and contravention of the law could lead anywhere from fines to permanent closure of performance spaces. Such regulations applied not only to tiatros (theaters) but also to café-concerts and salas (a more neutral term for the maligned cabaret). Representations on stage, proper audience behavior, and submission to safety requirements functioned together to shape a modern effendi.

In its review of Antun's play *Misr al-Jadida*, the journal *al-Ahali* depicted an opening scene of a boat in Alexandria's harbor focusing on three French and two Egyptian passengers coming to "suck Egypt's blood."[89] "The thing that we most fear for Egypt," the author claims, "is the sea that tosses these people upon us." Most reviews of the play concurred. *Al-Watan*'s critic wished "everyone could see it," as it "accurately reflected" events in the country.[90]

Early on, the audience is acquainted with the bloated character Muhafhaf Pasha, one of the boat's passengers. He turns to a fellow passenger, a married French woman named Pauline, and takes her hand: "I don't know if we'll meet again after we get off the boat," he tells her, and just in case that is so, he gives her his card with his home address written on it. He adds, however, that he spends most of his time at elite hotels: the Heliopolis Palace, Shepheards, or the Continental, all reputed for hosting primarily European patrons. "I'm there mostly every night. In case Mr. Etienne [her husband] asks about my whereabouts (and he gives her a suggestive look that indicates he means her, not Etienne), you'll find me in one of those places."[91]

Muhafhaf Pasha personified one of Antun's greatest concerns: self-indulgent local elites. He was very much a product and symbol of that world, one that Antun considered inimical to a new, modern Egypt. Muhafhaf, whose name is a humorous Arabic word meaning "flighty," is described as a man with a big body and bloated belly who speaks fluent French. His overuse of French was a symbol of unchecked Westernization, a form of excess that severed all ties to a stable, grounded, indigenous culture. Despite Antun's own love of French thought, culture, and language, he was concerned about its appropriate usage. Speaking French for personal gain and status enhancement as Muhafhaf Pasha did was suspect, whereas Antun's own use of French language to access new ideas that may be applied locally for the greater good was appropriate. Muhafhaf indulges his desires and squanders his wealth at Christo's coffeehouse to the point of bankruptcy, mirroring Egypt's own precipitous financial decline under the leadership of Isma'il. Though Muhafhaf is married, he uses Christo as a middleman to arrange for purchasing the French maid as a nanny for his children, though it is clear that his intentions are less innocent.[92] Such scenes reflected concerns among the larger population that local elites conspired with colonial powers for their own gain. Such leisurely self-indulgence and indifference to any responsibility to the *umma*, or nation, were anathema to Antun's New Egypt.

Overwesternization, overspending, and overindulgence would lead to both Muhafhaf's and Egypt's downfall. Similar errors had already made Egypt beholden to European economic and political occupation. In the late nineteenth and early twentieth centuries, the Egyptian upper class was shifting as indigenous major landowners (*a'yan*) increasingly intermarried with Turco-Circassian urban bureaucratic and military elites (the *dhawat*) to create a new Turco-Egyptian upper class (*ibn al-dhawat*). This often meant migration of *a'yan* to urban areas, despite the fact that large landownership remained central to their identities.

But more than landownership, wealth, and access to power characterized elites. While titles like "bey" and "pasha" distinguished them in one way, their lifestyles also set them apart from other Egyptians. Though it would be another decade or so before pashas gathered in exclusive social and sporting clubs like the Muhammad 'Ali Club and the Gezira Sporting Club, many vacationed abroad in Europe and Istanbul, smoked the *shisha* (water pipe), and played games in cafés and bars like the Soult Parlour and Splendid Bar.[93] They sometimes included their wives in entertainments by taking them out for nights at the opera or inviting guests into their homes for (gender-segregated) evenings of gambling and live musical performances.[94] As the center of Cairo developed, especially around 'Imad al-Din Street, dance halls and cabarets increasingly drew elites alongside other patrons, which created opportunities for their lavish spending, drinking, dancing, womanizing, and mixing with other classes.[95] Theatergoers were made to understand that prodigality—and those who engaged in it—could not lead Egypt into a modernity that retained political, economic, and cultural integrity.

Christo and Etienne unambiguously stood for those Europeans who exploited Egyptian resources for personal gain. Christo's establishment is described as a fancy coffeehouse in front with access to a casino/cabaret in the back. His income clearly derives not only from legitimate business but also from lending money to Egyptians at exorbitant interest rates.[96]

A number of scenes highlight the ways Christo exploits Egyptians in need of funds. In one case, a peasant couple approaches him for a loan. Christo says to them, "I don't have money right now because the *ibn-al-dhawat* [sons of the urban notables] held it." Saying "held it," instead of "took it," is a purposeful error written into the script. His foreignness, indicated by his poor Arabic, is a source of comic relief.

The wife responds: "Must the *ibn al-dhawat* always get in our way? They take our crops from the fields, and we have to go borrowing from here and there. We're the ones who plant and reap, and we get nothing. They also take the money that we need. Lord protect the fellahin from the *dhawat* [urban notables] and their children!" Christo appeases her: "You're right . . . we all depend on you . . . and without you we're no good." The husband, innocently laughing, responds: "And we, too, are nothing without you. You are our goodness and blessing, ya khawaga" [European foreigner]. Off to the side, a servant cleaning chairs acts as a type of Greek chorus, commenting on the main action of the play. "The lamb is praising the butcher," he says to himself. Christo tells the peasant couple to come back for money the next day, and as they walk out, trusting in Christo and praising his kindness, Christo mutters: "By God, the people of Egypt are pathetic."[97]

Shortly afterward, a wealthy customer, presumably one of the ibn al-dhawat referenced above, approaches Christo, also to borrow money. Christo respectfully stands to greet him, asking, "Honorable bey, you were waiting, and I didn't know?" The man responds, "I need 200 [Egyptian] pounds right away." Christo slowly replies, "At your service. But, you know that the amount now is 1500LE," indicating that the totality of the man's loans and interest accrued is significant. The man brushes it off. He needs the money immediately, and Christo complies, bowing to him as he exits. Despite the show of respect, Christo repeats the same sentiment: "By God the people of Egypt are pathetic."[98] To their faces, Christo treats people of means with greater respect than those without. But his refrain about the pathetic state of Egyptians gives credence to Antun's concern about vice and the dangers of European exploitation.

Between 1836 and 1907, Western European, Greek, and Armenian populations in Egypt jumped from 3,000 to 147,000; thus, concern about their influence was not surprising.[99] Many were British bureaucrats in Cairo, but others worked as missionaries, teachers, soldiers, merchants, journalists, amateur actors, business owners, and in various other capacities. British bureaucrats had their own exclusive social and sports clubs for recreation. In Alexandria, where Antun lived from 1897 to 1905, Greeks, Armenians, Italians, and others also effectively created their own communities, replete with schools, voluntary associations, hospitals, and even graveyards.[100] Legal structures contributed to the social separation of many European groups from the indigenous population, most notably the Capitulations that the Ottoman Empire had established in the sixteenth century to grant foreign merchants exemptions from local laws and taxes. Though the Capitulations originally were intended to encourage commercial activity, they became a source of great resentment among local populations as Europeans increasingly abused the system, using it to claim extraterritorial rights. In Egypt, the system fostered inequalities between European and Egyptian businesses and workers, as Europeans were paid more and Egyptian skilled labor was shunned in favor of European workers.[101] Furthermore, the Capitulations effectively blocked Egyptian jurisdiction over activities like drug trafficking and prostitution.[102]

Misr al-Jadida's representation of Europeans reflected these problems. The play depicted businessmen as exploitative and cast them as individuals who utterly lacked moral character or a sense of responsibility to the larger society. Christo's butchering of the Arabic language was a way to add some levity to the portrayal, and Antun's subplot of the victimized French maid was a nod to the fact that not all Europeans were evil, but his focus was on those who conceivably could ruin Egypt's future. At the end of the story, it is not only Fu'ad who is left standing—Christo and his establishment remain as well. They persist because those who indulge themselves in his café are powerless to destroy Christo so long as they give in to their base desires. Others, like the peasant (*fellahi*) couple who borrow money from him, are caught in a web of debt from which they cannot escape. Though Antun does not expressly state who is at fault, the implications are clear. Capitulations that enable Christo to run such an establishment unfettered by local laws, unchecked desires to which his patrons succumb, and economic conditions that victimize the fellahin are part of an old system that endangered Egypt's ability to renew itself.

The representation of fellah as victim was one of an evolving set of representations that appeared in the early twentieth century. From the mid-nineteenth century onward, the restructuring of agriculture to produce cotton as a single cash crop weakened peasant families. In the nineteenth century, the fellahin increasingly were forced to work as wage laborers or to migrate to cities as a result of the development of capitalist agriculture and a monetized rural economy. Though land laws supported fellahi ownership of land, indebtedness resulted in a high rate of land loss, and in order to pay for seed, animals, and monthly tax installments the fellahin were forced to borrow at high rates of interest.[103] The fellahin expressed their grievances in folklore, songs, jokes, and poetry, where issues related to land reform, old feudal lords, socialism, and contemporary events appeared.[104] Such cultural forms lightened hardships, entertained, celebrated the living, and lamented the dead.

For Egyptian nationalists, with whom Antun aligned himself in this period, the voice of the fellah was of less concern than the fellah as symbol. Though journals during the late nineteenth century commonly represented the fellah as ignorant, backward, and superstitious—in contrast to the effendiyya who published these journals—his image slowly evolved into a timeless symbol of the authentic Egyptian and the wise font of respectable folk tradition. The intricacies and difficulties of peasant life were rarely addressed in any meaningful, nuanced manner, as nationalist concerns never fully coincided with those of the fellah himself. Thus the fellahi couple who appear in *Misr al-Jadida* are depicted as victims of a system that is out of their control. The fellahin raise crops in a land dependent on agricultural production, and they are necessarily a part of Antun's "new Egypt," but their role in the play seems merely to remind audiences of their victimhood and the inhumane consequences of greed and exploitation.

Though he does not explicitly attend to how the problems of fellahi indebtedness might be addressed, Antun's views on economic advancement hint at his solutions. Antun distrusted Western capitalism, a system he felt was ready to devour the Arab region. For him, hope for the most equitable future lay in a form of socialism that featured more prevalently in his other writings, like *The Three Cities* (1901) and *Urushalim al-Jadid* (New Jerusalem) (1905), which he printed in his journal *al-Jami'a* in 1904. In *New Jerusalem*, the Christian promise of love and tolerance plays out in a secular, religiously tolerant context in which society is egalitarian, work is collective and nonexploitative, and the wealthy are responsible for helping the poor.[105] Though Antun does not develop any of these ideas in *Misr al-Jadida*, the call for audiences to work hard and "attend to the blessings of the country" might well have been a reference not only to the Nile, history, and surrounding land but also to the fellahin who long occupied and worked that land. As symbols of an eternal Egypt, and as a group that members of the effendiyya hoped to bring into the nationalist fold, the fellahin stood at the heart of effendi campaigns to unify Egyptians in the name of an independent Egypt.

The "woman question," too, was a fundamental effendi concern and was uniquely manifested in *Misr al-Jadida* in the character of Almaz. Likely named after the real-life performer and wife of the singer ʿAbdu al-Hamuli, Almaz's role as a singer of questionable virtue embodied preconceived notions regarding female cabaret performers in early twentieth-century Egypt.[106] Cabarets were only one of several sites in which women performed at the turn of the century. Women were actresses, singers, and dancers, and they performed in places as varied as the opera house, tiatros, people's homes, and the street.[107] The context, audience, and content of performances all figured in to the degree of respectability accorded to these female performers: women who performed in front of men in settings that permitted alcohol and drug use were among the least respected. Women who performed in cabarets typically sat and drank with customers between stints singing or dancing onstage. This practice of drinking with customers, known as *fath*, from the Arabic verb "to open," typically yielded the evening's greatest profits for both performer and cabaret owner. Female performers kept a certain percentage of the profits, often amounting to half the pay they took home every night, from the drinks they and their customers consumed.[108] Such remuneration promoted heavy drinking and creative strategies for encouraging wealthy men to spend lavishly on drinks. Though prostitution was not necessarily involved, women might consent to it in order to retain wealthy patrons and earn more money. Thus, despite the fact that women were not paid by cabaret owners to engage in prostitution, most female performers acquired reputations as morally dubious.

Antun's representation of Almaz, however, is more ambiguous. On the one hand, she appears as a seductress, one of many whom Christo uses to trap patrons, and she almost succeeds in tempting Fu'ad Effendi to destroy his family and personal honor to be with her. On the other hand, in conversation with a friend, Almaz expresses her happiness sharing a home with Fu'ad, secure in a life with a man who loves her. As she puts it: "I give away all types of freedom for this happiness."[109] Upon discovering that Fu'ad already has a family, Almaz's heartfelt statement about her own dreams and aspirations cast her as a lost soul, victim to the vices of Old Egypt. She was a woman who might have been saved. Rather than exhibit pride in her vocation, she grieves: "The home—the home is a woman's paradise and kingdom."[110]

In some ways, nationalist concerns with women's status in Egypt were reflected in their personification of Egypt *as* a woman who needed to be honored and protected.[111] This was complicated by the fact that effendis sought suitable female counterparts—women who shared similar values and common goals—to be wives and mothers to their children. Although Almaz, as an unmarried public performer, does not live up to those specific ideals, Antun uses her character to highlight the need for both Egyptian women and the figurative "woman,"—that is, Egypt—to be saved by the effendiyya.

In some ways, Antun's views on women correlated with those of the judge Qasim Amin, often designated the "father of Egyptian feminism."[112] Though the scholar Leila Ahmad has insightfully delineated the ways in which Amin merely substituted Western for Eastern patriarchy, Amin's widely read books on the status of women in Egypt articulated a perspective on the role and needs of women that many of his cohort shared.[113] His position called for reform in marriage and divorce, education for women, and unveiling.[114] The emphasis for Amin and others was on domestic vocations as opposed to work in a profession. And the scholar Beth Baron broadened this patriarchal history of feminism in Egypt by noting that female intellectuals in pre-1919 Egypt, too, were concerned with expanding and elevating the role of women, usually within the context of the family.[115]

Female intellectuals at the turn of the twentieth century, in fact, published a host of journals (and other writings) in which they articulated beliefs regarding the role of women in a modernizing Egypt. Though often conflated under the label of "feminists," the women embodied a range of perspectives and prescriptions that fell, broadly, into three major categories: secularist (mostly minorities who focused on language and education); modernist (those who promoted innovative interpretations of Islam to improve their status within the family); and Islamist (those who stressed the rights that Islam had given women in its "truest" form and called for a return to it).[116] Like the secularist feminists, Farah Antun, a member of an ethnic and religious minority, was less concerned about aligning changes to women's status with Qur'anic teaching and more interested in promoting education and skills women needed to properly care for home and family. He did not agree with a segment of women who defined feminism differently, who saw family as anathema to freedom and solely emphasized political, social, and economic equality for women. Though he contemplated the idea of women working outside the home, and his sister, Rose, was a teacher and journalist, his years in New York City aroused anxieties with regard to women who, in his eyes, behaved like men.[117] Even less would he embrace the cause of another segment of feminists who advocated stricter seclusion and heavier veiling to increase women's status.[118]

It appears, however, that the majority of female intellectuals and effendiyya could agree on a few prescriptions for women. Their writings commonly promoted education, companionate marriage, "scientific" domestic practices, and patriotism.[119] Thus Almaz's yearning for a home as "paradise and kingdom" reflected a shared ideal propagated by male and female intellectuals of the day. The problem, however, lay in Almaz's failure to acquire this respectable position in society. When she finds that Fu'ad has lied to her, Almaz leaves him and returns to her work for Christo. What does one make of the woman who yearns for a respectable life but cannot attain it? Is she merely a casualty in the process of "effendification," in the transition to a new Egypt; a victim; or an agent who should be held liable for her fate? After her relationship with Fu'ad ends, Almaz describes her appearance and voice as a "constant spring, but inside, eternal mourning . . . if only you knew how much I suffered."[120] As Antun's focus is on the effendi as prime agent, hope, and model for a modernizing Egypt, Almaz, like the fellah, is cast in a position where only someone other than herself can save her. In most intellectuals' writings, the limited financial and social resources available to lower-class women were sometimes addressed but rarely figured in to prescriptions for a respectable life. It was the effendi who had to marry her to save and deliver her to the home for which she longed.

And yet, her return to Christo's establishment was a triumph: "Egypt has turned upside-down because of her. Princes and pashas and the whole world come to hear and see Almaz. And so many gifts! And the papers praising her! And the photos! The people forgot 'Abdu."[121] Antun does not appear to portray this success in a negative light. Further, when Fu'ad returns after his sojourn in the Sudan, it is Almaz who puts the final end to their relationship. Fu'ad offers to marry her, to make her a second wife. But she responds, "What I tolerated, no woman could tolerate twice in her life," and Fu'ad accepts her decision. Despite all that she has lost, Almaz is a moral figure, almost noble in her suffering.

Once faced with the damage—moral, financial, emotional—that he inflicted upon so many, Fu'ad's determination to make amends leads him to atone for his indulgences. In a melodramatic moment, he successfully intervenes to save the French maid from prostitution. He moves his family to take a job in the Sudan, then returns to Egypt only after he earns back the fortune he lost in his transgressions. Fu'ad's redemption was primarily a rededication to hard work and economic self-sufficiency, and the Sudan—considered a place of exile but also a source of economic opportunity—was a site for self-inflicted punishment and reform.[122] Desiring to thank the nation that provided him this opportunity for renewal, Fu'ad tells Almaz that he has returned to Egypt with two Sudanese boys he intends to raise in Egypt.[123] Framing this patriarchal undertaking as an act of charity, Antun echoes ambiguous Egyptian nationalist conceptions of Sudanese people as siblings in need of civilizing.[124]

As was apparent in Fu'ad's characterization, the effendi was more defined by his values and lifestyle than his background. Both Fu'ad and Muhafhaf Pasha came from the same wealthy family, but it was Fu'ad's decision to work for a living, focus on his family, and help others in need that set him apart as a member of the effendiyya, a leader of New Egypt. For Antun, Fu'ad and others like him were Egypt's only hope for escape from the decadence that Muhafhaf Pasha, Etienne, Pauline, and Christo embodied. Together, elite and foreign exploitation represented poison and decay, the danger in Egypt's succumbing to all things foreign. In the early twentieth century, as the Egyptian woman and the fellah were rendered into symbols of the Egyptian nation, the devotion, respectability, and protective role of a faithful effendi was both literal and figurative. In the context of the family, the effendi was to encourage his wife's education, consider her a companion in the home, and remain monogamous.[125] Outside the family, the effendi was expected to speak and act publicly on behalf of the umma (nation). As the historian Michael Gasper notes, "to be civilized meant to act decisively and in public . . . to redress problems in society through reform."[126] For Antun and many others, modern theaters offered public spaces in which to perform this effendi identity and to use performance to improve the greater society.

For all its talk, the government was limited, at best, in its support of Arabic theater in Egypt. In 1907, the nationalist paper *al-Liwa'* published a harsh criticism of an Egyptian government "which professes such pious zeal for the spread of education by means of Arabic [and] can afford to subsidise [*sic*] French Opera in Cairo but has not a cent to bestow upon developing Arabic drama or Arabic music."[127]

Theater faced other problems as well. There was always the chance that the representation of vice on stage and the mixing of male and female audience members might have unintended negative effects. The assumed merits of theater were, conversely, potential sources of danger. If the theater could be a school for progress and morality, then might it not also school audiences in the vices performed on stage? As Tahtawi warned, the exemplary, didactic benefits of Parisian theater did not preclude it from offering "Satan's temptations."[128]

The writer Muhammad al-Muwaylihi's fictional romance *Hadith 'Isa Ibn Hisham* (The Narrative of 'Isa Ibn Hisham) encapsulated such concerns in his chapter on the theater.[129] In his book, which first appeared between 1898 and 1900 as a serial in the journal *Misbah al-Sharq*, Muwaylihi addresses his contemporaries' concerns about the growth of new Arabic theaters, their educational role, and their potentially hazardous dissemination of the worst elements of Western culture. The story's main character, ʿIsa Ibn Hisham, narrates a series of episodes describing and critiquing life in turn-of-the-century Cairo. One of the final chapters of the book recounts an evening at the Arab theater, and in it, ʿIsa richly details the physical space and audiences who attended the show:

> Having reached the theatre where plays are performed, we mingled with the people as they went in, men and women of all shapes and sizes. . . . [T]hey were all raising a hue and cry; joking and laughing, sharing abuse, and punching and kicking each other. On looking upwards at the boxes and tiers, we saw various compartments with curtains drawn back to reveal beautiful women wearing pearls and gems on their necks, queens of the women's quarters in palatial mansions.[130]

In the balcony seats at the top of the theater, the "mob" were "boxed in, horde upon horde, like traders at a sheep market where people never stop arguing and fighting."[131] He depicts a tremendous range of theatergoers—rich and poor, male and female.

ʿIsa describes the play onstage, an overwrought love story; the first act ends with actors speaking about "stealing, fraud, betrayal, treachery and murder at one moment, and then about committing various other crimes, such as embezzlement and kidnapping."[132] Its final scene involves a dramatic standoff between the young man and his lover's father in which the characters get wounded, cry, and faint. ʿIsa and his friend leave during the second intermission when police arrive to break up a fight in the smoking room.

During the first intermission of the play described in al-Muwaylihi's story, ʿIsa Ibn Hisham and his bored companion, the Pasha, debate the merits and vices of the theater, with ʿIsa explaining that the theater "among Western peoples is acknowledged as being a basic aspect of education and culture, a rich source of virtues and worthy traits. . . . It's regarded as the twin of the press."[133] ʿIsa and the Pasha's discussion echoed persistent notions among elites and the effendiyya of theater as a "civilizing tool" for the wider Egyptian population.

The Pasha, however, is unconvinced. To him, Western society does not appear to have benefited much from the moral education of theater, and he suspects that may be due to its method of illustrating vice to convince audiences to disavow it. In doing so, "robbers and other cunning rogues have received an excellent training by attending performances of plays." Rather than uncritically importing this form of theater, he advises that "plays performed in front of audiences made up of Eastern people must be relevant to the conditions in which they live"—in terms of both content and circumstances surrounding performance.[134]

Arabic theater's success ultimately depended on the participation of indigenous patrons, a supportive press, and local audiences.[135] Discourse on the moralizing and civilizing power of theater did not always align with reality, since performers had audiences to please. Dramatic actors and playwrights soon learned that their successes or failures were very much connected to commercial realities. Audiences had viewing preferences, and performers who ignored them simply could not succeed. Though the play *Misr al-Jadida* gained a measure of respectability by opening in the Khedivial Opera House, it attracted local audiences in Arabic theaters only by adding the famed singer Salama Hijazi to the performance.[136] Hijazi sang between acts, and, as Antun noted, his voice was what people came to hear. The lead actor, Jurj Abyad, was respected, but Hijazi was the draw.[137] Effendi playwrights and actors quickly recognized that audience demands did not always align with the ideals that certain of their members promoted. Less overtly didactic forms of theater—vaudeville, cabarets, and folk theater—appealed to greater numbers.

To make a living, Antun turned increasingly to writing more popular, vaudeville-style plays that appealed to audiences, drawing the ire of fellow playwrights who saw this as a vulgarization of an art form. His work included approximately twelve adaptations of European light entertainments—plays and operettas that he sold for approximately 100 Egyptian pounds apiece.[138] One of his critics was the esteemed playwright Muhammad Taymur (1892–1921) who, over the course of his short lifetime, contributed much to debates on the purpose of theater. Taymur had spent three years studying law in Paris, where he became a regular theater attendee.[139] His time abroad was cut short by World War I, which broke when he was vacationing in Egypt and blocked his return to France. Before his untimely death at a young age, Taymur wrote a number of essays and articles on theater in which he enumerated what he considered the criteria of a good play. His critique of the quality of Egyptian theater was less about morality and more about principles of drama to which he felt Egyptian playwrights did not subscribe. For him, Egyptian theater repeatedly fell short of European theater. To help overcome this, he advocated the Egyptianization of foreign (especially French) literature to adapt it to local conditions. His interest in Egyptianizing literature was matched by his distaste for melodrama, vaudeville, revues, and other types of seemingly trivial performance that relied on emotion rather than sound characterization and plotlines.[140] Each of the plays that he wrote raised social concerns—elite and middle-class problems, drug and alcohol abuse, generational conflicts, artificial Westernization—and ended with a moral imperative for the audience.[141]

In 1920, Taymur published a series of articles in his journal, *al-Sufur*, that put various playwrights "on trial" for the quality of their contributions to the theater.[142] One of those playwrights was Farah Antun, who, according to a cohort of esteemed Western playwrights including Shakespeare, Molière, Goethe, and others, had become lazy in his later years and wrote bad plays simply to make money. The judge accuses Antun of producing poorly written plays that neglected poetic language in favor of vulgar prose. He charges Antun with forcing the respected dramatic actor Jurj Abyad to sing and recite prose, both of which, the judge argues, contributed to the death of Abyad's career. Furthermore, he condemns Antun's plays as Arabicized forms of vaudeville, a form of entertainment that Taymur held in very low esteem. The fictional Antun pleads for mercy, conceding that his plays were inappropriate for Abyad and not true art. He argues, however, that "this is the type of work that appeals to the larger population's tastes."[143] At the trial's end, Antun is banned from writing plays for ten years "in hopes that the time will be long enough for the Egyptian public to forget this unprofitable type of play."[144] The punishment could have been more severe but was reduced in recognition that Antun's early plays, including *Misr al-Jadida*, had edified society.

Concern with the vulgarization of theater points to a larger issue within and among the effendiyya. As they worked to define and differentiate themselves from other Egyptians, effendis were battling not only external influences but also the ambiguities of their own complex, diverse, and changeable identities. Plays that too closely resembled elements of street theater—with traditional music and scatological humor—threatened to identify the effendiyya too closely with folk culture, a culture not fitting with effendi notions of a modern Egypt, but also one to which many of them were rooted by birth. Thus, performances of musical vaudeville and women's cabarets, in particular, were dangers on two fronts. On the one hand, they offered seemingly mindless entertainments connected to what were considered imported Western vices of alcohol, public women, and drug use. On the other, they celebrated elements of *sha'bi*, or popular (the implication being "unmodern") culture, in spaces intended to offer modern lessons and entertainments.

As Egyptian effendi nationalists cultivated a sense of unity within their own social group, as much as in broader Egyptian society, the openness and fluidity of the category "effendi" became more constrained. Characteristics of Egyptianness were circumscribed to create the myth of a single Egyptian identity; inevitably, voices that did not fit in were excluded. Thus "dissonant cultures and voices—women, minorities, social outcasts, the poor"—had to be minimized, neglected or erased.[145] Trivializing their interests and concerns could do this; elevating them to stand as symbols of the unified nation could as well.[146]

Ironically, Syrians like Antun, who had effectively pioneered the indigenous press and contributed much to debates over Egyptian identity, came to be numbered with other "intruders," that is to say, as people who exploited Egyptian wealth and openness.[147] In effect, Antun's critique of foreigners in *Misr al-Jadida* was effectively turned into an accusation against him and his compatriots. Though the fluidity of the category "effendi" initially allowed Antun and other Syrians to participate in imagining New Egypt, the narrowing conception of who embodied that New Egypt ultimately came to exclude them.

CHAPTER 3

The Story of Ahmad the Rat

After the evening prayer, the wedding music started. It was Cairo, 1909, and the twelve-member improvisational troupe led by Ahmad al-Far was tasked with getting the wedding party on its feet. One member held a torch to light the area while others played the *tabla* and *zummara*, a traditional drum and flute. A performer dressed as a woman encouraged the male guests to dance.

Soon, troupe leader al-Far (aka The Rat) arrived, a short man carrying a big stick and wearing his trademark enormous *ʿimma*, or turban, with a southern Egyptian cloak called a *zaʿbut*.[1] "Hey lads," he called out, "inhabitants of Cairo!" And with that, men gathered around al-Far in a circle called a *samer*, awaiting a short play.[2] On that day it was *Riwayat al-Saʿidi* (The Upper Egyptian's Story), and the actors' wordplay and quick pace bent to the whims of an audience that called out encouragement, critique, disgust, and pleasure. Refusing any linear trajectory, rational dialogue, or polite language, the play irreverently mocked everything and everyone it could, not least the new Western-educated professional and intellectual strata of Egyptian society, the *effendiyya*. In short, the play was the opposite of everything *effendis* cast as "modern." This was precisely the point.

Depending on the host family's financial resources, a wedding celebration like this might last for several days, and troupes like al-Far's were central to the diversions. Festivities might involve singers, dancers, and actors who entertained guests in different areas of the house. Upstairs, female performers fêted the women of the party who celebrated separately from the men, while in front of the house, or in its courtyard, male musicians, actors, and sometimes women who sang from behind a screen entertained the men.[3] Mimics, or *muqallidin*, were some of the most popular types of performers, and the *muqallid* al-Far was known for cleverly mimicking village life, women, and animals. He performed most often at private weddings, but also in tents for religious celebrations (*mawalid*) and in neighborhood coffeehouses. In the early twentieth century, the more famous mimics even began performing on the proscenium stage at the end of, or during the intervals between, more serious, reputable Arabic plays.

Most of al-Far's audiences comprised people collectively referred to as the "*shaʿb*," a loose term meaning "the people" that included trade merchants, craftsmen, and the broader working, urban population. Over time, it would also include a growing number of factory workers and urbanites living in older sections of the city considered to be *shaʿbi* quarters.[4] Whereas for much of the nineteenth century elites saw the great majority of Egyptians as nothing more than an undifferentiated mob in need of reform, by the turn of the century they became, to effendis, "a potential constituency to be mobilized."[5] As the number of effendis grew, they established a network of people's night schools (*madaris al-shaʿb*) to teach things like literacy, arithmetic, ethics, hygiene, and history to workers and artisans.[6] The goal was to turn them into good Egyptian nationalists.

How the shaʿb experienced these interventions is less clear.[7] Generally speaking, everyday concerns and realities of shaʿbi existence—family life, faith, joys, hardships, hopes—have received little attention, chiefly due to the difficulty of accessing a segment of the population whose forms of communication were primarily aural and oral. Scholars like Liat Kozma and Hanan Hammad have demonstrated that court and police records are invaluable sources to access the realities of nonelite lives, but because such sources record instances of transgression, their utility for illuminating a fuller sense of everyday life, imagination, and humor are limited.[8]

For these reasons, closer examination of *fasl mudhik*, or farcical playlets, performed at weddings, coffeehouses, and theaters offers a rare and provocative glimpse of the shaʿb who enthusiastically attended and engaged with them. Such skits raised social issues and invited audience members' active engagement in the shaping of storylines.[9] The few existing records of these popular entertainments offer an illuminating point of entry into the social concerns, interests, humor, and imagination of a subaltern sociocultural stratum that has been largely understood from the perspectives of cultural and political elites.

Street performances—versions of which appeared in private celebrations and local coffeehouse stages—had long been channels to mock foreign and local elites, but in the early twentieth century the presence of European colonial officials, along with the new personage of the effendi, who claimed authentic Egyptianness and authority to speak for "the nation," became a fresh focus of critique. While the effendi rooted his authenticity in his unique blend of tradition and modern science and education, shaʿbi performers questioned his validity and challenged what they interpreted as his posturing.

To these performers—and presumably their audiences—effendis were an ambitious group that had become unmoored from their origins and thus lost their authenticity. Instead, the shaʿb were, in the anthropologist Walter Armbrust's words, "Egyptian[s] who depended less obviously, if at all, on the modernizing foreign order than did functionaries of the bourgeoisie."[10] In short, the shaʿb were the real *awlad al-balad*, the real Egyptians, the salt of the earth.[11]

Unofficial folk culture, seen in street and private performances, functioned as what the Russian philosopher Mikhail Bakhtin termed a "second culture," "the antithesis of elite and official culture . . . at the center of intellectualism."[12] Its language and subject matter engaged with and opposed both British colonial power and an increasingly hegemonic form of Egyptian nationalism being cultivated and disseminated by effendis.[13] As the shaʿb were losing socioeconomic power in a changing context that favored foreigners and elites, the emphasis on cultural identity became even more important. The stage was a place of conscious self-representation, a space to depict the realities of life but also to offer possibilities for alternatives. In other words, it was a space in which to play with and forge a modern identity. The extent to which any sort of consensus was cultivated is less important than the possibility—or the threat—the shaʿb posed for doing so. An increasingly nationalist effendiyya, one that was constructing itself in the very same period, was concerned with limiting the expression of the shaʿb whom they were busily co-opting into their own historical narrative.

Effendis had an ambivalent relationship to shaʿbi performances. The plays were, after all, witty and certainly had a transgressive appeal. Performers used colloquial and coarse slang rather than the high Arabic (*fusha*), knowing full well that they were provoking the elites they lampooned, and intellectual, cultural, and political elites were both drawn to and disgusted by the vulgarity of shaʿbi performances. Certainly, when shaʿbi skits were incorporated as entr'actes in more serious plays, the formality of the stage, along with its typically effendi audiences, framed and controlled content that might offend bourgeois tastes. Outside the middle-class theater, however, street performance was not under the same constraints. It had the threatening potential of offering alternative views of identity and modernity to a growing number of urban workers who would slowly see themselves as a unique—and powerful—stratum of society.

Yet even as shaʿbi performance challenged and mocked effendi norms and narratives, it validated them by naming and representing them. Enacting effendi norms gave them life.

The dialogue between shaʿbi and effendi norms and ideals was quite literal in the cases discussed in this chapter. In hopes of softening or elevating shaʿbi performance messages, some effendis engaged in a kind of passive sabotage, inserting their own lines and dialogues into written scripts of shaʿbi plays. Regardless of intent, such actions reclaimed some element of control of the overall message and literally inscribed an emerging effendi narrative onto alternatives that challenged it.

Just like the term "effendi," the term "shaʿb" does not map easily onto a particular socioeconomic class. One's place of residence and way of life were the primary elements in the designation, more so than religion, occupation, education, dress, or speech.[14] To describe something as "shaʿbi," as the anthropologist Walter Armbrust describes, is to say it is "'of the people' . . . local, vernacular, and from the proverbial 'street' . . . a virtual synonym of 'folkloric.'"[15] Depending on who uses the term, "shaʿbi" might "suggest authenticity, savvy, cleverness, and an engaged connection to one's humble yet honoured origins and social environment . . . [or] it can imply being poor-quality, grossly impoverished, unsophisticated, and downright uncouth."[16]

The composition of individuals associated with the shaʿb would shift as urbanization and industrialization transformed Egyptian society. By 1907, the labor force in Cairo was approximately a half-million people.[17] In relative numbers, the population of laborers was a minority, but the historians Joel Beinin and Zachary Lockman argue that there emerged "an embryonic labor movement, which was to make its presence increasingly felt, politically as well as economically" in the early decades of the twentieth century.[18]

Urban workers' numbers increased due to economic shifts in Egypt over the second half of the nineteenth century, and especially in the two or three decades before World War I. In that period, foreign and Egyptian state investment promoted the rise of large-scale industrial and transport enterprises. Investments centered on the development of goods and services for a European and Europeanized urban population. They also supported the processing of agricultural raw material and the growth of a transport infrastructure. Changing agrarian relations between peasants and the state over the nineteenth century meant that *fellahin* (peasants) increasingly needed to rent land, work for large landholders, or hire themselves out as wage laborers to survive.[19] Thus, *fellahi* workers began to migrate in large numbers from the countryside to towns in search of work in the emerging free-labor market.[20] At the same time, urban artisans and craftsmen experienced the decline of a guild system that formerly had protected them and their crafts. The transition to a capitalist economy meant that certain handcrafts, such as copper vessels, wooden latticework, and woven materials, declined due to competition with urban and foreign industries.[21] Following these shifts, many artisans found it necessary to turn to wage labor to make a living. Such changes increased the number of people included in the "shaʿb" category.

The pace of change was gradual, and any sense of unified social identity was limited in the late nineteenth century. Many peasants still had ties to land and only worked in industry seasonally or indirectly. Linguistic and other differences between Egyptian and foreign skilled workers who toiled alongside each other divided them. Industrial development was complex and uneven, and the embryonic working class was heterogeneous.[22]

Spurred by events such as the 1906 Dinshaway incident, urban intellectuals and political leaders began to reach out and include artisans, merchants, and workers in their demand for an independent "Egypt for the Egyptians." By 1908, the word "shaʿb" underwent a semantic shift, as Egyptian nationalists increasingly used the word with more specific connotations. As the historian Zachary Lockman explains, "It was not quite identical with 'the nation,' but nevertheless suggested its great majority, its 'authentic' core, was the repository of its nation-ness."[23] The change marked a shift in nationalist thinking that perceived the great majority of Egyptians as something more than an uncivilized mob. Instead, they became "a potential constituency to be mobilized."[24] Muhammad Farid, the leader of the Nationalist Party, for example, started to publicly criticize terrible working conditions and the absence of labor laws in Egypt in 1908. At the same time, the party's newspaper, *al-Liwa'*, published articles in support of labor struggles. Members of the party also helped to establish the network of madaris al-shaʿb, the night schools teaching literacy, arithmetic, geography, religion, ethics, hygiene, and history to workers and artisans.[25] By 1910 there were eight of these schools in Cairo and more in provincial cities. Thousands of workers and artisans were connected to the schools in their first two years.

Night schools were not the first attempts to educate and mobilize workers, but the rise of mass politics in the early twentieth century propelled concern about the shaʿb to the forefront of arguments favoring mass education. Effendis were not the only ones concerned with bringing an educated shaʿb into their fold. Individuals of various ideological persuasions, including communists, socialists, and anarchists, also attempted to diffuse messages and mobilize workers in support of their particular social prescriptions.[26]

Theater was intimately connected to projects to educate workers. From as early as the 1870s, the Egyptian nationalist ʿAbdullah al-Nadim used school plays to help poor and orphaned children.[27] The scholar Ilham Khouri-Makdisi has shown how the Francisco Ferrer play of 1909 disseminated radical socialist ideology to its effendi and shaʿbi audience.[28] When the Syrian actor Iskandar Farah formed a new acting troupe, a writer for the journal *al-Hilal* reported that it was "a venture whose educational fruits will not be less valuable than the establishment of a big school that educates youth for free."[29] Theater was deemed an appropriate educational tool for all of society, but the underlying assumption was that effendis and elites would author the scripts.

Shaʿbi performers did not always deliver what effendis had in mind. Popular entertainments often contested both colonial power and an increasingly hegemonic form of nationalism that was trying to absorb everyone into a uniform narrative of Egyptian resistance.

Some of the most important everyday spaces where such concerns were enacted were coffeehouse stages. As alternatives to mosques and taverns, coffeehouses were neighborhood gathering spaces that offered men a place to meet any time of day. Their patrons would drink coffee and tea, smoke water pipes, and catch up on news and gossip. These were men from many walks of life, individuals from all over the Ottoman Empire. Yet by the turn of the twentieth century, neighborhoods and, by extension, coffeehouses were changing. As newly developing western sections of Cairo grew, they attracted elites and rising middle classes, who left their old neighborhoods—and coffeehouses—to the urban workers who stayed behind.

By the early twentieth century, men who spent evenings with friends in coffeehouses not only smoked and drank tea and coffee. They also enjoyed musical performances, local comedians' acts, and farces performed on raised platforms. Comedians, jesters (*muhabbizun* or *Awlad Rabiya*), and mimics (*muqallidin*) like Ahmad al-Far performed in such coffeehouses. Many performers started careers in shaʿbi neighborhoods, performing in theater-cafés like Dar al-Tamthil al-Zaynabi, Dar al-Salam, and the Egypt Club. They mimicked street vendors and famous singers but also staged original, colloquial plays where they excelled at mimicking regional accents and dialects. Fluid categories meant that an individual player might be either a muqallid, a muhabbiz, or both.

The earliest and most detailed accounts of muhabbizun appear in European Orientalists' and travelers' writings. The Victorian Orientalist Edward Lane's impressions of muhabbizun provide important insight into their satirical content and popularity, as he was deeply concerned with representing Egyptian life with accuracy and detail.[30] In his description of a wedding party, Lane observed that men and boys played the roles of women, and shows opened with music and dance followed by a skit that might critique anything from the oppression of work to corrupt tax collectors.[31] In one case, he described a play that was staged in a *samer*, a circle of spectators in the midst of which muhabbizun performed, much like Al-Far's wedding entertainments. The skit included stock characters: a provincial governor (*nazir*), a village chief (*shaykh al-balad*), his servant, a Coptic clerk, a peasant (fellah), his wife, and five musicians. In the story, the poor peasant ʿAwad is flogged and thrown into prison for failing to repay the government a thousand piasters of debt. He asks his wife to bribe the Coptic clerk with food in order to secure his release, and she agrees. She arrives at the Copt's house and asks:

> "Where is the ma'llim Hanna, the clerk?" They answer, "There he sits." She says to him, "O Ma'llim Hanna, do me the favor to receive these, and obtain the liberation of my husband." "Who is thy husband?" he asks. She answers, "The fellah who owes a thousand piasters." "Bring" says he, "twenty or thirty piasters to bribe the Sheykh el Beled [*sic*].

The wife takes the bribe to the Shaykh, who accepts it, then suggests that she go the nazir. In preparation, she applies kohl (a thick black eyeliner) to her eyes and henna (a red dye) to her hands and feet. After completing the beauty ritual, she sets off to see the nazir:

> "Good evening, my master" she says to him. "What does thou want?" he asks. She answers, "I am the wife of Awad who owes a thousand piasters." "But what does thou want?" he asks again. She says "My husband is imprisoned and I appeal to thy generosity to liberate him" and as she urges this request, she smiles, and shows him that she does not ask this favor without being willing to grant him a recompense.[32]

Though Lane described the skit as "vulgar farce" and found it inferior to European performance for its lack of costumes, set text, and logic, its social commentary surely did not escape him. The satire alerted its audience, most notably the Ottoman governor of Egypt, Mehmed ʿAli Pasha, to the suffering of the shaʿb in the face of such corruption.[33] The skit's concern with contemporary social problems was not unique. As the historian Philip Sadgrove notes, "The depiction of the misfortunes of the downtrodden masses, the players' attacks on corrupt officialdom, the high and mighty ruling classes and excessive taxation" all appeared in puppetry (*karagoz*) and other farce well before the turn of the century.[34]

Egyptian performers practiced what Dina Amin refers to as the "politics of a-realism," meaning that performances embraced absurdism, the fantastical, the humorous, and the cathartic. Such elements were prominent in street performances that were termed *luʿbat* (playlets, skits) before the term *masrahiyat* (dramas or plays) entered the Arabic lexicon in the twentieth century.[35] In the late nineteenth and early twentieth centuries, the term for a play shifted from *luʿba*, with a root that meant to play, toy with, act fraudulently, to *riwaya* (narrative or story), with a root that meant to tell, to relate, to give an account of.

The change of labels reflected a shift in relations between actor and audience: A "luʿba" implied communal and physical participation, whereas a "riwaya" indicated that an audience was told a story but did not actively participate in it.[36] Such evolution in theatrical language marked a shift that occurred in late nineteenth- and early twentieth-century theater, when a curtain was introduced between players and audiences. Previously, theater had integrated audience and players in performances that involved the creation of a communal, imagined story. Audiences sat or stood in a circle around actors and voiced opinions about storylines, demanding changes when they were unsatisfied with performances.[37] The Danish traveler Carsten Niebuhr commented on this in the late eighteenth century when he attended a farce in the courtyard of a house in Cairo. He wrote:

> The story is that of a woman (played by a man), who lures one traveler after another to her tent, and who after robbing them of their belongings chases them away with a stick. Incidentally, the audience grew so tired of the repetition of this absurd situation that they forced the actors to stop their performance halfway through.[38]

Muqallidin offered different sorts of entertainment. Muhammad Idris, for example, earned his reputation by perfecting his mimicry of a famous and beloved Egyptian singer named Shaykh Salama Hijazi. Hijazi was Idris's contemporary, a man from a poor family whose voice had propelled him to fame in the world of effendi stage theater. Idris's mimicry of Hijazi started as a hobby but soon became a full-time career, testifying to Idris's (and Hijazi's) broad appeal.

Idris's work in the shaʿbi Sayyidna al-Husayn neighborhood began with a successful engagement in 1912 at the Egypt Club. When a new improvisational group invited Idris's troupe to sing between acts of their performances, Idris was captivated when he "found they performed without a play [script] and without a prompter."[39] Within the year, Idris was performing not only between acts but also as a player with the troupe. Alongside him, the head comedian, Hafiz ʿAbbas, played the recurring role of a servant who wore pajamas in fifty colors, a pointy *tarbush* that looked like a fool's cap, and a mustache with one half drawn to point upward. Audiences would have known that the character and look were at the very least a nod to the well-known player Georges Dakhul, who also played the role of a servant with a half-upturned mustache. Dakhul's performances became so popular among the shaʿb that they inspired several muqallidin of their own, many of whom modified his plays to be even more ribald and licentious. They forced Dakhul to refer to his Syrian stage character, Kamil, as Kamil the Original, or Kamil al-Asil, so as not to be mistaken for a copy.

Mimics seem to have been common features of shaʿbi performance. Idris, for example, performed in Rawd al-Farag's small, cheap theaters, in the countryside, and at weddings. He acted with a number of well-known muqallidin—most notably, Ahmad Fahim al-Far. The added name "Fahim," however, indicates that he was not the same al-Far as the wedding performer mentioned earlier. In fact, just like Dakhul, there were multiple Ahmad al-Fars, and it is unclear whether Fahim al-Far was the "original" or a "copy" of the wedding performer al-Far.[40] As performers and copies of performers like Idris, Dakhul, and al-Far moved through Egypt, they were part of a process of cultural circulation that would shape shaʿbi notions of themselves and their place in a larger Egyptian society.

Arabic stage theater and shaʿbi performance were not entirely discrete events. The influence of Arabic musical stage theater, for example, inspired Idris to perform music from the actor and singer Salama Hijazi in coffeehouses in shaʿbi neighborhoods. Georges Dakhul also incorporated elements of musical melodrama in his troupe's coffeehouse shows.[41] Equally, shaʿbi performance influenced the formal stage. Professional actors and writers, like Muhammad Hosni (a member of Hijazi's troupe) and the Egyptian playwright and journalist Yaʿqub Sannuʿ, attended and were influenced by shaʿbi performance.[42] Exposure to shaʿbi skits led Syrian playwrights in Egypt, such as Abu Khalil al-Qabbani, to Egyptianize their plays by including music, singing, and puppet theater on stage.[43] The comedians Najib al-Rihani and ʿAli al-Kassar both derived their early plays from street farce.[44] Indeed, Al-Kassar's biography mentions the critical influence of muhabbizun, whose performances captivated him in childhood.[45] In general, Arabic stage performance, particularly comedies, incorporated the shaʿbi imitation of dialects, accents, manners, and tics into shows.

Simple plotlines, like those in puppetry and shadow play (*khayal al-zil*), made them familiar to audiences, although they were also improvised and therefore variable. Loosely episodic stories had no apparent rational sequence, and action in the skits centered on main characters' exploits and changes of fortune, not their character development.[46] The humor in the fasl mudhik satirical skits came from imitation of dialects, accents, and manners, and costumes were minimal.[47] Actors juxtaposed the serious to the comic, and audiences were expected to sing with the characters, curse villains, and freely interact with performers, voicing their approval or disapproval as street performance had long practiced.[48]

In the years before World War I, fasl mudhik was increasingly incorporated into Arabic stage theater in between acts or at the end of more serious plays. The popular genre drew from traditions of puppetry and *khayal al-zil*, but it reflected local concerns and used contemporary language and humor. It was a type of irreverent social and political satire performed in a mixture of colloquial Arabic and gibberish. Stock characters, like the Matchmaker, the Foreigner, the Fellah, the Turk, the Copt, and the Trickster, populated these playlets.[49] Though the plays first appeared in street performances and in coffeehouses, ads for Arabic theater that appeared daily between 1900 and 1914 often boasted a traditional music interlude and fasl mudhik as part of the production.[50] Ads usually listed the names and dates of plays, the troupes performing them, and the names of musicians and fasl mudhik players. Journals, including the Coptic *Misr*; the government-supported *al-Watan*; the British-backed *al-Muqattam*; and the nationalist *al-Mu'ayyid*, encouraged readers to attend shows. Traditional musical interludes involved the use of instruments like the *rababa* (a two- or three-stringed guitar), *tabla* (drum), and *riq* (tambourine).[51] Some performers sang improvised tunes or imitated those of more famous singers. Salama Hijazi often incorporated fasl mudhik into his troupe's plays. His versions of *Hamlet* and *Aida* ended with a fasl mudhik, presumably to lighten the mood.[52] Fasl mudhik also appeared in ads for plays by the Arabic Acting Society, Iskandar Farah, the Coptic Society, the 'Akasha troupe, and even for amateur student performances.[53] The Syrian troupe leader Sulayman al-Qabbani, too, incorporated a fasl mudhik at the intervals or ends of his formal plays.[54]

The decision to present a fasl mudhik at the end of a play had cultural and commercial incentives. Troupes knew that comedies drew bigger audiences than did tragedies.[55] To satisfy audiences, playwrights like Tanyus 'Abdu who adapted European drama for Egyptian audiences stated that they had to alter plays to give them happy endings. In 'Abdu's version of Shakespeare's *Hamlet*, Hamlet lives and is victorious in regaining the Danish throne.[56] Including a fasl mudhik at the end of a serious play was conceivably another way to divert audiences from tragic endings. It also, perhaps unwittingly, integrated elements of shaʿbi culture into effendi conceptions of authentic Egyptianness. Fasl mudhik brought shaʿbi humor to the effendi stage, and audiences loved it.

Audience members sometimes attended plays for the fasl mudhik and not for the main performance. An extremely popular fasl mudhik performer named Muhammad Naji, for example, often appeared on stage at the end of Hijazi's and Shaykh ʿAtta Muhammad's plays. His fans commented that they explicitly attended plays to see him and would not leave until he performed.[57] Naji's popularity meant that he was included in the troupes' trips to Damascus and Beirut when they toured the region.

Ironically, if Arabic stage theater was as much about effendification of spectators as it was about entertainment, then the fasl mudhik contradicted the process at nearly every turn. Its disordered vulgarity and fantasy were diametrically opposed to the ordered, textual rationality of the effendi theater. Arabic stage theater was very much invested in establishing, representing, espousing, and promoting certain Egyptian bourgeois norms. Effendi contributors consciously set themselves and their plays apart from shaʿbi influences while establishing new modes of performance that embraced modern elements of European stage theater, integrating them with what they considered to be authentic Egyptian traditions. The distinction was tenuous but critical, as the effendiyya used the theater to shape and define themselves, just as they sought to shape and define Egyptians and Egyptianness in their image. Theater was to teach spectators about the merits of work and serve as a physical antithesis to the coffeehouse, which increasingly was derided by effendis as a debauched space where Egyptian labor and capital were wasted on drugs and idleness. By contrast, the theater was a place for personal improvement, a space where families could attend performances that were informative and edifying.[58]

In street and café theater, audiences knew they were integral to performances. They interrupted with shouts of praise and disapproval, and players spoke back to them throughout their scenes. Although this type of interaction went out of fashion once the proscenium stage was introduced and audience behavior became more passive, it persisted among the shaʿb. The opportunity—indeed, demand—for active engagement in the performance meant that they were never passive viewers but vital insiders whose voices and opinions not only mattered but were deemed essential to the outcome of a scene. This iterative process could translate in many ways. Performances might offer escape, an outlet to subdue passions. But it could also bind audiences together in common cause as agents of change. If "popular cultures and comedy have a capacity for both 'containment and resistance,'" as the cultural theorist Stuart Hall claims, what would stop the shaʿb from transferring that sense of power to the public sphere?[59]

At the turn of the twentieth century, at least three Ahmad al-Fars existed around Cairo. Each "Rat," as the name "Al-Far" is translated, was famous for imitating animal noises, playing instruments like the rababa, delivering comedic monologues, and performing original plays.[60] The most famous al-Far took the title "effendi" and the middle name "Fahim" to distinguish himself.[61] Much of the information about him comes from his contemporary, the prominent writer Mahmud Taymur, who praised the effendi al-Far's natural acting talent and noted that he performed with Iskandar Farah and Salama Hijazi's troupes, both of which were popular and respected at the turn of the twentieth century. A contemporary cultural critic, ʿAli al-Raʿi, added that the effendi al-Far "wore Frankish clothes and drank with the aʿyan [wealthy landowners] . . . he would negotiate contracts in Bar al-Luwaʾ." He was "very good at playing the *mizmar*, the *qarba* (bagpipe), and the *rababa* in the neighborhood, delivering comedic monologues and acting" in satirical and farcical original plays.

References to at least one of the al-Fars started to appear in journals in 1907. One advertisement for an al-Far performing a fasl mudhik on the Arabic stage makes no mention of "Fahim" or "effendi" and therefore may refer to the noneffendi al-Far. The ad promoted a special night of plays, singing, and moving pictures.[62] A few other ads, however, refer explicitly to an "al-Far, effendi." On August 13, 1907, for example, the effendi performed between acts of the play *Zenobiya Malikat Tadmor* (Zenobiya, Queen of Palmyra) for Sulayman al-Qirdahi's troupe.[63] He also "made people laugh" in the interval between acts of the play *Opening the Andalus*, written by the then-deceased leader of the Nationalist Party, Mustafa Kamil.[64] An original play in Alexandria by the effendi al-Far received a bit more coverage. In 1910, he performed in a casino at the old Raml train station, a place that attracted "elegant men and those who love humor," according to the journal *al-Muʾayyid*. That evening, al-Far presented a "very funny" three-act play titled *The Obstinate Shaykh*. The enthusiastic listing continues: "Tomorrow he will perform another play much like it" and the writer "urge[s] the people to seize the opportunity to see the priceless farce."[65]

Less is known about the wedding performer known as al-Far. Beyond a few notes that describe his troupe of twelve, huge ʿimma, and zaʾbut, he is harder to locate in historical memory. Thus the discovery of two sets of printed scripts—one in the Leiden Library and the other in the private papers of the mid-twentieth century Orientalist Kurt Munzel—of five of his plays offers a rare a glimpse into al-Far's world and that of everyday shaʿbi performance.[66]

Since impromptu theater is largely nontextual, the fact that these skits were recorded at all is unusual. Both contain text for the same five plays, but the Leiden (L) version is bound and much lengthier than the Munzel (M) version. Manfred Woidich and Jacob Landau, the scholars who assembled and published the scripts together, surmise that a scribe for the shorter M version may have simply summarized parts that he was told about but had not seen, or that he abbreviated what he saw.[67] The M manuscript is clearly marked as a collection of Al-Far's playlets (*liʿb*) for weddings, whereas the L manuscript is marked as al-Far's *baladiyyat*, an uncommon word that, based on its root, probably means "folk stories."

The scripts all share certain characteristics. All have prologues that begin and end abruptly, purposely leaving audiences wanting more. Puns, errors, misunderstandings, crassness, and innuendos pepper the dialogue, all of which are central to the skits' humor. They also each incorporated musical and/or dance interludes.

All of the playlets also use prototypes already well-established in shadow plays. *Riwayat Ibn al-Balad* (The Story of Ibn al-Balad), for example, is set in Cairo and involves characters like al-Gharib, literally "the stranger," who is from Alexandria. The term is different from *khawaga*, which referred to European strangers. Al-Gharib is mainly interested in hashish, cocaine, and attractive women, and one of the women he meets easily swindles him out of his money. Later in the skit, the audience meets a policeman who is more interested in flirting with the same woman than doing his job. His attempted seduction involves him underscoring his simplicity, stating he prefers "lentils and falafel" to meat and rice.

Characters in al-Far's other plays include a shaykh who offers to help a husband deal with his problematic wife. The husband complains that during his lunch break, he bought vegetables and meat and brought them home, only to find his wife was not there. When she returns with inconsistent stories about where she had been, he beats her, but soon finds that she's become possessed by an *ʿafrit* (a powerful jinn, or spirit). The shaykh fails to exorcise her, but he agrees to help grant her a divorce. The skit ends with huge fights between an obscenity-spewing mother-in-law, the wife, and the husband.

In al-Far's skits, everyone is a target of mockery. Police officers are negligent but charming, Bedouins savage, Europeans exploitative but foolish, women seductive victims. The stories tend to revolve around interpersonal relationships in (mostly) everyday situations: marriage, love, divorce, lust, stealing, cheating, and haggling. These were issues relatable to the audience.

The play *Riwayat al-Shaykh al-Turuqi wa al-Mar'a wa Zawjaha* (The Story of the Shaykh Turuqi and the Woman and Her Husband) includes a reference to the changes wrought by technology. The wife in the skit says that "there are no ʿafrit in this *hara* [neighborhood]." Al-Far adds: "Since the tram was built, they've dispersed all over the city."[68] The squeaking metal from the tram was frightful enough to disenchant the metropolis.

The al-Far texts raise a host of questions, not least being: Why were they recorded? Who recorded them, and for whom? And how do the scripts compare to one another? Undoubtedly, printed texts offer only a glimpse of what was actually performed, as actors took cues from audiences and improvised lines and endings. As the scholar James Scott notes, oral culture has no primary text from which it deviates or with which it is consistent. Consequently, it achieves "the anonymity of collective property, constantly being adjusted, revised, abbreviated or, for that matter, ignored."[69] Its improvisational nature made it adaptable to a variety of sites and situations, from the stage to private courtyards. As audiences and contexts changed, the content of the fasl mudhik differed as well. Its plasticity meant that it could be shaped to suit an array of tastes. Thus, the text of a fasl mudhik must be considered fluid and open-ended (just as muhabbizun and muqallidin would have used them) rather than as a rigid text. Despite this, a close reading of the playlets yields details about shaʿbi desires, fantasies, humor, and frustrations.

The fasl mudhik *Riwayat al-Saʿidi* (The Upper Egyptian's Story) opens with a Saʿidi, a man from southern (Upper) Egypt, in Cairo complaining about the city's lack of hospitality. Soon, however, a Bedouin woman invites him to stay in her home, and several disconnected and rather circular and nonsensical conversations follow between the Saʿidi, the woman, and her husband. In one, the Saʿidi reveals that he formerly worked on boats but could no longer do so because "there is no water left in the sea."[70] He explains that he has spent all his money, he knows seven languages, and he is in Cairo because his wife is taking him to court to divorce him.[71] He then suddenly and inexplicably falls sleep, but the husband (played by al-Far) abruptly awakens him to accuse him of stealing money. "French or silver coin?" the Saʿidi asks, leading to another round of nonsensical and fast-paced insults between the two.

The subject somehow shifts to a discussion about what the Saʿidi is wearing. Al-Far's character haggles with the Saʿidi to buy some of his clothes but refuses to pay unless there is a guarantor for the sale. The Saʿidi agrees and sets out to find one, returning with a man who turns out to be a thief and former associate of his. Together, the two conspire to steal back the clothes from the husband.[72] Eventually, the Saʿidi wants out of the situation. "Let's go listen to the leader," he says, and the play concludes with a song.[73]

A summary of the play fails to capture the absurdist strain that runs through it. In a preface to the play *Ya Taliʿ al-Shajara* (The Tree Climber), the Egyptian playwright Tawfiq al-Hakim (1902–1986) explicated the importance of absurdism in premodern Egyptian performance. As he defined it, absurdism was "the expression of reality without realism, and the attainment of the ridiculous and the illogical in every artistic expression. It is the creation of abstraction in order to arrive at new rhythms and influences."[74] He went on to explain how the use of language figured into such performance: "When a play consciously departs from realism, it loses any justification for using realistic language with its characters. Therefore, what becomes more suitable for its unrealistic events is an unrealistic language, in other words a language other than the language of conversation."[75] Nonsense and wordplay are hallmarks of the fasl mudhik, and other absurdist elements, such as repetition and cyclical dialogue, are central as well.[76] In the Saʿidi play, there is no particular reason why the story unfolds in the sequence it did. There is little by way of linear narrative and no clear progression of time. And there does not seem to be much sense in most of the dialogue. But this was not solely for entertainment purposes. As al-Hakim suggests, these devices were powerful vehicles for expressing the realities, frustrations, and desires of their popular urban audiences. Skits like *Riwayat al-Saʿidi* reveal unique shaʿbi perspectives on identity and cultural authenticity.

This was different from representations of the shaʿb as repositories of unchanging folk culture to be preserved as heritage. Instead, this skit, and others like it, challenged the rationality and discipline of effendi modernity. The shaʿb, particularly those who were factory workers, encountered effendi modernity in physical and material ways. The transition from a peasant-based, handcraft economy to factory organization and hierarchy would take off about two decades after the performance dates indicated for the al-Far plays, but changes were already afoot.

The ideal of state-sponsored, effendi-led modernization required that the shaʿb be educated in the ideals of self-discipline, punctuality, and efficiency. But this new relationship to time did not necessarily replace the older temporal markers of prayer time and religious festivals, for example, that broke up the days into meaningful components. The shaʿb responded to effendi attempts to educate them in ways that ranged from imitation to manipulation to evasion. The reality is that effendi prescriptions for modern life—especially in the context of industrialization and, later, proletarianization—

would undoubtedly transform urban life, but not necessarily in ways they prescribed.

As effendis celebrated scientific and technological progress while repeatedly critiquing popular knowledge, beliefs, and conceptions of time, they conjured what the historian On Barak terms "countertempos," or nonlinear reactions against modernizing currents. These responses came out of "discomfort with clock time and disdain for European standards of efficiency."[77] Shaʿbi performances played with the countertempos of circularity, superstition, and irrationality. These were not necessarily conscious assertions of any unified shaʿbi identity, but they matter in that they represented alternative conceptions and experiences of contemporary life.

Perhaps the most distinctive marker of the Upper Egyptian in *Riwayat al-Saʿidi* is the Saʿidi's accent and use of language. Audiences would have heard al-Far's character speak with an exaggerated Saʿidi accent. In Upper Egypt the letter *qaf* (a throaty "k" in formal Arabic but a glottal stop in Cairene dialect) is pronounced as a soft "g." When the Saʿidi says the word *foog* (up), instead of *foq* or *foʾ*, he is instantly recognizable as someone from outside Cairo.[78] Colloquial language varied considerably based on the region in which it was spoken, the class, and even the occupation of those who spoke it. Thus, the type of Arabic used and the ways it was pronounced could mark and mock social class, origins, and even religion.

In this period of significant cultural production (journals, plays, novels, and vocal music, among other examples), the colloquial language that was specific to Lower Egypt, that is, from Cairo north to the Nile Delta, became the dominant national dialect. The historian Ziad Fahmy points out that "only an 'authentic' *ibn* or *bint al balad* [son or daughter of the country] ... would use Egyptian Arabic and grasp its multiple meanings and nuances and hence participate in this new mass-produced colloquial culture." Political cartoons and comedic performances included unsympathetic foreigners who mispronounced words and contrasted them to the proper pronunciation of jovial Egyptian characters. Fahmy contends that "Cairo's dialect and culture were overwhelming—colonizing, if you will—the multitude of other localized dialects and cultures in Egypt. Thus, Cairene Arabic was the primary tool for nationalist, anti-imperialist discourse, and simultaneously ... imposed its own culture on the 'nation.'"[79]

Portraying Upper Egyptian Saʿidi characters that spoke exaggerated dialect as "dimwitted and backward" showcased Cairene dialect as the proper standard of speech.[80] Saʿidis were cast as an internal "other," "unintelligent, hardheaded, and culturally inferior."[81] In al-Far's playlet, the Saʿidi plays the Fool—a naïve character who is unable to keep pace with urban society.[82] In other moments, however, he is the Trickster—a quick wit and clever bargainer who gets the better of those around him.[83] Despite his long, insult-ridden dialogue with the husband, for example, it is never entirely clear whether the Saʿidi actually stole the money he is accused of stealing. He spends considerable time talking his way out of the situation and is successful enough to distract the husband from the theft, at least for some time.[84] As the scholar James Scott observes: "It doesn't take a great deal of subtle analysis to notice that the structural position of the trickster hero and the stratagems he deploys bear a marked resemblance to the existential dilemma of subordinate groups."[85]

At the same time, there is slippage between the characterizations of Trickster and Fool, in that they are not always discrete categories. The exchange of insults is one place where this is evident. In some cases, it is unclear whether the Saʿidi is insulting himself or the other character. An exchange in the Saʿidi play demonstrates this.:

Husband: Pig!
Saʿidi: Son of a pig, *ya buuy*! [Saʿidi expression indicating trouble or irritation]
Husband: Pimp!
Saʿidi: Son of a pimp, my son![86]

It is possible in this exchange that the Saʿidi is accepting the insult. But it is equally plausible that he is hurling it back. The humor lies in the ambivalence between those two possibilities. Trickster stories invert social relationships by allowing the protagonist to triumph over others who are usually his social superiors, but the Saʿidi's simultaneous identity as both Trickster and Fool makes his position less clear. In turn, he is less threatening.

Undoubtedly, humor is the main ingredient of the fasl mudhik, and much of it derived from "the ridiculous and the illogical," as the playwright Tawfiq al-Hakim claimed. Prose, poetry, and song intermingled in each of the skits, and humor came from misunderstandings of identity, unexpected situations, mistaken assumptions, obscenity, and lewd (sometimes oblique, other times blatant) conduct. It also came from slapstick and futile attempts to get the better of someone via matchmaking, cheating, stealing, and wordplay.

Inverted gender roles were a favorite theme. For example, it is the wife of the couple that the Saʿidi lodges with—not her husband—who insists the traveling Saʿidi stay with them in their home.[87] Considering that all women in al-Far's troupe were played by men, this would have been funny on several levels. To an audience accustomed to a norm of gender segregation, the woman's actions were transgressions of propriety. Her behavior was "masculine" in that it involved public engagement with an unrelated man.[88] But because a man played the role, it turned a situation that was a real concern in a changing Egypt into something funny rather than threatening.

Humor also came from exaggerated use of colloquial expressions. The Arab woman, for example, repeatedly invokes the Prophet Muhammad in her dialogue with the Saʿidi. This common colloquialism would have sounded familiar to the shaʿb in attendance and could serve to appease more pious audience members. At the same time, the wife's deliberate overuse of it bordered on the ridiculous. When she pleads with him to stay at her house, for example, she says, "I see that you're tired, and the prayers of Muhammad." Likewise, when she reprimands him, she says, "The neighbors and walls are tired of your snoring, and the prayers of Muhammad."[89]

Sometimes an exchange of insults added to the hilarity. In one interchange between the husband and the Saʿidi, for example, the husband swore at him by calling him the "son of 100 prostitutes." "I'm the son of 100 prostitutes?" the Saʿidi deadpans. "Yes," answers the husband. "No, son," the Saʿidi replies, "I'm the son of ONE prostitute."[90] This was quite blatant, but not all insults were. Those who took themselves too seriously as arbiters of modern Egyptianness were targets of mockery.

The Saʿidi takes aim at effendi identity in another exchange about origins. When the husband attempts to insult the Saʿidi by referring to him as a fellah (peasant), the Saʿidi responds: "I'm not denying that I'm a fellah, you contrarian. I AM a fellah, and the son of a fellah. You think you're the son of a soldier? You're a fellah like me."[91] The fellah stood for many urbanites as backward, ignorant, oppressed, and submissive.[92] But the Saʿidi reminds the husband that his roots—just like most Egyptians'—were also fellahi. The Saʿidi embraces the roots that the effendi rejects and reminds him that Egypt's modern vanguard, though distancing themselves from their own rural, fellahi roots, owed their existence to it. This was a critique of their posturing.

In a memorable exchange, the husband expresses keen interest in purchasing the Saʿidi's cloak, a southern Egyptian wrap called a zaʿbut, and his tarbush, a hat worn by effendis to mark their social status. The husband asks the Saʿidi if the zaʿbut is good for anything more than being worn, and the Saʿidi answers: "It's good for the effendiyya; they can wrap it around their necks and [the lice in it] will scratch them instead of them using their hands."[93] He then asks the Saʿidi what the tarbush is good for and how it stays on one's head. The Saʿidi replies: "You put on the tarbush, then you tie the lace around your neck . . . then it will be just right."[94] "Priceless," the husband responds. Though the tarbush—which has no laces—is a marker of effendi status, the husband makes a mockery of it by having no idea how it is to be worn or even what it stands for. At the same time, the zaʿbut, a marker of an Upper Egyptian, becomes desirable when the husband learns that an effendi might find it useful for scratching his neck. For an effendiyya negotiating between their rural origins while shaping modern urban identities, one's choice of clothing mattered. The idea of wearing a zaʿbut with a tarbush was a total contradiction, and it indicated that the husband, a Bedouin and outsider to urban Cairo, was attempting to behave as an effendi without any real understanding of its meaning.

Even as the purpose of such exchanges was to evoke laughter at effendi pretentions, the performance also affirmed the existence of the effendiyya as a bounded, unified social group. In broad brushstrokes, the playlet paints the effendi as a serious personage, one who places greater emphasis on his urban identity than his rural roots and whose sartorial choices mark him as separate from the crowd. Shaʿbi skits that represented effendis enacted elements of the effendi ideal, even as they mocked them.

Success in comedy, the anthropologist Susan Seizer argues, "assumes everyone's familiarity with moralizing discourses of propriety, vulgarity, and the ideology of separate spheres . . . not normally laughing matters."[95] Indeed, the skits assumed audiences had considerable local knowledge in order to understand their humor. Transgression of social conventions—the assertive Bedouin woman, thievery, and use of crude language—also reasserts the importance of those conventions.[96] Layers of meaning complicated the Egyptian comedy writer Amin Sidqi's theory that "a joke is not humorous unless it is completely understood by everyone."[97] Instead, humor might derive from any of several levels of comprehension, some less accessible than others.

The manipulation of language is a case in point. Al-Far's use of double entendres made some exchanges between characters both offensive and funny.[98] To understand them, however, required a higher level of facility with colloquial Arabic language than did the more direct curses. In one instance of double (or triple) entendre, the Saʿidi attempts to compliment the husband by asking, "You clever fellow [*dahiya*], where are you from?" But the word "dahiya" also means catastrophe or calamity, and the husband, who understands the word in this way, responds angrily: "The same calamity that will send you back to your village!" "Oh, thank you," the Saʿidi replies, once again understanding the word "dahiya" in a different way: "Traveling on a cursed flying carpet [dahiya] would be much better than traveling by sea."[99] The humor in the exchange exists on several levels, the most obvious being the Saʿidi's naiveté and the clever manipulation of language. On a deeper level, it was funny because it came from a transgression of appropriate conversational language. Using the terms without explanation assumed that the audience was familiar with the words, understood they were rude, and sometimes vulgar, yet still found them funny. Audience members were in on the joke because they were well aware that conventions were being transgressed. To be an authentic Egyptian, one had to see through elite pretensions. And one also had to get the jokes.

Something odd happens in the longer L manuscript. In the middle of the play, the Saʿidi (only here referred to as "Ahmad") and his friend Hanafi meet in a shop. At one point, Ahmad, or Al-Far, asks Hanafi: "Don't you see how backwards we are and how people laugh at us? We've become inferior—that's what foreigners say. Isn't that humiliating?" Hanafi replies: "But what have we done to deserve that? We're just living our lives . . . we keep to ourselves . . . why don't they leave us alone? So they want us to involve ourselves in the world like they are? Crazy, running around, complaining that the papers wrote this or that . . . do they think they're immortal?" Ahmad disagrees: "Forgive me, but it's our attitude that's held us back." Hanafi isn't convinced, and Ahmad is angry when Hanafi mentions the joys of smoking hashish: "If only you would forget the stuff and pay attention to what matters," he scolds. "Try to mingle with foreigners . . . understand how they do their trades, open a store like them, wouldn't that be better?" He calls on an urban vanguard to navigate these reforms. Egyptians, according to al-Far, needed to learn from Europeans.

Over thirteen pages of text, the humor vanishes and a moral message emerges: work, order, and discipline, not hashish, would make the country—and its people—modern and civilized. Hanafi's satisfaction with passing time in the limited world of friends, family, work, and hashish was, according to Ahmad, the reason for Egyptian backwardness. In order to progress, Egyptians needed to emulate rather than critique Europeans. And then, abruptly, the skit returns to its absurdist, circular humor. How does one reconcile this message with the rest of the play?

One might argue that the improvisational nature of shaʿbi performances made it impossible for two performances to be exactly the same; thus it is logical that manuscripts of two separate performances of the same play would deviate from one another. But the inclusion of a lengthy, moralistic, didactic element in one of the scripts is too divergent to ignore. To better understand it requires some interrogation of who wrote the manuscripts and for whom they were intended.

The L manuscript, as Woidich and Landau explain, is bound and recorded on high-quality paper that bears the watermark of the Egyptian government. Red colloquial Arabic markings in the margins provide stage directions and explanations at various points. A sticker on the back cover bearing the bookbinder's name (Rudolf Preller) suggests that the L manuscript was recorded for an Orientalist audience in Europe. The M manuscript was not bound, but it was found in the library of a British Orientalist named Kurt Munzel who lived in Cairo in the mid-twentieth century. Landau and Woidich conclude that commissioned Egyptian scribes must have recorded both texts.[100]

The content of the L manuscript's additional thirteen pages contradicted the rest of the play, in both tone and message. The L scribe's decision to add dialogue about the merits of hard work echoed effendi prescriptions for modernizing Egypt. In fact, the scribes lifted the moralistic passages in these pages directly from the writings of the reformer, political activist, and pioneering journalist Abdullah al-Nadim.[101] In the late nineteenth century, al-Nadim's satirical writings and plays famously critiqued social, economic, and political inequalities in Egypt. He used his writings, along with his charity work, to raise Egyptians' awareness of internal problems while promoting resistance to Khedive Isma'il and, later, British occupation.

Both al-Nadim and the scribes who recorded al-Far's plays were educated urban professionals—the embodiment of the effendi. Thus, the scribe's decision to insert al-Nadim's words into al-Far's play, regardless of intent, quite literally wrote effendi prescriptions and respectability into a sha'bi narrative. There is hardly a clearer illustration of the extent to which crafting and representing Egyptian identity was a dialogic process in the Bakhtinian sense: it was dynamic and relational.[102]

Sha'bi performers who became stars contributed to the conversation in other ways. Individuals like the effendi version of Ahmad al-Far and two of Egypt's most renowned comedians, 'Ali al-Kassar and Najib al-Rihani, started work in coffeehouses performing fasl mudhik before moving to the Arabic proscenium stage.[103] The effendi al-Far recorded several 78s with the Baidaphon recording company.[104] Recordings undoubtedly expanded the reach of the effendi al-Far's voice to audiences beyond those who were physically present at the live shows. Meanwhile, both Kassar and Rihani performed up and down 'Imad al-Din Street and acquired enough fame and wealth to eventually open their own theaters across the street from each other. Audiences cheered their recurring characters, Osman al-Basit and Kish-Kish Bey, Trickster-Fools that drew from stock characters in sha'bi performances. The recurring representation of effendis in these skits added the Effendi to the known list of stock characters that audiences easily recognized and knew to expect. Shows blended fasl mudhik, farce, and vaudeville in the new context of the proscenium stage and appealed to shaʿb and effendi alike. Performers' fame and mobility—from street and coffeehouse to proscenium stage—allowed shaʿbi voices and humor to infuse effendi spaces, thereby assimilating them into effendi ideals of Egyptian identity. They demonstrate that modern Egyptian identities were never simply applied from the top down. In mocking hegemonic ideals, shaʿbi performers both wrestled with and amplified the conflation of effendi and Egyptian identity.

Shaʿbi performers' bawdy, clever lines were intended to shock bourgeois sensibilities and provoke laughter from audiences that encompassed everyone from private patrons to the urban working classes. Their loose scripts were frameworks for improvisations that muqallidin and muhabbizun adapted to local contexts and the mood and makeup of their diverse audiences. Drawing on elements such as collective history, humor, and mythology—in addition to contemporary social and political situations—muhabbizun and muqallidin did more than offer release from the frustrations of lived realities; they provoked audience members' imaginations as to what *might be*.

Though shaʿbi performers borrowed from older performative conventions, a script's content engaged with and implicated itself in the modern world, even as it critiqued and rejected elements of that same world. By framing contemporary problems, responding to audience demands to shape performance to local tastes, and offering viewers a range of common cultural symbols, shaʿbi performers cultivated a unique view of modernity grounded in humor, social critique, and fantasy. It was a life full of unknown and unexpected turns; it required clever and imaginative use of language; it was rooted in an interactive community, cognizant of its shared rural heritage; and, perhaps most important, it was managed with a sense of humor. It was a rejection of the order, logic, and rationality of effendi modernity and concern with the shaʿb as a target of social reform. The refusal to incorporate Western theatrical conventions of performance, as well as the persistence of the a-realism of shaʿbi performance, were certainly a part of this. Ultimately, it located cultural authenticity with the shaʿb, not the effendiyya.

In this context, effendi attempts to absorb, co-opt, and manipulate shaʿbi plays make sense. Shaʿbi audiences recognized that outcomes changed as a result of their input. Emboldened, it was possible to imagine these participants setting sights on engaging and debating issues outside of the theatrical space. Such was the fear—and hope—of effendis seeking to control shaʿbi voices and terms of engagement.[105]

CHAPTER 4

Cabarets and the Mothers of the Nation

At a prearranged time one afternoon in March 1919, Cairo's actors, actresses, and playwrights shut down their theaters and gathered in front of the Khedivial Opera House. There, they joined massive anti-British street protests erupting throughout the city and countryside triggered by the arrest and exile of the nationalist leader Saʿd Zaghlul. The actresses Dawlat Abyad and Zaynab Sidqi donned pharaonic and Arab clothing and led actors on a long procession that started at Station Square, passed through Opera and Qasr al-Nil Squares, and ended at Bayt al-Umma, the home of the exiled Zaghlul. Alongside them marched leaders of the Egyptian women's movement, including Huda Shaʿrawi and Sayza Nabrawi, who were veiled in *yashmak* and shawls, clothing worn by elite women of the era.[1] Actors who followed the women were dressed in the costumes of Napoleon Bonaparte, Harun al-Rashid, and Othello, a combination of real and fictional political and military leaders.[2] All the way, they demanded "freedom from occupation or death!"[3]

In the era of 1919, theatrical performance spilled into the streets, and events on the streets fed back to the stage. People from all walks of life poured into boulevards and squares, democratizing, at least for the moment, spaces that elites had constructed to symbolize the modern state nearly a half-century before. The area around central Cairo's Azbakiyya became a revolutionary space, reclaimed by the Egyptian people Ismaʾil had sought to modernize, and they now made their own demands for Egyptian independence, justice, and freedom.[4] Egyptian actresses helped to lead the call.

Women were central to anti-British protests.[5] Some 350 elite women from Alexandria, Fayyum, and elsewhere marched in Cairo's anti-British demonstrations, and peasant women in rural areas worked alongside men to tear up railway tracks, destroy telegraph lines, and pillage and burn the countryside.[6] Those who led the women's movement in Egypt were some of the first to march in protest after Zaghlul's exile—a striking image of female political engagement and visibility in a public sphere where they had previously been involved only in limited degrees.[7] In the context of a political march for independence, female involvement was considered not only acceptable but admirable.

In late nineteenth- and early twentieth-century Egypt, expanded educational opportunities that included the new field of home economics alongside a new prescriptive literature taught women how to be "new women," within bounded categories of mother, wife, consumer, and citizen.[8] The Egyptian women's movement, consisting mostly of middle-class and elite participants, worked closely with Egypt's nationalist leaders to support this view. Together, they cultivated a concept of "maternal citizenship," which, as the historian Laura Bier explains, "glorified women's roles . . . as mothers and custodians of a reformed domestic sphere based upon bourgeois models of companionate marriage, scientific childrearing, and rational household management."[9] The maternal citizen discourse, as an ideal, portrayed Egyptian women in this period of rapid social expansion as disciplined guardians of the nation's moral purity.

The exile of Egypt's nationalist leaders at the end of World War I created a space for women from which to claim a (potentially independent) public identity. Members of the Wafdist Central Women's Committee organized economic boycotts and public demonstrations, and they served as liaisons between British officials and nationalist leaders in exile. Women, they argued, had a duty to participate both inside and outside the home in the everyday struggle against colonial domination and local "backwardness."[10] That call to struggle provided women from all walks of life a path to respectable engagement in the public sphere. Social reformers argued that, to properly perform their roles as maternal citizens, poor and working women in particular would need help and training. To this end, they established job-training sites that focused on cultivating women's roles in the home. But in the end, no matter how morally superior she may be, the maternal citizen would remain for nationalists a "category of manly possession and protection."[11]

There were other limits as well. The classed domesticity that reformers supported neglected to address the challenges women faced in the workplace.[12] Female performers in particular did not fit neatly into idealized roles, and many lived outside the boundaries of honor-protection usually provided by males of a family. Performing in commercial establishments like cafés, theaters, and music halls meant that women interacted with men they did not know and, in the case of music halls and casinos, in the presence of alcohol. As Farah Antun illustrated in his play *Misr al-Jadida*, for effendis the potential for moral depravity made such establishments damaging and dangerous leisure spaces for both the individual and the trajectory of the nation. In allowing their bodies to appear physically in front of male audiences and provoking male desire and consumption, performing women were by definition marginal and transgressive. This posed a problem, as the model of a disciplined woman was epitomized by her controlled sexuality and impulses. This was also true of the model man/effendi.[13]

New media technologies in the early twentieth century both exacerbated and mediated concerns about the propriety of performing women. Records and popular journals allowed for women's voices and images to proliferate in both the public sphere and private homes. But recordings allowed for the dissemination of women's voices without the physical appearance of their bodies. Performers like Munira al-Mahdiyya—an actress, singer, and dancer—addressed concerns regarding women's visibility in different ways. They mobilized the tension between the roles that male and female reformers prescribed for women—mothers in the domestic sphere and national subjects in the public sphere—to create a space and a language onstage and in popular journals to legitimize their public presence. Representing themselves as patriotic, bourgeois wives and mothers, performing women wove narratives of the self that claimed respectability in both a stigmatized profession and in the broader public sphere, all the while smoothing over more complex, sometimes chaotic lives. Commercial success provided financial power, fame, and status that allowed some performing women to push the boundaries of modern Egyptian womanhood, yet many still chose to represent themselves as abiding by hegemonic norms propagated by effendis and women reformers.

The desire to embody and disseminate effendi ideals was not a simple capitulation to a top-down imposition. In the fight for Egyptian independence and the period of nation-building that followed, women across the board elevated and focused on what they understood to be the concerns of the nation. Even after Britain gave Egypt nominal independence, effendis who populated the newly elected parliament had to negotiate with the interests of the British (who never really left), as well as the authority of the Egyptian king. They fought to create a functioning state while still trying to prove themselves worthy of the independence they were attempting to claim. For them, a failure to present a unified, modern Egyptian identity, as personified by the effendi, was a threat not only to effendi leadership but also to the very existence of the independent nation-state. Many female reformers and performers alike recognized what was at stake and played their part in embodying unity and love of nation above all else.

In truth, even as audiences enjoyed their provocations, female performers' embrace of nationalism and the maternal citizen ideal was good for business. Those who were talented and navigated their positions well became commercially successful, signing record deals and performing in the more respectable *salas*, or music halls, on ʿImad al-Din Street. In contrast, those whose talents or reputations were considered questionable either chose or were relegated to the realm of performance in the types of cabarets that Farah Antun castigated as being vulgar and unedifying. In some cases, the families of female performers—both successful and not—found the stigma too great to bear and actively purged themselves by casting out the performer and/or the memory of her profession from their family's history. Pressing the limits of the nationalist paradigm and the maternal citizen ideal might be appealing, but going too far threatened the integrity and good morals of the Egyptian nation that effendis expected of themselves and others and that they looked to women to uphold.

Taken together, the experiences of and reactions to female performers in early twentieth-century Egypt created significant challenges and alternatives to effendi norms. Yet even as they broadened the parameters of what the "new woman" might be, their participation in—even touting of—effendi norms meant that they validated more than upended them. The career of Umm Kalthum, arguably the most famous and successful Arab female performer of the twentieth century, is a case in point.

In the early years of World War I, an influx of British soldiers and newly enriched Egyptian landowners supported a flourishing vaudeville theater in Cairo.[14] Everyone from village *ʿumdahs* (leaders) whose cotton crops were booming, to British soldiers who descended upon Cairo once war broke out, found distraction in the cafés, casinos, and music halls nestled between ʿImad al-Din Street's retail stores and Arabic-language theaters. Vaudeville, comedy, and musical theater attracted larger audiences than the moralizing effendi theater, and performers responded to the demand. Egyptian poetry, jokes, and songs were ways to vent wartime anxieties.[15]

The outbreak of war posed a dilemma for the British, as Egypt was still a province of the Ottoman Empire. Once the Ottomans officially allied with Germany, the British government moved quickly to declare martial law, making Egypt a formal British protectorate and instituting rigid limits on the press and freedom of assembly, along with various forms of political and economic control. Urban dwellers initially benefited from the growth of local wartime industry, but this changed over time. Peasants increasingly migrated to cities to escape their many burdens and subsequently put pressure on an urban infrastructure already stressed by housing shortages and increasing rents. Stagnant wages, massive inflation, rising crime rates, prostitution, and drug use also plagued cities.[16]

For performers who catered mostly to effendi audiences, business was difficult during the war, when curfews designed to curb carbon use and keep people off the streets meant that theaters had to shut down early, at 11 P.M.[17] Many troupes could not find urban audiences large enough to support themselves, so they supplemented work in Cairo and Alexandria with provincial tours and private jobs. Despite such efforts, many went bankrupt.[18]

As places like Cairo became garrisons for the hundreds of thousands of fighting units from Australia, India, New Zealand, Malta, and other parts of the British Empire, troops' rowdy behavior in the streets contributed to what was already a litany of Egyptian resentments. Dismal economic, political, and social conditions created a situation ripe for revolt. Elite landowners resented British artificial controls on the cost of cotton and other production; the middle classes were angry with the increasing numbers of British bureaucrats taking what they believed should be their civil service jobs; peasants had had enough of economic colonialism, forced labor, and the requisitioning of their resources; and nearly everyone suffered due to spiraling inflation and stagnant wages.[19]

Performance and politics converged in the most visible and literal ways at the end of the war. One of the most beloved of Egypt's contemporary composers, Sayyid Darwish, wrote a number of stage pieces that echoed the sounds and concerns of everyday people. His song "Salma Ya Salama," for example, celebrated the return of men recruited for the Egyptian Labor Corps. These were Egyptian civilians whom the British conscripted in numerous, often brutal, ways. The Egyptian intellectual Salama Musa wrote about the forced recruiting of peasant men in his memoirs. He recalled: "Men [were] bound with thick ropes around their waists and put in a long row with their fellow victims and marched like that to the village office where they were confined in the room for the accused to be deported to Palestine."[20] One-third of Egyptian men between the ages of seventeen and thirty-five either volunteered or were forced to participate in the Egyptian Labor Corps.[21] They laid railway lines, dug trenches, and performed other menial labor for miniscule pay.[22] A report to the British government stated that Egyptian laborers "died like flies due to the ill treatment they received."[23]

Egyptian nationalists had taken notice of the American president Woodrow Wilson's call for self-determination of all nations and chanted his name in anti-British protests.[24] With great hope in what seemed to be an internationally binding, legal basis for independence, a delegation of nationalists led by the former vice president of Egypt's defunct Legislative Assembly, Saʿd Zaghlul, sought a place at the table in Versailles to demand Egyptian sovereignty. Egypt's British High Commissioner, Reginald Wingate, refused to grant their request to represent Egyptian interests at the Armistice conference, and this set in motion a series of revolutionary events. Zaghlul and the others created a delegation, or *wafd*, under Zaghlul's leadership and traveled to collect signatures (*tawqilat*) from all over Egypt as proof of their mandate to speak for Egyptians. In effect, the Wafd created itself at the very same time it promoted itself as a legitimate voice of the people.[25] Despite their success in amassing large numbers of signatures, the Wafd was denied permission to travel abroad. Worse yet, on March 8, 1919, several of the Wafd's key members, including Zaghlul, were arrested and exiled to Malta. The British not only denied the delegates access to Versailles but also forced them out of the country.

Decades of frustration with colonial rule, coupled with the effects of war and the exile of Wafd leaders, triggered an explosive response. Initiated by students, demonstrations against British occupation and demands for the return of Zaghlul and company soon included Azhari sheiks, Coptic priests, Jewish rabbis, Nubians, Sudanese, urban and rural elites, effendis, workers, peasants, and women of multiple social classes. This convergence made visible a plurality of Egyptian society that famously coalesced in common cause, determined to force the British out of a country exhausted and exploited by war.

The walls between theater and street dissolved as performers transcended bounded private performance stages to play a part in the drama outside. The actress Fatma al-Yusuf described her experience participating in the protest of 1919. Yusuf gathered with a host of Cairo's actors, actresses, and playwrights in front of the Khedivial Opera House, where she and fellow actress Mary Mansur got in a buggy with the editor-in-chief of the journal *al-Ahram* and wound their way through the theater district with a massive Egyptian flag in hand and a group of costumed actors following in their wake.[26] In her autobiography, Yusuf describes how what had started as a spirited protest ended in a terrifying moment. At one point along the route, a British soldier emerged from the shadows and leveled a weapon directly at her. She recounted the experience in the third person: "One of the soldiers raised his rifle and aimed it at the young artist carrying the flag, and she froze as terror flooded her body. . . . [S]he felt as if a bullet had pierced her back, so she clung to the flag as if to lean on it. . . . [The feeling] was not, in reality, anything more than the consequence of her terror."[27] As she watched in shock, an Egyptian revolutionary crept up and shot the British soldier, saving Yusuf's life. The electrifying experience moved her to participate even more fully in anti-British work. It would eventually lead her to establish a career in journalism, providing her a forum to serve as a leading critic of Egyptian politics.[28]

The social consequences of 1919 were complicated, for regardless of the solidarity of popular protest against the British, Egyptians in the streets were from an array of backgrounds and experiences, and their concerns varied considerably.[29] Urban workers, for example, had organized and led strikes for higher wages and to protest poor working conditions from at least as early as 1882, and women had been advocating for reform since the 1890s.[30] Political demands for independence, freedom, and justice resonated differently among people who experienced subjection and injustice in very different ways.

It is unsurprising, then, that the anticolonial uprising did not resolve social problems but instead unleashed a torrent of protests by groups who agitated for social change. On this, the historian Husayn Fawzi observed:

> The [Azbakiyya] Garden Kiosk turned—after the superficial calming down of the waters of the revolution—into something reminiscent of the syndicates' hall in socialist countries. The 1919 Revolution was in appearance and in essence a movement against occupation, which then revealed an even deeper essence: it was also a movement of great social change. It started in the form of professional groupings demanding their rights from those monopoly companies which controlled much of the country's services. . . . [The] Kiosk acquired a daily "agenda" of meetings for which it was the venue: tramway workers; gas and electricity company workers; water company workers; café waiters; unemployed casual workers; cigarette company workers . . . drop-outs of the *kafa'a* [matriculation] certificate; old system eighth-grade civil servants; women workers in garment workshops; *sufur* [unveiling] women activists; pensioners; ex-convicts; *'utuf* [alley] dwellers to protest the squalor of their quarters, and dwellers of alleys overlooking the royal stables in Bulaq to protest the smell of the cattle, etc. This or that group is invited to convene on Saturday, Sunday, or Monday the 12th . . . to deliberate upon their affairs or to demand such and such or to protest against this or that.[31]

Participation in meetings such as the ones at the Azbakiyya Kiosk was one example of women's active and multifaceted engagement in Egyptian life. Educated women had been writing about their experiences and concerns since the 1870s and 1880s, publishing books and contributing to literary journals, among them *Anis al-jalis* (1898–1908), *Al-ʿafaf* (1910–1922), and *Fatat al-Nil* (1913–1915). In the following decades, they founded intellectual organizations that drew from a variety of traditions, some from Islamic thought such as the Society for the Advancement of Women, and others with secular leanings, such as the Intellectual Association of Egyptian Women (1914). Huda Shaʿrawi and the writer May Ziyada founded the latter.[32] Women participated in the growing state educational system as teachers and administrators.[33] They also initiated and participated in a number of social services such as dispensaries, nursery schools, and charitable associations that involved care for poor women and children.[34]

Intellectual and organizational activity in the early twentieth century soon led to increased political involvement for women as well. They became more visibly active in politics as they collaborated with prominent male politicians and participated in debates about the appropriate role of women in a burgeoning modern Egyptian society.[35] Safiyya Zaghlul, wife of Saʿd Zaghlul, served in both a symbolic capacity as the "Mother of Egyptians" and also in a practical sense as a link between Zaghlul and other Wafdist leaders when Zaghlul was exiled. In his absence, Safiyya hosted Wafdist meetings in their home.[36] Women also created parallel political organizations, such as the Wafdist Women's Central Committee and New Woman Society, which supported men's organizations. The "new women" of Egypt organized boycotts of foreign goods and participated in public demonstrations during the revolution.[37]

In France, the fin-de-siècle new woman referred to urban, middle-class women who blurred gender boundaries in various ways, from choosing not to marry to entering masculine professions like medicine and law, outside the home.[38] In the context of a colonized and, shortly thereafter, newly independent nation, however, the Egyptian new woman looked quite different. Nationalists and female intellectuals stressed the role of women as mothers of the nation, holding them responsible for raising proper citizens while also standing as symbols of Egyptian authenticity.[39] Male and female nationalist writers attempted to carve out a space for women as educated mothers whose role as custodians of morality and educators of their children put them at the center of nation-building while also keeping them in the home.[40] Not all reformers were in lockstep. For some, like Nabawiyya Musa, liberation included training women to work in particular fields, such as teaching and nursing.[41] For most leading female reformers, however, ideals of modern Egyptian womanhood meant being educated and patriotic, a virtuous wife and mother, skilled in the proper raising of future citizens.

Women hoped to guide the transition of home life to a more rationalized, nuclear, European bourgeois ideal, one that accommodated the shift to a new agrarian capitalist class.[42] Reformers like Shaʿrawi were concerned with issues such as seclusion, veiling, and child-rearing by nannies (or servants of bad character) instead of mothers—all practices common among Ottoman-Egyptian elites of the time. In neglecting working and rural women's issues and focusing on addressing their own concerns, reformers effectively bolstered the role of elite women in society. As the scholar Laura Bier contends, "Elite women accepted the paternalism of liberal-nationalism, in part because it gave them authority over subaltern women."[43]

The disconnect between elites and working women's concerns were stark. Secular and leftist reformers' concern with unveiling as well as ending seclusion had little relevance to women who did not live in seclusion and whose relationship to veiling was more complex (or who did not veil at all). Poor and working women were deemed a particular problem for reformers, and many articles that focused on household economy also debated different means to "uplift" poor women in order to raise productive, moral, intelligent, clean, healthy children.[44] Members of the Egyptian Feminist Union and other women's organizations embraced the struggle against "local backwardness" by providing an array of social services to poorer women. They focused on teaching basic literacy, principles of hygiene, and child care to "enable working-class and rural women to be better wives and mothers."[45] For male and female reformers, instruction in the "proper pedagogy of children, the cultivation of the body, and the moral education of the self" drew from indigenous concepts of *adab* (a combination of valued intellectual, moral, and social characteristics that reflected proper upbringing and education) and *ʿafaf* (which described a woman of virtue and integrity, purity, and honesty), both of which were foundational to the creation of a modern Egyptian nation.[46] Literature on child-rearing argued that poor, uneducated mothers raised unclean, superstitious children in harsh living conditions.[47] Though reformers established some job training sites for those who had to work outside the home, most of their efforts lay in elevating the authority and status of women within the home.[48] These beliefs complemented nationalist discourse that stressed the critical role of the mother in raising patriotic Egyptian children.[49]

The revolution was significant for all types of women because it turned civic engagement into national responsibility. As pioneering Egyptian feminist Huda Shaʿrawi put it, "The Egyptian women, from the moment of the first spark of the revolution of 1919, entered public life from the most honorable door, the door of national struggle for freedom and independence."[50]

Language about the role of women as mothers of the nation homogenized women rhetorically by turning them into symbols.[51] But many women used nationalist rhetoric and patriotic language to create new spaces for themselves and to advocate for their own needs. They argued, for example, that proper mothering required proper education. They also sought greater access to public life that would grant them greater equality in society.

Women like the actress Bahia Hafiz not only did not fit into the paradigm of appropriate womanhood; they also actively rejected it. In response to frequent criticism for her choice of a profession in singing and acting, Hafiz responded:

> Many have criticized me for having chosen this profession, calling it a great scandal! But have they ever considered the difficulties of all kinds thrown in the way of a woman alone, who is without resources but wishes to remain independent? What pushed me toward the cinema therefore was not mere whim nor a simple wish to appear before the public but my need to create a condition that would guarantee my freedom.[52]

Hafiz's position was undoubtedly a challenge to liberal-nationalist womanhood. Like other female performers, she resisted prescriptions that she work within parameters that made the family her primary concern. Instead, she stressed the importance of her freedom. This was a radical stance: even reformers who fought against female seclusion did not think that women's unrestricted public presence was an acceptable alternative. An article by the editors of the journal *al-Hilal*, for example, argued that, despite the dangers of seclusion, unrestricted "freedom is more dangerous for young women, so what is best is the middle ground."[53] Ibrahim ʿAli Salim, a secular advocate of premarital acquaintance (the opportunity for a man and woman to get to know each other before engagement), indignantly stated that "some narrow-minded people . . . hide their daughters from their fiancés but show them in theaters, amusement parks and . . . stores [practically] naked!"[54] Clearly, Salim felt female visibility was appropriate only within certain parameters.

Female performers had long pushed boundaries of acceptable female engagement in the public sphere, though the circumstances surrounding their engagement shifted over time. Throughout the nineteenth century, women in Egypt provided entertainment for various special occasions, such as saints' holidays, weddings, and other events. Some also performed in coffeehouses from behind curtains or fully covered by veils and wrapped in *malayat* (long, black coverings) to perform in what was deemed acceptable fashion in front of men whom they did not know. In private homes, performers recited Qur'anic verse, danced, and sang religious repertoires, usually for other women. Though families hired them for private occasions, people from the neighborhood were welcome to participate in the festivities. While some performers worked locally, others traveled to perform at events throughout Egypt. Most received remuneration for their performances and were recognized for their remarkable musical skill.[55] The most accomplished were in great demand, respected, and well paid.

Professional female singers, called *ʿawalim*, participated in their own trade guild and often came from mostly Muslim (but also some Jewish and Christian) working-class families in Cairo. Groups of ʿawalim commonly lived together and worked under an experienced female performer, or *usta*, who taught them the trade. Muhammad ʿAli Street, which was lined with coffeehouses and music shops, was a popular neighborhood for musicians and ʿawalim, and ustas often visited its coffeehouses to learn the latest songs.[56] Individuals seeking entertainers for specific occasions would head to Muhammad ʿAli Street and negotiate with an usta, or her male assistant, in offices on the ground floor of their living spaces or in one of the cafés. Though some ʿawalim married local tradesmen, others made matches that offered them some degree of upward social and economic mobility.[57] The royal court patronized the most exceptional performers, the most famous being Almaz, whom Khedive Isma'il retained. The court rewarded them richly until it was determined that their looks and talent no longer sufficed. At that point, ʿawalim became increasingly dependent on their spouse—if they had one—for financial support. Alternatively, they went to work in the new and less respectable music halls.[58]

Toward the end of the nineteenth century, acting guilds started to decline, and individual actors and actresses increasingly negotiated their own wages with theater troupes, recording companies, and theater managers. Such agreements lasted for entire performance seasons, or even years, as opposed to the older practice of only negotiating individual engagements.[59] In the early twentieth century, a shift toward professionalization created distinctions between fields of singing, dancing, and acting, privileging specialization over diversified talents. Though men tended to specialize in one specific form over another, women often needed to participate in all fields to remain viable entertainers.[60] Distinctions between professionalized male artists and less-professionalized female performers further entrenched negative biases against women already considered to be of doubtful repute and questionable talent.

Still, professionalization offered unique opportunities for women. The mastery of numerous repertoires and types of performance made women highly desirable additions to acting troupes in need of talent. Their diverse skills made them popular and appealing to audiences. By the early twentieth century, especially after World War I, individual singers and actresses contracted by themselves or via agents, with institutions (not individuals) like theater companies, recording companies, and theater management. Contracts were no longer for single events but for seasons or years. The change was largely due to the spread of commercial entertainment (which proliferated in urban areas) and commercial recording.[61]

Between 1890 and 1920, theaters and European-style cabarets sprung up in Egypt. In Cairo, the main areas were Rawd al-Farag, a shaʿbi area where admission to shows was usually free, and ʿImad al-Din, which catered to more effendi audiences.[62] By the mid-1920s, ʿImad al-Din had more than thirty theaters, silent movie cinemas, coffeehouses, and cabarets. Performers from all over the Arab world and top foreign artists, including Isadora Duncan, Pavlova, and Sarah Bernhardt, included Cairo in their tours.[63]

From the mid-1910s, Egyptian actresses and singers like Munira al-Mahdiyya broadened their activities to include theater management, commissioning music and plays, and composing their own music. Successful performers like Umm Kalthum, Naʿima al-Misriyya, Fathiyya Ahmad, and Badiʿa al-Masabni were among the highest-earning women in the 1920s, in some cases making more than male singers and musicians.

As entertainment districts developed around ʿImad al-Din Street and in the Rawd al-Farag district in the late nineteenth and early twentieth centuries, women increasingly performed in their cafés, music halls, and theaters. The shift from private entertainments to performance in commercial establishments created new dilemmas for women. In many cases, audiences were larger and unknown to the performers. Alcohol fueled rowdy behavior, and, in some music halls and cafés, female performers were expected to sit and drink with audience members. Consequently, despite their popularity, the most commonly expressed concern was that entertainments—and by extension performers—were tainted by drunkenness, gambling, drugs, undignified behavior, and prostitution.[64]

Religious leaders and effendis vociferously critiqued women's cabarets for their repertoires and their performance environments. Some requested that publishing and distribution houses scour record company catalogs to ban "dirty and vulgar songs that offended the public morals."[65] Performers were blamed for a host of problems, including promoting divorce. In 1923, Egyptian religious leaders went so far as to issue a fatwa banning all "indecent and immoral nightclubs" like Rawd al-Farag, al-Busfur, Alhambra, and Sala Badiʿa.[66]

Around the same time that the 1919 street protests erupted, the actress and singer Munira al-Mahdiyya opened her troupe's performances in a new way. Before the curtain was raised to signal the start of a show, the first Muslim-Egyptian actress stepped out and sang the following song:

> Depending on her adab
> She keeps the laws of decency and ʿafaf
> She suppresses her emotion
> For the sake of her nation and honor[67]

Mahdiyya's choice of language was no accident; it drew from Egyptian anticolonial nationalist discourse about respectable womanhood. Adab was an indigenous concept that referenced a combination of valued intellectual, moral, and social characteristics that reflected "proper upbringing and education (*tarbiyya*)." For secular nationalists and Islamic modernizers, adab was central to modern Egyptian womanhood, and that modern woman was a symbol and lynchpin for the modern nation.[68] Similarly, ʿafaf was a concept that described a woman of virtue and integrity, purity and honesty. For reformers, both adab and ʿafaf were integral characteristics of the modern Egyptian woman. What did it mean for a performing woman, involved in what was considered a morally dubious profession, to sing about womanhood in this way?

By using concepts like adab and ʿafaf in her opening song, Mahdiyya linked public performance to honor and national duty. This was one of many strategies women used to demonstrate a commitment to increasingly prevalent expectations of a loyal female citizenry. Just like the women marching in the streets in 1919, Mahdiyya made her presence in the public sphere a commitment to "nurturing the nation."[69] But her story also illuminates the contradictions of a performing woman claiming to uphold the ideals of maternal citizenship.

Mahdiyya had a penchant for singing early in life (see figure 4.1).[70] Born sometime between 1877 and 1895, she attended a convent school in Zaqaziq but neglected her studies in favor of singing with friends or sneaking out to hear a popular singer, al-Lawandiyya.[71] Before long, her singing supplemented her family's meager income. She first performed at a coffeehouse in Zaqaziq known for its dancers, and by 1913 she moved to Cairo, where she sang at the Nuzhat al-Nufus coffeehouse, a place that British authorities routinely shut down for its anti-imperialist performances.[72] This may well have been a place where she first encountered nationalist thought in the context of theater.

The actor and troupe/vaudeville manager ʿAziz ʿId became enamored with Mahdiyya's voice and encouraged her to take her singing to the theatrical stage. When the coffeehouse where she sang was once again a target of police repression, Mahdiyya took ʿId's advice and joined the theater.[73] For a time, she performed and sang between acts of ʿId's plays at the Printannia Theater. The newspaper *al-Akhbar* took note of her opening night, titling its article "The First Egyptian Actress." It continued: "The evening of Thursday the 26th, in the Printannia Theater, will be a night to celebrate the entry of the famous singer [*mughaniyya*] lady Munira al-Mahdiyya, into Arabic acting." That evening, she sang an opening song, composed by Kamil al-Khaliʿi, and performed the role of William in the third act of the play *Salah al-Din al-Ayyubi*.[74] Between 1915 and 1916, she sang Salama Hijazi's songs in ʿAziz ʿId's productions, playing male roles such as Romeo (*Romeo and Juliet*) and William (*Salah al-Din al-Ayyubi*). Her performance in male roles may well have tempered public objections to her as one of the first Muslim women to remove the veil and perform publicly before a mixed audience. Despite—or, perhaps, because of—the controversy that this generated in the press, she attracted huge followings. Tickets for shows in which she performed sold out well before curtain time.[75] Mahdiyya's name was clearly a draw, as evidenced by its prominent placement in advertising posters. A journal article advertising a program at the Kursaal Theater listed Mahdiyya as one of several headliners who made up "the most famous actors and actresses of the era." The article described the evening as "one of the most miraculous and astonishing at the Kursaal."[76]

Though most theater audience members in the early twentieth century were men, Mahdiyya further bolstered her reputation by borrowing an innovation from fellow-singer Badiʿa al-Masabni.[77] Mahdiyya explicitly made space available in many of her performances for women. In some cases, ads made clear that ticket prices applied equally to both men and women. Others indicated that separate seating areas would be available for women.[78] One ad explained that "the second floor is entirely for Egyptian women, and they have a special door [for entry]. No one should be kept from seeing this performance; ticket prices are reduced."[79] Regardless of the number of people who took advantage of this, welcoming women to her performances allowed Mahdiyya to intimate that her shows were appropriate for everyone.

Mahdiyya's name and voice became increasingly recognizable due to her success in both live singing and recordings with the Gramophone, Odeon, and Baidaphon companies. Recording companies of the early twentieth century provided new options for female performers who wished to share their talents widely. Records allowed for the dissemination of the female voice without the presence of the female body, circumventing concerns about the propriety of women performing unveiled in front of men. People in coffeehouses and private homes across the region heard Mahdiyya's voice, making her—and other female singers—recognizable in places where physically they had never been. Recordings popularized their songs with broad audiences.

In the new era of mass media, singers like Mahdiyya could use material success to bolster their positions in society. Mahdiyya wielded great power in the world of commercial recording, as she was a highly desirable performer, and at the turn of the century record companies built their reputations on the caliber of the singers they signed. Odeon, which started recording Egyptian artists as early as 1905, signed popular singers like Salama Hijazi and Bahiyya al-Mahalawiyya, while Gramophone signed an exclusive contract with the musician Dawud Husni and the singer Ahmad ʿAshur.[80] Baidaphon's success in eventually signing an exclusive contract with Mahdiyya was a boon for the Lebanese company. It was also a coup for Mahdiyya, as it allowed her a great deal of artistic and economic power and freedom.

On the one hand, commercialism and mass production freed performers from the limits of patronage by khedives or wealthy patrons. In this way, their repertoires were not entirely determined by benefactors' tastes. On the other, record sales and commercial sales increasingly defined repertoires. While the company employed its own composer, Ahmad Ghunayma, Mahdiyya was permitted to compose her own songs and, later, gave final approval when Baidaphon hired Yunis al-Qadi to be her primary songwriter. She supplemented income from her recordings with revenue from her coffeehouse and theater performances.[81] Financial security enabled her to flourish as a performer. And her knowledge of various types of performance prepared her to take on proprietary roles as troupe director, as well as theater and cabaret manager. With female artists working outside the bounds of conventional womanhood, commercial success made women power brokers in a way that challenged their stigmatized position in society.

Before long Mahdiyya's popularity led her to form her own theater troupe. Though the composition of the troupe changed each season, it typically included a mix of men, women, Muslims, Christians, and Jews.[82] In January 1916, ads first appeared for performances by "Lady Munira al-Mahdiyya's troupe" and listed the dates, names of plays, and theaters where it would perform.[83] Typically, a season began with the performance of musical theater from previous seasons and/or borrowed from other companies. Her repertoire included a combination of plays adapted from European productions and original pieces written expressly for her troupe.[84] In that first season, the troupe performed the plays *Salah al-Din al-Ayyubi*, *Dahiyyat al-Ghawaya* (Victim of Seduction), *al-Sariqa* (The Raven), *'Aida*, *Romeo and Juliet*, *Hamlet*, *'Ali Nur al-Din*, *Shuhada' al-Gharam* (Martyrs of Love), *Sidq al-Akha'* (The Brotherhood's Faithfulness), and *Carmen* in Cairo; and *Anis al-Jalis* (The Sociable Companion) in Cairo, Tanta, and Alexandria.[85] Ads for her shows highlighted her role as lead actress, emphasizing the number of songs she would sing.[86] Like other effendi theater troupes, Mahdiyya's sometimes included *fasl mudhik* (farcical skits) in her programs.[87] Until she had her own theater, Mahdiyya performed in a number of theaters in Cairo and outlying provinces. Provincial tours were a regular feature of her calendar, and in September 1919 her troupe even began to travel outside of Egypt to perform in Syria.[88] Though commercial recordings paved the way, Mahdiyya's physical appearance in various locations increased her fame and exposed large numbers of people to her troupe's theatrical performances, eventually earning her the title "Sultanat al-Tarab" (Queen of Tarab) in contemporary magazines.[89]

As the first woman to form her own troupe, she personally assumed its management duties. Responsibilities included negotiations with theater owners, singers, composers, and lyricists. It also meant meeting payrolls, planning schedules, and performing on stage.[90] Yet she was bound to a male benefactor, as it was Mahdiyya's first husband, Mahmoud Gabr, who rented the theater Dar al-Tamthil al-'Arabi for Mahdiyya, and it was Gabr who initially bankrolled it.[91] His name was often listed alongside hers as the troupe manager, among other capacities.[92] Together, Gabr and Mahdiyya maintained full theatrical seasons, which ran each year from October through August/September of the following year. This lasted until 1924, when their marital estrangement and later divorce created a rift in the troupe and forced Mahdiyya to leave the theater that Gabr rented.[93]

The writers, musicians, and lyricists for all of Mahdiyya's troupes were men, who, along with her husband, formed a coterie of male supporters, especially in her early career. They included playwrights such as Farah Antun and Yunis al-Qadi and composers such as Sayyid Darwish. The relationship of male mentor to young female artist was a common one, seen repeatedly in the world of Egyptian theater.[94] Newspaper articles and biographies of male and female performers often recounted such relationships, which were of particular importance due to the legitimacy they bestowed upon the young upstarts, especially if they were women.[95] Certain themes recurred in such accounts—stories of humble roots, early involvement with religious music, and tales of discovery by famous performers—and these stories allowed performers to claim a place in a lineage of singers. In many ways they echoed Islamic traditions of *isnad/tasnid*, which sought to assure the trustworthiness of a statement by building on previously authenticated statements.[96] As a form of cultural tasnid, performers' discovery stories implied that their legitimacy was guaranteed due to their recognition by and association with an older, reputable mentor and patron. Thus isnad, together with humble religious origins that made them authentic *awlad al-balad* (literally, "children of the country"), accorded them some degree of respectability.

Mahdiyya continued to perform in different theaters in the 1920s and eventually opened her own sala (music hall) in 1931.[97] In this era, more female performers started to run their own troupes and cabarets.[98] After a number of years singing in local weddings, provincial music halls, and major theater districts in Cairo, the singer al-Masriyya bought her own casino, the Alhambra, in 1927 and managed it herself. Other female singers, including Mary Mansur, Fatma Qadri, ʿAliya Fawzi, Ansaf, and Ratiba Rushdi, also opened their own music halls in the 1920s and 1930s.

In her performances, Mahdiyya blended old and new markers of respectability to push the acceptable boundaries of womanhood. Her training in Qurʾanic recitation and mastery of what was considered the more distinguished male song repertoire gave her more credibility than the female repertoire for which she was famous. The *qasida*, for example, set to music classic literary texts that alluded to historical or religious events. For contemporary cultural critics, mastery of the qasida, and other types of music connected to the male repertoire, demonstrated "musical and vocal skill or virtuousness, seriousness (*dadd*), enchantment (*tarab*), heritage and tradition (*turath*), and [may] be passed down from master to pupil."[99] Her background legitimated her talent and was a foundation upon which to craft a respectable identity as a female performer.

Mahdiyya specialized in a type of song called the *taqtuqa*, a short, ostensibly light, catchy piece sung in colloquial Arabic by a solo singer accompanied by a small *takht*, a small ensemble of musicians playing classical instruments used in Arabic music. Record companies favored *taqatiq* (plural of *taqtuqa*), as they were much shorter than other genres (such as the *wasla*, which lasted two or more hours) and therefore fit easily in the three-minute-per-side limit of the early 78 rpm shellac records.[100] Egyptian critics, however, considered the taqtuqa frivolous and superficial and expressed alarm at its popularity. Its mass appeal may partly explain largely effendi cultural critics' disapproval of the genre, since it violated their standards of artistic musical forms. The industry's insistence on shorter, precomposed songs with little or no improvisation was commercially viable but considered by critics to be an inauthentic adaptation. Nationalist historiography of music sees the "taqtuqa era" as an "all-time low in Egyptian music: vulgar lyrics, bad music, unrefined musicians, dissolute singers, drunken British soldiers roaming the streets of Cairo for cheap entertainment in ill-reputed cabarets."[101]

While nationalist women were calling for things like the right to education, an end to polygamy, and banning prostitution, early taqatiq focused more on frivolity and material pleasure. In 1927, Muhammad Isma'il wrote lyrics for the singer Ratiba Ahmad. The song was titled "Adi al-gamal wa adi al-gammal" (This is the camel, and this is the cameleer, or Take your responsibilities).[102] In it, Ahmad is a seductive young woman who directly lists her demands to a prospective groom, thereby ignoring the usual practice of allowing families to negotiate marriage. In the comical song, she claims she'll need one Egyptian pound of pocket money each day in addition to fifty extra pounds per month and an open account at the Bon Marché. "My conditions are clear," she sings, "and if your income is not sufficient, take a girl of your class."[103] Both funny and concerning, the song may well have represented the anxieties of men facing the demands of modern women. Male and female reformers engaged similar topics, but taqtuqa singers presented them in a coy, flirtatious manner that pushed the boundaries of acceptable behavior.

In the late 1920s, taqatiq and other recorded musical genres like monologues and dialogues continued to engage contemporary issues, some more serious than others. Issues of particular concern to women—debates about the nuclear family model, the dangers of polygamy, the right of a woman to get acquainted with a suitor before marriage, the minimum marriage age, how to deal with a spouse's misconduct, and the roles and dangers of women working in the public sphere—all found their way into song lyrics.[104]

One dialogue titled "Qabadan, Qabadan" (Never, never, with a longer title translating to "Never, never, Mr. Ticket Inspector, do not take from this lady the ticket's fee"), Ahmad sings about a religious man, or shaykh, on a bus who is accosting her. The shaykh's pomposity is evident in his ridiculous mixing of colloquial and classical Arabic to invent made-up words that sound impressive.[105]

Despite their successes, Mahdiyya, Ahmad, and other female performers could never fit neatly into the "maternal citizen" framework. Recording technology raised a host of new social dilemmas. Playing records in private homes increased the possibility that mixed-sex audiences would hear songs dealing with risqué subject matter and that young girls might listen to lyrics detailing marriage, love, and other subjects considered inappropriate to their age and social status.[106] Additionally, cultural critics eyed commercialism and consumer society suspiciously. In his critique of Mahdiyya's opera *Carmen*, for example, the reviewer Mustafa Ismaʿil al-Qashash fixated on the problem of deceptive advertising:

> We read about *Carmen* in long ads before its performance on March 22 at Kursaal [Theater] . . . that it was the first Egyptian opera, expenditures on clothes were hundreds of pounds, that 40 actors and 50 actresses would perform, so much that people were convinced to see it. . . . [B]ut how quickly their hopes were dashed, how soon they realized they had been fooled . . . when the curtains rose, there were not 40 actors and 50 actresses . . . nor were there 180 tunes.

In the end, al-Qashash warns, "the truth is that we must make ourselves aware because we were deluded by the embellishments of advertising and we believed what biased people wrote, which is debasing to precious wisdom."[107] His concern with the deceptions of advertising and the sense of being fooled was one shared by many. Thus, while commercial success made possible some women's financial independence, it could not on its own secure their respectability.

Performing women's physical comportment, personal life, and performance content raised questions in the press. A cartoon of Munira al-Mahdiyya, for example, illustrated her power to seduce and emasculate men who, in states of ecstasy, could not resist offering her flowers, jewelry, even themselves (see figure 4.1). Instead of educating future citizens, Mahdiyya wreaked havoc among young men—the nation's leaders—thereby posing a threat to ordered society.

The singer and dancer Badiʿa al-Masabni was the subject of much gossip due to her divorce from the actor Najib al-Rihani.[108] The press was also captivated by a paternity scandal involving the singer Fatma Sirri and Muhammad Shaʿrawi, the son of Huda Shaʿrawi. He fiercely denied Sirri's claims that he had married her and fathered her daughter.[109] The press followed the case for several years. And Ratiba Ahmad was known for her alcohol consumption, romantic liaisons, and divorces.[110] Her repertoire, in addition to those already discussed, included songs that addressed controversial issues in marital life (such as polygamy and alcoholic husbands) and single life (boasting of her youth, beauty, and sexual experience). The combination of Ahmad's conduct, independence, and provocative songs made her a favorite subject of gossip columns and the target of criticism.[111] Perform-

Figure 4.1. "Munira al-Mahdiyya. All the members of the play should be in love with her," *Ruz al-Yusuf*, December 31, 1929. Courtesy of the Rare Books and Special Collections Library, The American University in Cairo.

ing women's ostensible lack of dignity and restraint violated nationalist and feminist ideals of disciplined bodies representing a modern nation.

But the popular press also became an important tool for crafting positive images of glamorous celebrities, bourgeois mothers, and patriotic citizens. In the 1920s and 1930s, images of performing women dressed in costume or dazzling attire graced the covers and interiors of a host of popular magazines.[112] Actresses, singers, and dancers were pictured wearing expensive jewelry, elegant dresses, full makeup, and sophisticated hairstyles. Though readers' responses are difficult to gauge, the proliferation of these journals indicates that there was a market for them. In some cases, fans wrote letters to magazines sharing their opinions. When Mahdiyya first appeared unveiled onstage, for example, a contemporary magazine reported that it received "tens of letters written from women who supported her and wished they could stand beside her."[113] Audience interest also fueled *Ruz al-Yusuf* magazine's yearly referendum asking readers to vote on their favorite singers from a choice of those they deemed the top three. In 1926, it reported an "Amazing Win" by the singer Fathiyya Ahmad, against Mahdiyya and the rising star Umm Kalthum.[114] The journal followed with a series of articles about her, including a flattering one titled "Who Is Fathiyya Ahmad?"[115]

Around the same time, photo spreads of female performers in the context of home and family were published, demonstrating respectability in the context of both public and private lives.[116] Illuminating home life played on an old trope that married women symbolized a sublimated and controlled sexuality. This was of particular importance, as nationalist rhetoric insisted that those who threatened norms of respectability were threatening not only themselves but also the health of the nation.[117] Restraint and control were intimately tied to nationalism because nationalist leaders justified their demands for total Egyptian independence by rejecting British insistence that Egyptians' lack of restraint (along with a host of other indications of "backwardness") justified their prolonged presence.[118]

In an article titled "I Battled the English with My Singing," published before Egyptian independence, Munira al-Mahdiyya described how she covertly expressed patriotic sentiment in one of her songs. She noted that all lyrics had to be:

> insinuation and ambiguous critique because of English censorship of theater, cinema, and entertainment at that time. Censorship made us have to hide our hatred of the English, so it [that hatred] surfaced in plays and songs. In the theater where I worked, I introduced... a play entitled "Kulaha Yumayn," and in that play I was a butter seller, so I carried my wares on my head and shouted out singing this song:
>
> *Maker of fresh butter*
> *My country, the choicest cream*
> *Children of my country*
> *Butter, my children*
> *Buy and weigh it*
> *At your place, store it*
> *Beware of selling it*
> *Do not give it up*
> *To he who betrays,*
> *Else you live treated unfairly.*
> *How can it be of so little importance to you my country?*
>
> And these words, of course, had nothing for the censor to remove ... but the audience understood the song's meaning very well and its goal was to incite hatred and distaste for the usurper/colonizer.[119]

Mahdiyya appeared regularly in theater magazines that captured not only her costumes and home life but also her charitable work, another marker of effendi respectability.[120] Mahdiyya enhanced her reputation by raising money for others at various points in each acting season. Beneficiaries included Maronite, Roman Catholic, and Muslim charities and victims of a fire in a cloth factory.[121] She was praised for her benevolent work. An article in the journal *al-Basir* commented that she had used "talent and compassion . . . to help the meager victims of poverty."[122] The same article reported on one of her philanthropic nights for Roman Orthodox charities: "She wrote to us to say that she is prepared to do this with all the charities of all the religions so long as the societies let her know four days in advance."[123] For Mahdiyya, as for female activists, charity work was part of her civic responsibility.

Despite all efforts, journals had only limited power to promulgate the respectability of women performers. This was highlighted by an incident in which Huda Shaʿrawi refused to be pictured in the former actress Fatma al-Yusuf's magazine. As one of the leading figures of the women's movement, Shaʿrawi supported local artists and hired traditional musicians to perform for her fundraisers. She saw nationalism as an honorable door by which women could enter public life.[124] Yet she refused to have her photo appear in *Ruz al-Yusuf* magazine, fearing that it would taint her image by linking it to photographs of female performers.

Mahdiyya drew audiences that included ministers and political leaders such as Saʿd Zaghlul, Rushdi, and Tharwat Pashas.[125] Her sala inspired the slogan "*Hawa' al-huriyya fi Masrah Munira al-Mahdiyya*" (There is love of freedom in the theater of Munira al-Mahdiyya).[126]

But at the same time performing women were entertaining, they had to be kept in check. Though they consciously represented themselves as embracing maternal citizenship, their suggestive sexuality and flouting of social norms regarding alcohol consumption, multiple marriages, and appearing publicly while unveiled in front of men belied their efforts. The freedom that performing women represented was quite different from the freedom that effendis and women's rights activists demanded in 1919. It posed a threat to the stability of an effendi patriarchal leadership that depended on the support of a unified nation. That particular iteration of freedom also posed a threat to the ideal of maternal citizenship that made women custodians of the nation's moral purity. Female performers' provocations held the potential to overturn the myth of the patriarchal moral order.

And yet, even as they threatened effendi hegemony, most performing women embraced its basic assumptions. Perhaps it is not so difficult to understand why. For one thing, it made good business sense. The most successful performers appear to have practiced a type of *disciplined transgression* that pushed boundaries and participated in the creation of desire, but they did so within certain limited parameters. With some talent, they could make a living singing in the moderately respectable salas of ʿImad al-Din Street and make a good income from record sales.

But to understand why audiences rewarded performing women who pushed limits without overthrowing those limits requires a broader look at the political stakes involved. In interwar Egypt, effendi leaders were caught in the postcolonial dilemma of trying to prove themselves and all the Egyptians they stood for as "modern enough" to be worthy of the independence Britain had only partially granted. Though "new women" in Europe and the United States were testing social boundaries, they did not have to grapple with the legacies of imperialism, the fragility of national independence, and the question of balancing authenticity with modernity in the ways that "new women" in Egypt and other Arab nations did.[127] In the case of the latter, they shaped their advocacy to elevate the needs of the nation over demands for individual political rights, at least for a time. A concern with unifying the nation in the face of such challenges was central to the appeal of effendi hegemonic ideals and the maternal citizens who would uphold them.

New media and the stardom it promoted benefited a few, but it also created a schism between different kinds of female performers. During that era of social mobility, commercial success could provide a path to elevating one's social status. But most women did not achieve such goals. Some maintained their positions as ʿawalim, signing individual contracts and performing in private homes. Others who tried and failed to achieve commercial success found themselves performing in Rawd al-Farag, a shaʿbi area hosting what effendi critics considered to be tasteless, talentless, cheap entertainments. They offered the type of leisure that Farah Antun critiqued in *Misr al-Jadida* as threatening to the health of the nation.

Even those who achieved commercial success found themselves in a rather ambivalent social position. Stardom may have allowed them to push social and cultural limits, but the stigma of public performance persisted, and their presence on stage was itself a subversive act. The actress and filmmaker Bahia Hafiz's family was so offended by her public visibility that they disowned her and "accepted condolences for her death."[128] She tried to explain her position: "I am for freedom for women, freedom to do menial jobs instead of remaining locked in the house. If I followed the advice of my family I would not be anyone, but today I have learned the languages and the arts that I like. I was born a man in a woman's body."[129] It seems she could not escape prescribed gender norms, even as she rejected them.

The story of the singer Naʿima al-Misriyya followed a different trajectory, but it also illuminates the depth to which hegemonic ideals had penetrated individual Egyptians' lives. Misriyya's singing career spanned twenty-six years, from 1911 to 1937. The daughter of a Moroccan merchant and a wealthy Egyptian landowning family, Misriyya started singing at weddings at age seventeen and, despite her family's disapproval, managed to save enough money to open her own music hall, the Al-Hambra, on ʿImad al-Din Street. She continued her career through five marriages. Her daughter's marriage to a conservative Egyptian accountant forced the end of Misriyya's career, as he insisted she decline further invitations to perform. In time, all of her recordings and evidence of her singing career were given away or destroyed in an effort to erase her stigma from the family's legacy.[130] Only her granddaughter's efforts to reconstruct a family history revived her story.

The attempt to erase evidence of Misriyya's career illuminates both the provocation of performing women as well as the limits of the alternative identities they offered. There may be no greater example of the ways performing women navigated hegemonic ideals and their own position within them than the story of the renowned Egyptian singer Umm Kalthum. Kalthum's career began in the 1920s, when her father, recognizing his daughter's talent, brought her to Cairo to perform with him and her brother and male cousin. Seen initially as an unsophisticated country girl who was trained in Qur'anic recitation and who sang old religious songs, Kalthum endeavored to reverse her image. She learned new musical styles and worked her way up to perform in major music halls and theaters. Her reach was massive once her concerts were broadcast over the then-new technology of radio, and her recordings were also extremely successful. In 1926, Baidaphon paid Kalthum fifty pounds per record when they paid Mahdiyya only forty.[131] Eventually, record sales earned enough to provide her an annual income, and she assumed personal control over all of her own finances. Kalthum never married, and she kept her private life out of the public view—an increasingly difficult task as fan magazines proliferated. In the press, she cultivated a dignified demeanor, most often pictured in long, elegant dresses and with the trademark handkerchief she held in her hand while performing. Kalthum sang for political leaders, kings, and presidents, openly professing her patriotism. Her fierce control over her public persona allowed her to curate a pristine image that set the standard for female performers.[132]

In her lifetime, critics occasionally voiced anxiety about the intoxication her concerts inspired in her audiences, but after her death, those seem to have been forgotten. Cast as a national mother, a symbol of the nation and its honor, accounts in memory of Umm Kalthum reinterpreted the unconventional elements of her life. Never marrying or having children and her decision to be a public performer became examples of the sacrifices she made, and ultimately her transcendence of her gender, to uphold the honor of the nation.[133]

Onstage, the rhetoric surrounding the revolution of 1919, despite its mixed political outcome, provided a language for women to link their increased public presence to the well-being of the nation. Advancing the nationalist cause allowed Mahdiyya and her peers to shape her modern career using local idioms, within an expanding and changing definition of respectability. She blended nationalist rhetoric with older forms of female respectability in the context of a burgeoning sphere of commercial performance to create a new prototype for what a modern woman could be. In some ways, Mahdiyya supported a model of Egyptian womanhood that nationalist leaders and leaders of the movement for women's rights promulgated. Her work in the public arena might be seen as a logical extension of women's demands for more public participation. The language of patriotism offered Mahdiyya and other performing women a means to be independent and free—political and social concepts strongly linked to modernity—while retaining some sort of authenticity and concern with adab and ʿafaf. Engaging such language, while also navigating local concerns regarding a female performer's respectability (having a male protector, mastering the male musical repertoire, and her use of commercial recording, which allowed the dissemination of her voice without the appearance of her body), allowed her to appear as a modern presence in the public sphere.

Mahdiyya's career, and those of her peers, threatened the parameters of the ideal Egyptian woman, and by extension they could be considered threats to the stability of the nation. Performers' visibility and their public voice in questionable spaces in front of mixed audiences flouted the idealized female roles as wives and mothers in Egyptian society. The new category of "celebrity" further mediated the tension between the domesticated woman and the performing woman. It made female performers models of womanhood that diverged from and disrupted the ideal proffered by nationalists as well as by participants in the elite women's movement.

But female performers and their families' self-censorship demonstrated how persuasive the ideal of the effendi—supported by the model maternal citizen—was by the interwar period. Thus even as performing women threatened the stability of the nation, they also expanded and contributed to the meaning of the respectable modern Egyptian women. As an exceptional figure, Umm Kalthum's status and authority allowed her to shape the patriotic maternal citizen ideal in perhaps the most clear light. Even as she sang publically, Kalthum's patriotism, comportment, and cultivated public persona allowed her to sustain and balance a public career while epitomizing the respectability of the modern woman and the unity of the modern nation.

Conclusion

Theater writers, performers, and audiences played critical roles in the shaping of class and nation in Egypt. Bolstered and complemented by the Arabic press, theatrical spaces of many kinds were essential spaces where individuals contested the authority of their occupiers to frame history and situate Egypt and Egyptians in the contemporary world. It was also a place for them to mirror and debate conversations about what it meant to be modern and Egyptian.

But the message was not unified, and identity was not defined in a single way. For elites, the construction of an Italian-designed opera house in central Cairo presented Egypt as a modern, commanding force, independent of the Ottoman Empire and commensurate with contemporary European powers. The specially commissioned opera *Aida* instantiated this by representing Egyptian identity as rooted in its ancient history. But elite modernity never translated, nor was intended, to include fully the broader mass of Egyptian society. *Effendis* who worked within the middle-class Arabic theater circuit represented their own lifestyles and mores on stage as models for how to be both modern and "authentically" Egyptian even as they increasingly circumscribed how they defined themselves. At the same time, the *shaʿb*, a significant target group for "effendification," navigated effendi prescriptions while retaining what they considered a more authentic Egyptian identity. Mockery reduced those more powerful and made those who understood the jokes superior in their real understanding of the messiness of the world. Meanwhile, female performers challenged old stigmas by borrowing language from the nationalist and women's reform movements to create modern Egyptian identities. As they benefited from new technologies and entered new public spaces, they tried to temper their threatening visibility and independence by using new technologies to demonstrate respectability.

Ultimately, the *effendiyya*'s social, cultural, and political concerns would come to dominate conversations about modern Egyptianness. Effendis managed to harness concerns of diverse groups in the service of independence, and they benefited from the synergy of various new media—like theater and, later, cinema—in the first two decades of the twentieth century. Indeed, the effendiyya as a social group emerged contemporaneously with the rise of modern theater in Egypt. The fact that a small number of colloquial songwriters and scriptwriters dominated the entertainment sector contributed to effendi success in developing a coherent repertoire of words and ideas denoting shared identity and common language. Though not all Egyptians attended theaters, the most popular songs from the stage were also recorded on phonographs, part of a burgeoning new industry that disseminated voices, music, and the ideas contained therein to a wide and diverse listening audience. The relationships that performers forged as they moved through these new social spaces encouraged them to see themselves as critical players in constructing the ideal of Egypt as a "bounded moral-political entity."[1] Their use of new technologies helped performers to shape consumers, national tastes, and modern identities even as audiences spoke back to them.

Political realities unified the populace but also seemed to eclipse the interests and concerns of women, the shaʿb, and others who did not conform to effendi ideals. The suffering brought by World War I coupled with the clear existence of a common British enemy made independence seem to be the panacea for all social problems, and a protracted negotiation for independence only bolstered a sense of shared Egyptian identity in opposition to the British enemy. By providing a forum for the critique of society, encouraging vocal and invested audiences, and infusing the revolution itself with music and song, theater culturally undergirded the unfolding of 1919. Nevertheless, in its aftermath, as the effendiyya attained political power and effendi culture became increasingly hegemonic in Egypt, women and workers were disappointed in effendi leadership and disenfranchised from a country that neglected their concerns. Modern Egyptian identity may have appeared uniform in rhetoric, but it was not so in reality.

Questions about what a modern Egypt should be persisted in both politics and theater in the era often referred to as Egypt's "liberal experiment."[2] The 1920s and 1930s in Egypt were an era of semi-independence and nascent liberal political institutions. But they were also a time of economic crisis and political stalemate, as Britain's continued dominance in Egyptian affairs hindered any real autonomy. As social problems multiplied and fascism gained some Egyptians' sympathies, extraparliamentary organizations like the Muslim Brotherhood, the fascist Young Egypt, and numerous communist organizations increasingly challenged the effendi, liberal-nationalist vision of Egypt.

Challenges to national identity emerged in the artistic arena as well.[3] The rise of the professional artist coincided with the rise of the effendi, and as effendis moved into political leadership roles, artistic value was increasingly measured by artists' contributions to the construction of a national heritage. Artists' work adopted signifiers of national identity, most notably elements of Egypt's pharaonic past, to create a canon of "authentically" Egyptian art, and the state patronized their work by championing cultural organizations like the Egyptian Association of Fine Arts and the Société des Amis de l'Art.[4]

In response, a number of independent artists' collectives emerged to play with and challenge the normative nationalist and bourgeois art world. One of the most theatrical was the Art and Liberty collective, which the art historian Sam Bardaouil explains rejected the "conflation of art with national sentiment."[5] Concerned with social problems of poverty, the plight of women and working classes, and local profascist sentiment, the group announced its creation in a manifesto, *Vivre l'Art Dégenéré* (Long Live Degenerate Art), which was published on December 22, 1938. Its presumed author, Georges Henein, wrote: "It was mere idiocy and folly to reduce modern art . . . to a fanaticism for any particular religion, race, or nation," and it championed Surrealism and its uninhibited freedom of artistic expression as a fitting counterpoint to tyranny and a means to instigate social change.[6] Between the 1930s and late 1940s, the group hosted five exhibitions of its emancipatory, spontaneous art, and produced multiple publications that challenged what members saw as bourgeois rigidity in art and thought while making visible the horrors of war, prostitution, and neglect.[7]

The Art and Liberty group's critiques highlight several points. As but one example of groups who challenged hegemonic effendi ideals, it is clear that alternatives to dominant effendi conceptions of modern Egyptian identity persisted well into the interwar period. As effendis took the reigns of power and became the storytellers of Egyptian history, they crafted a narrative that aimed at a unified authenticity even as Egypt and its relationship to the rest of the world was changing. But a look beyond the official archive reveals that identity is always in process. In the dynamic between its repeated performance and reception there lies a multitude of alternative renderings and interpretations.

Notes

Introduction

1. *Al-Muqattam*, 7 July 1906, rpt. Ahmad Sakhsukh, ed., *Al-Masrah al-Misri, 1906–1910* (Cairo: Dar al-Zaʿim li al-Tabaʿa al-Haditha, 1998), 48.

2. Amira Sonbol, ed., *The Last Khedive of Egypt: Memoirs of Abbas Hilmi II* (Reading, UK: Ithaca Press, 1998), 158.

3. The Earl of Cromer, *Modern Egypt* (New York: MacMillan, 1908), vol. 1: xvii–xviii.

4. Mohammed Wahid, letter to Sir Edward Grey, 4 Sept. 1907, FO 371, British National Archive [hereinafter BNA], London, England. Mustafa Kamil responded to the accusations of a larger Muslim conspiracy by openly declaring that "that so-called threat was . . . a ploy to legitimize the recent atrocities and other atrocities that may be perpetrated in the future. But that danger of Muslim fanaticism does not exist although such atrocities might create it" (*Al-Mu'ayyid*, 6 July 1906, rpt. *Egyptian Gazette* [9 July 1906, 3]).

5. "The Denishwai Affair. Trial of the Accused. Description of the Court," *Egyptian Gazette*, 25 June 1906, 3. I've retained the spelling of "Denishwai," as it was written. The issues of the paper that covered the Dinshaway trial were so popular that the *Gazette* could not keep up with requests for copies.

6. "The Denishwai Affair. Continuation of Trial. The Closing Stages," *Egyptian Gazette*, 26 June 1906, 3.

7. BNA, Confidential paper 8842.

8. The effendiyya were split in their positions with regard to British occupation; some preferred a more moderate, evolutionary stance toward British withdrawal (exemplified by al-Sayyid and his newspaper *al-Jarida*) while others supported shifts in the Watani Party as it increasingly promoted revolution. See, for example, Muhammad Farid, *The Memoirs and Diaries of Muhammad Farid, an Egyptian Nationalist Leader*, intro., trans., and anno. Arthur Goldschmidt (San Francisco: Mellon University Research Press, 1992), 25.

9. Kamil, "The Dinshaway Affair: To the English Nation and to the Civilized World," *Le Figaro*, 11 July 1906, rpt. Sonbol, ed., *The Last Khedive*, 166.

10. BNA, Confidential paper 8842; "The Denishwai Affair," 3; Ahmad Lutfi (al-

Sayyid) would later start the moderate political journal *al-Jarida*. Sonbol, ed., *The Last Khedive*, 166. Other members of the court were Fathi Bey Zaghlul, William Ahmad Goodenough Hayter, M. Bond, and Lieutenant-Colonel Ludlow (Judge Advocate).

11. "La Chasse Aux Colombes ou L'Affaire de Denshawai," *Revue du Monde Musulman*, Nov.-Dec. 1907, 504–509.

12. "La Chasse," 508.

13. "La Chasse," 509.

14. "La Chasse," 509.

15. *Al-Mu'ayyid*, 12 July 1906, rpt. Sakhsukh, ed., *Al-Masrah al-Misri 1906–1910*, 49; *Wadi al-Nil*, 15 Dec. 1909, rpt. Sakhsukh, ed., *Al-Masrah al-Misri 1906–1910*, 9.

16. For more on the relationship between space and audience, see, for example, Marvin Carlson, *Places of Performance: The Semiotics of Theatre Architecture* (Ithaca and London: Cornell University Press, 1989); Yi-Fu Tuan, "Space and Context," in *By Means of Performance: Intercultural Studies of Theatre and Ritual*, ed. Richard Schechner and Willa Appel (Cambridge, UK: Cambridge University Press, 1990).

17. An *Egyptian Gazette* article titled "Story of the Outrage" referred to the fellahin as "a very savage and criminal people" (18 June 1906), 3.

18. Wilson Chacko Jacob, *Working Out Egypt: Effendi Masculinity and Subject Formation in Colonial Modernity, 1870–1940* (Durham, NC: Duke University Press, 2011), 46.

19. Jacob, *Working Out Egypt*, 46; Lucie Ryzova, "Egyptianizing Modernity Through the 'New *Effendiyya*': Social and Cultural Constructions of the New Middle Class in Egypt Under the Monarchy," in *Re-Envisioning Egypt, 1919–1952*, eds. Arthur Goldschmidt, Amy J. Johnson, and Barak A. Salmoni (New York: American University in Cairo Press, 2005), 124–163.

20. Jacob, *Working Out Egypt*, 5–6, 62–63.

21. On Barak, *On Time: Technology and Temporality in Modern Egypt* (Berkeley: University of California Press, 2013), 5.

22. Hanan Hammad, *Industrial Sexuality: Gender, Urbanization, and Social Transformation in Egypt* (Austin: University of Texas Press, 2016), 11.

23. Nandi Bhatia, *Acts of Authority, Acts of Resistance: Theater and Politics in Colonial and Postcolonial India* (Ann Arbor: University of Michigan Press, 2004), 3.

24. See, for example, Kelly M. Askew, *Performing the Nation: Swahili Music and Cultural Politics in Tanzania* (Chicago: University of Chicago Press, 2002); Bhatia, *Acts of Authority*; Joshua Goldstein, *Drama Kings: Players and Publics in the Re-creation of Peking Opera, 1870–1937* (Berkeley: University of California Press, 2007); Susan Seizer, *Stigmas of the Tamil Stage: An Ethnography of Special Drama Artists in South India* (Durham, NC: Duke University Press, 2005).

25. T. J. Jackson Lears, "The Concept of Cultural Hegemony: Problems and Possibilities," *American Historical Review* 90:3 (June 1985): 591.

26. Barak, *On Time*; Beth Baron, *Egypt as a Woman: Nationalism, Gender, and Politics* (Berkeley: University of California Press, 2005); Yoav Di-Capua, *Gatekeepers of the Arab Past: History and History Writing in Twentieth-Century Egypt* (Berkeley: University of California Press, 2009); Ziad Fahmy, *Ordinary Egyptians: Creating the Modern Nation through Popular Culture* (Stanford: Stanford University Press, 2011); Nelly Hanna, *In Praise of Books: A Cultural History of Cairo's Middle Class* (Syracuse: Syracuse University Press, 2003); Michael Ezekiel Gasper, *Power of Representation: Publics,*

Peasants, and Islam in Egypt (Stanford: Stanford University Press, 2009); Hammad, *Industrial Sexuality*; Jacob, *Working Out Egypt*; Hussein Omar, "'And I Saw No Reason to Chronicle My Life': Tensions of Nationalist Modernity in the Memoirs of Fathallah Pasha Barakat," in *The Long 1890s in Egypt: Colonial Quiescence, Subterranean Resistance*, ed. Marilyn Booth and Anthony Gorman (Edinburgh: Edinburgh University Press, 2014); Lisa Pollard, *Nurturing the Nation: The Family Politics of Modernizing, Colonizing, and Liberating Egypt, 1805–1923* (Berkeley: University of California Press, 2005); Eve M. Troutt Powell, *A Different Shade of Colonialism: Egypt, Great Britain, and the Mastery of the Sudan* (Berkeley: University of California Press, 2003); Mona Russell, *Creating the New Egyptian Woman: Consumerism, Education, and National Identity, 1863–1922* (New York: Palgrave Macmillan, 2004); Lucie Ryzova, *The Age of the Effendiyya: Passages to Modernity in National-Colonial Egypt* (Oxford: Oxford University Press, 2014); Keith David Watenpaugh, *Being Modern in the Middle East: Revolution, Nationalism, Colonialism, and the Arab Middle Class* (Princeton: Princeton University Press, 2006); Hoda A. Yousef, *Composing Egypt: Reading, Writing, and the Emergence of a Modern Nation, 1870–1930* (Stanford: Stanford University Press, 2016).

27. Nancy Reynolds, *A City Consumed: Urban Commerce, the Cairo Fire, and the Politics of Decolonization in Egypt* (Stanford: Stanford University Press, 2012), 7.

28. Stuart Hall, "Who Needs Identity?" in *Questions of Cultural Identity*, ed. Stuart Hall and Paul du Gay (London: Sage Press, 1996), 2–3.

29. Marvin Carlson, *Performance: A Critical Introduction* (London: Routledge, 2003), 44. For literature on the relationship between social performance and social roles, see Friedrich Nietzsche, *Human, All Too Human*, trans. Marion Faber (Lincoln: University of Nebraska Press, 1984), 18. For a more positive take, see William James, *The Philosophy of William James* (New York: Random House, 1925); Michel de Certeau, *The Practice of Everyday Life*, trans. Steven F. Rendall (Berkeley: University of California Press, 1984), xix.

30. Hall, "Who Needs Identity," 4.

31. Stuart Hall, "The Question of Cultural Identity," in *Modernity: An Introduction to Modern Societies*, ed. Stuart Hall, David Held, Don Hubert, and Kenneth Thompson (Oxford: Blackwell, 1996), 617.

32. Hall, "The Question of Cultural Identity," 618.

33. Roger Caillos, *Man, Play, and Games*, trans. Helen Iswolsky (Cambridge, MA: MIT Press, 1965), 9–10.

34. Victor Turner, *From Ritual to Theatre* (New York: *Performing Arts Journal* Publications, 1982), 20–60.

35. The director, theorist, educator, and editor Richard Schnechner stressed the social experience of theater, highlighting "the importance of the underlying social event as a nest for the theatrical event," in *Performance Theory* (London and New York: Routledge, 1988), 195.

36. Erika Fischer-Lichte, "Culture as Performance," *Modern Austrian Literature* 42:3 (2009): 3–4.

37. Fischer-Lichte, "Culture as Performance," 3. This diverges somewhat from Erving Goffman's development of the concept of "framing." He describes performance as a circumscribed sequence of activity before an audience, whose duty it is to observe at length the activities of the performers without directly participating in those activities (Erving Goffman, *Frame Analysis* [Garden City, NY: Doubleday, 1974]).

38. Mikhail Bakhtin, *Rabelais and His World*, trans. Helen Iswolsky (Cambridge, MA: MIT Press, 1965), 122–123. For more on the disruptive potential of performance, see Bertolt Brecht, *Brecht on Theatre: The Development of an Aesthetic*, ed. and trans. John Willet (London: Methuen, 1964); Judith Butler, *Gender Trouble: Feminism and the Subversion of Identity* (London: Routledge, 1990); Helene Cixous and Catherine Clement, *The Newly Born Woman*, trans. Betsy Wing (London: I. B. Tauris, 1996).

39. *Al-Muqattam*, 12 April 1900, rpt. Ramsis 'Awad, *Al-Tarikh al-Sirri li al-Masrah Qabl Thawrat 1919* (Cairo: Mutba'a al-Kilani, 1972), 6.

40. Turner, *From Ritual to Theatre*, 45.

41. "Reglement sur les theatres promulgué par arrête du Ministère de l'Intérieur," *Recueil des Documents Officiels du Gouvernement Egyptien* (Cairo: n.p., 1911).

42. Nevill Barbour, "The Arabic Theater in Egypt," *Bulletin of the School of Oriental Studies, University of London* 8:1 (1935): 182.

43. "La Chasse Aux Colombes," 504.

44. "La Chasse Aux Colombes," 504–509.

45. Marvin Carlson, *Performance: A Critical Introduction* (London: Routledge, 2003), 196–197.

Chapter 1

1. See 'Arafah 'Abdu 'Ali, *Al-Qahira fi 'Asr Isma'il* (Cairo: Dar al-Misriyya al-Lubnaniyya, 1998), 70.

2. Clyde T. McCants, *Verdi's* Aida*: A Record of the Life of the Opera On and Off the Stage* (Jefferson, NC: McFarland & Co., 2006), 22. Auguste Mariette, letter to Camille Du Locle, 28 April 1870, rpt. Hans Busch, ed., *Verdi's* Aida*: The History of an Opera in Letters and Documents* (Minneapolis: University of Minnesota Press, 1978), 12. Verdi's conditions for signing a contract appear in Giuseppe Verdi, letter to Camille Du Locle, 26 Aug. 1870, rpt. Busch, ed., *Verdi's* Aida, 57.

3. Mabel Caillard, *A Lifetime in Egypt, 1876–1935* (London: G. Richards, 1935), 19.

4. Caillard, *Lifetime*, 19; Max Rodenbeck, *Cairo: The City Victorious* (New York: Alfred A. Knopf, 1999), 133. The cost of the production exceeded 650,000 Egyptian pounds sterling. Draneht, letter to Riaz Pasha, 28 April 1871, File 3, Mahfuza 80, 'Asr Isma'il (Dar al-Watha'iq al-Qawmiyya, [hereinafter DWQ: Egyptian National Archives] Cairo, Egypt).

5. De Kusel was British controller-general of Egyptian customs. Samuel Selig De Kusel, *An Englishman's Recollections of Egypt, 1863–1888* (London: John Lane, 1915), 90.

6. Filippo Filippi, *Le Perseverenza*, Dec. 1871, rpt. Michel Boctor, *Le Centenaire de L'Opéra Aida, 1871–1971* (Alexandria: Les Cahiers d'Alexandrie, 1972).

7. Trevor Mostyn, *Egypt's Belle Époque: Cairo 1869–1952* (London: Quartet, 1989), 79–82.

8. Michel Boctor, *Aida, 1871–1971* (Alexandria: Les Cahiers d'Alexandrie, 1972), 23; Giuseppe Verdi, letter to Giulio Ricordi, 26 Dec. 1871, rpt. Busch, ed., *Verdi's* Aida, 269.

9. Initially, Isma'il had asked Verdi to compose a hymn in celebration of the opera house's opening, but Verdi refused, considering the job beneath him. *Aida*'s storyline,

however, captured Verdi's imagination. His interest in the story, along with rumors that Verdi's rival, Wagner, was Isma'il's second choice, may well have encouraged his acceptance of the charge. Paul Draneht, letter to Giuseppe Verdi, 28 April 1870, Opera House Documents (Opera House and Music Library, Cairo, Egypt). McCants, *Verdi's* Aida, 22. Auguste Mariette, letter to Camille Du Locle, 28 April 1870, rpt. Busch, ed., *Verdi's* Aida, 12. Verdi's conditions for signing a contract appear in Giuseppe Verdi, letter to Camille Du Locle, 26 Aug. 1870, rpt. Busch, ed., *Verdi's* Aida, 57.

10. Auguste Mariette, letter to Camille du Locle, 27 April 1870, rpt. Busch, ed., *Verdi's* Aida, 11.

11. Auguste Mariette, letters to Paul Draneht, 15 July 1870, 8 Aug. 1870, and 30 Aug. 1870, rpt. Busch, ed., *Verdi's* Aida, 300–301; Auguste Mariette, letter to Barrot Bey, 28 Aug. 1870, File 5, Mahfuza 80, 'Asr Isma'il (DWQ, Cairo, Egypt); Donald Malcolm Reid, *Whose Pharaohs? Archaeology, Museums, and Egyptian National Identity from Napoleon to World War I* (Berkeley: University of California Press, 2002), 129.

12. *Aida* was supposed to have premiered during the inauguration of the Suez Canal, but the Franco-Prussian War created obstacles to its completion in good time. In *Aida*'s place, the opera house staged *Rigoletto* instead.

13. Isma'il's involvement in the creation of *Aida* included instruction on the scenery, décor, and costumes to be used. Auguste Mariette, letter to Barrot Bey, 28 Aug. 1870, File 5, Mahfuza 80, 'Asr Isma'il (DWQ, Cairo, Egypt).

14. Reid, *Whose Pharaohs?*, 12.

15. Edward Said, *Culture and Imperialism* (New York: Vintage Books, 1994), 119, 125.

16. Janet Abu-Lughod, *Cairo: 1001 Years of the City Victorious* (Princeton: Princeton University Press, 1971), 105.

17. Cairo's domestication of foreign influence was much like other Ottoman cities in the same period. See Zeynep Celik, *Empire, Architecture, and the City: French-Ottoman Encounters, 1830–1914* (Seattle: University of Washington Press, 2008), and *The Remaking of Istanbul: Portrait of an Ottoman City in the Nineteenth Century* (Berkeley: University of California Press, 1986).

18. James Scott, *Seeing Like a State: How Certain Schemes to Improve the Human Condition Have Failed* (New Haven, CT: Yale University Press, 1998); Timothy Mitchell, *Colonising Egypt* (Berkeley: University of California Press, 1988), xiii.

19. Accounts differ with regard to the time frame of completion. See Trevor Mostyn, *Egypt's Belle Epoque: Cairo 1869–1952* (London: Quartet, 1989), 50; Otello Iolita, "Training and Stylistic Background of Italian Architects and Planners in Modern Egypt," in *Le Caire-Alexandrie* (Cairo: Institut Francais d'Archéologie Orientale, 2004), 184–185.

20. Sources list different seating capacities for the opera house, ranging from 750 to 1,000. See, for example, 'Arafah 'Abdu 'Ali, *Al-Qahira fi 'Asr Isma'il*, 70; P. C. Sadgrove, *The Egyptian Theatre in the Nineteenth Century: 1799–1882* (Berkshire, UK: Ithaca Press, 1996), 52–53.

21. Caillard, *Lifetime in Egypt*, 18; Paul Draneht, letter to Riaz Pasha, 1 January 1870, File 7, Mahfuzah 80, 'Asr Isma'il (DWQ, Cairo, Egypt). A letter from Emanuele Muzio (Verdi's former student and friend who conducted the opera house's inaugural performance of *Rigoletto*) to Verdi mentioned a fire that broke out in the clock above the proscenium. 7 January 1870, rpt. Busch, ed., *Verdi's* Aida, 6.

22. Mashrabiya screens had been outlawed by Mehmed ʿAli during his time as governor. See Nihal S. Tamraz, *Nineteenth-Century Cairene Houses and Palaces* (Cairo: American University in Cairo Press, 1994), 38–39.

23. Jean-Marcel Humbert, "Les Expositions Universelles de 1867 et 1878 et La Création d'Aida," in *La France et L'Égypte à l'Époque des Vice-Rois 1805–1882*, ed. Daniel Panzac and André Raymond (Cairo: Institut Francais d'Archéologie Orientale, 2002), 298–299.

24. The *salamlik* was a domestic space typically found in upper-class and upper-middle-class homes.

25. Mitchell, *Colonizing Egypt*, 64.

26. Isma'il had studied in Paris as a boy and later served a diplomatic role there under the previous Egyptian governor, Said. P. J. Vatikiotis, *The Modern History of Egypt* (New York: Frederick A. Praeger, 1969), 79.

27. See, for example, Abu-Lughod, *Cairo*, 104; Hubert, "Les Expositions Universelles," 290; Reid, *Whose Pharaohs?*, 129.

28. See, for example, Abu Lughod, *Cairo*, 105–110; Blanchard Jerrold, *Egypt Under Ismaʿil Pasha* (London: Samuel Tinsley and Co., 1879), 28; David S. Landes, *Bankers and Pashas: International Finance and Economic Imperialism in Egypt* (New York: Harper & Row, 1958), 154; Reid, *Whose Pharaohs?*, 215–217.

29. Michel Carmona, *Haussmann: His Life and Times, and the Making of Modern Paris* (Chicago: Ivan R. Dee, 2002), 389, 391, 404.

30. See, for example, Khaled Asfour, "The Domestification of Knowledge: Cairo at the Turn of the Century," in *Muqarnas: An Annual on Islamic Art and Architecture*, vol. 10, *Essays in Honor of Oleg Grabar* (Leiden: E. J. Brill, 1993), 127–129. Asfour argues that it wasn't until the 1890s that there was a shift in Egyptian architecture away from "blind faithfulness to the French model" to what he terms a "domestification" of architectural theory. As he defines it, domestification meant "modifying the original model so that it became just one component of a new product, the other components of which would spring from the peculiarities of the local culture." In effect, "negotiation and compromise" with local people and conditions became the norm. Asfour acknowledges, however, that from the beginning Egyptian engineering students were taught theory but also environmental conditions in Egypt that had to be taken into account when importing "Western" techniques.

31. See Mercedes Volait, ed., *Le Caire-Alexandrie: Architectures Européennes, 1850–1950* (Cairo: Institut Francais d'Archéologie Orientale, 2004).

32. J. C. McCoan, *Egypt As It Is: 1829–1904* (New York: H. Holt, 1877), 49.

33. McCoan, *Egypt As It Is*, 50; André Raymond, *Arab Cities in the Ottoman Period* (Burlington, VT: Ashgate, 2002), 160–162, 260.

34. Isma'il spent approximately 3 billion French francs on engineering during his reign. See Vatikiotis, *Modern History of Egypt*, 84–85; Volait, *Architectes et Architectures*, 108; Abu-Lughod, *Cairo*, 107–108; Mohamad Refaat Tarek, *Early 20th Islamic Architecture* (Cairo: American University in Cairo Press, 1993).

35. William L. Cleveland, *A History of the Modern Middle East* (Boulder: Westview Press, 1994), 94.

36. Landes, *Bankers and Pashas*, 111.

37. David Levering Lewis, *Race to Fashoda: Colonialism and African Resistance* (New York: Henry Holt & Co., 1987), 26.

38. Abu-Lughod, *Cairo*, 105.

39. McCoan, *Egypt*, 50; Sadgrove, *The Egyptian Theatre*, 46–47.

40. Nina Nelson, *Shepheard's Hotel* (London: Barrie and Rockliff, 1960).

41. Reid, *Whose Pharaohs?*, 97, 105.

42. See, for example, Karl Baedeker, ed., *Egypt* (Leipsic: Karl Baedeker, 1885); Thomas Cook, *Cook's Tourists' Handbook for Egypt, the Nile, and the Desert* (London: Thomas Cook and Son, 1876).

43. Tamraz, *Nineteenth-Century Cairene Houses*, 24–27.

44. Tamraz, *Nineteenth-Century Cairene Houses*, 35.

45. Rita Abrahamson, "African Studies and the Postcolonial Challenge," *African Affairs* 102 (2003), 205–206.

46. Mitchell, *Colonising Egypt*, xii.

47. For more on legibility and the modern state outside of Egypt, see Scott, *Seeing Like a State*, 9–84.

48. Mitchell, *Colonising Egypt*, xiv.

49. Mitchell, *Colonising Egypt*, xv.

50. Mara Naaman, *Urban Space in Contemporary Egyptian Literature: Portraits of Cairo* (New York: Palgrave MacMillan, 2011), 24.

51. Naaman, *Urban Space*, 28.

52. Nelly Hanna, "The Urban History of Cairo Around 1900," in *Historians in Cairo: Essays in Honor of George Scanlon*, ed. Jill Edwards (Cairo: American University in Cairo Press, 2002), 192. Hanna argues that the "core area" changed over time. In the mid-nineteenth century, the "core" was the Azbakiyya and surrounding districts.

53. Hanna, "Urban History of Cairo," 193.

54. Ministry of Finance, *The Census of Egypt Taken in 1907*, vol. 1 (Cairo: National Printing Department, 1921).

55. Hanna, "Urban History of Cairo," 198–199.

56. De Kusel, *An Englishman's Recollections*, 78; Volait, *Architectes et Architectures*, 105.

57. McCoan, *Egypt As It Is*, 49.

58. Caillard, *Lifetime in Egypt*, 17.

59. John C. Van Dyke, *In Egypt* (New York: C. Scribner's Sons, 1931), xxii–xxiii.

60. McCoan, *Egypt As It Is*, 48.

61. Alfred Butler, *Court Life in Egypt* (London: Chapman & Hall, Scribner & Welford, 1887), 116–117.

62. James McDougall, *History and the Culture of Nationalism in Algeria* (Cambridge, UK: Cambridge University Press, 2006).

63. Paula Sanders, *Creating Medieval Cairo: Empire, Religion, and Architectural Preservation in Nineteenth-Century Egypt* (Cairo: American University in Cairo Press, 2008); Nezar AlSayyad, Irene A. Bierman, and Nasser Rabbat, eds., *Making Cairo Medieval* (Oxford: Lexington Books, 2005).

64. Elliott Colla, *Conflicted Antiquities: Egyptology, Egyptomania, Egyptian Modernity* (Durham, NC: Duke University Press, 2007), 135.

65. Drahnet Bey, letter to Riaz Pasha, June 1870, File 7, Mahfuza 80, ʿAsr Ismaʿil (DWQ, Cairo, Egypt).

66. Budgets from 1869 onward are available in File 3, Mahfuza 80, ʿAsr Ismaʿil (DWQ, Cairo, Egypt). Notably, the opera *Aida*'s budget and all other expenses con-

nected to it were always listed separately in ledgers. Not being lumped together with other performances for 1869, it was set apart, even financially, from the others. Paul Draneht, letters to Riaz Pasha, June 1870; 13 July 1870; and 27 Aug. 1870, File 7, Mahfuza 80, 'Asr Isma'il (DWQ, Cairo, Egypt). Alfred Butler complained that, during the opera season, "one actress alone got 1200 l. a month; all had money and jewels showered on them at leaving" (Butler, *Court Life*, 61).

67. Drahnet Bey, letter to Barrot Bey, 24 Nov. 1871, File 3, Mahfuzah 80, 'Asr Isma'il (DWQ, Cairo, Egypt).

68. Draneht, letters to Riaz Pasha, 27 Aug. 1869; 24 May 1870; June 1870, File 7, Mahfuza 80, 'Asr Isma'il (DWQ, Cairo, Egypt); Draneht, letter to Barrot Bey, 21 April 1875, File 1, Mahfuza 80, 'Asr Isma'il (DWQ, Cairo, Egypt). After the turn of the century, the *Egyptian Standard*, an English-language version of nationalist Mustafa Kamil's *al-Liwa*, called for more government subsidies for the opera house as it was undeniably an important tourist destination: "What about the foreign tourists who come here to pass a season, a month, or a fortnight," the author asks. "If Cairo wishes to compete with the Riviera and other winter health-resorts, the opera must be patronised and strongly subventioned by the Government" ("Opera Season," *Egyptian Standard* [13 Sept. 1907]: 1).

69. Paul Draneht, letter to Eram Bey, 27 Nov. 1869, File 4, Mahfuza 80, 'Asr Isma'il (DWQ, Cairo, Egypt); Budget for 1871–1872, File 4, Mahfuza 80, 'Asr Isma'il (DWQ, Cairo, Egypt).

70. "Theatre de l'Opera, Note des abonnements pour compte de S. A. le Khedive," Nov., Dec. 1869, 12 March 1872, File 4, Mahfuza 80, 'Asr Isma'il (DWQ, Cairo, Egypt).

71. Sadgrove, *Egyptian Theatre*, 13; 'Abd al-Rahman al-Jabarti, *A History of Egypt* (Stuttgart: Franz Steiner Verlas, 1994).

72. Butler, *Court Life*, 179.

73. Butler, *Court Life*, 282.

74. Sadgrove, *Egyptian Theatre*, 66–67.

75. 'Abd al-Rahman al-Jabarti, *'Aja'ib al-Athar fi al-Tarajim wa al-Akhbar* (Cairo: Bulaq Press, 1879), 200, rpt. Thomas Philipp and Moshe Permann, eds., vols. 3 and 4 (Stuttgart: Franz Steiner Verlag, 1994), 224.

76. Some performers like Salama Hijazi, Ahmad Abu Khalil, and Sulayman al-Qirdahi were able to perform on the opera house stage, but only for a limited number of shows. See, for example, Rouchdy Pasha, letter to Council of Ministers, 24 Dec. 1884, Mahfuza 1/2, Al-Magmu'a al-Ashghal, Majlis al-Wuzara' (DWQ, Cairo, Egypt).

77. Sulayman al-Qirdahi, letter to Lord Cromer, No. 464, File 141, Foreign Office (BNA, London, England).

78. See, for example, James H. Johnson, *Listening in Paris: A Cultural History* (Berkeley: University of California Press, 1995).

79. This was similar to the function of the opera house in eighteenth-century France. As James Johnson writes, "like the balls, banquets, coronations, and ceremonies of absolutism, musical experience in the Old Regime served the ideological function of temporarily illuminating the invisible power structure of the system." Johnson, *Listening in Paris*, 34.

80. C. A. Bayly, *The Birth of the Modern World, 1780–1914: Global Connections and*

Comparisons (Malden, MA: Blackwell Publishing, 2004), 11–12. The American diplomat Thomas Skelton Harrison made note of one M. Turnères's visit to his loge, or box, during the intermission of *Rigoletto*. In another entry, he writes at greater length about his secretary's experience being "invited into Lord Granville's loge" where he "had much politeness generally offered to him" (Thomas Skelton Harrison, *The Homely Diary of a Diplomat in the East: 1897–1899* [Boston: Houghton Mifflin Co., 1917], 52, 80).

81. "Subventions to Theatres," *Egyptian Gazette*, 27 Oct. 1906: 3.

82. " L'Opéra Khédivial du Caire," *Egyptian Gazette*, 23 Jan. 1893: 3.

83. " L'Opéra Khédivial du Caire," *Egyptian Gazette*, 23 Jan. 1893: 3.

84. Roger Owen, *Lord Cromer: Victorian Imperialist, Edwardian Proconsul* (Oxford: Oxford University Press, 2004), 332.

85. Magda Baraka, *The Egyptian Upper Class Between Revolutions 1919–1952* (Reading, UK: Ithaca Press, 1998), 19–20.

86. F. Robert Hunter, *Egypt under the Khedives, 1805–1879: From Household Government to Modern Bureaucracy* (Cairo: American University in Cairo Press, 1984), 54.

87. An oft-recounted anecdote about the first Chamber meeting illustrates the limited scope of the delegates' powers. When the shaykhs were told to form three groups following European parliamentary models—a "right" to support government, a "left" opposition, and a moderate middle—all of them scrambled to take a place on the right. (Alexander Scholch, *Egypt for the Egyptians: The Sociopolitical Crisis in Egypt, 1878–1882* [London: Ithaca Press, 1981]), 16.

88. Hunter, *Egypt under the Khedives*, 102.

89. See, for example, Huda Sha'rawi, *Harem Years: The Memoirs of an Egyptian Feminist* (Cairo: American University in Cairo Press, 1998), 88–91.

90. Hunter, *Egypt under the Khedives*, 101.

91. Toledano, *State and Society*, 249 (emphasis in original).

92. De Kusel, *An Englishman's Recollections*, 90.

93. Mostyn, *Egypt's Belle Epoque*, 79–80.

94. Mostyn, *Egypt's Belle Epoque*, 81–82.

95. Ellen Chennelle, *Recollections of an Egyptian Princess by Her English Governess* (London: William Blackwood and Sons, 1893), 59.

96. Ronald Storrs, *Orientations* (London: Ivor Nicholson & Watson, 1937), 27.

97. Leslie P. Pierce, *The Imperial Harem: Women and Sovereignty in the Ottoman Empire* (New York: Oxford University Press, 1993), 10.

98. For more on this, see Jurgen Habermas, *The Structural Transformation of the Public Sphere: An Inquiry into a Category of Bourgeois Society*, trans. Thomas Bürger (Cambridge, MA: MIT Press, 1962).

99. Pierce, *The Imperial Harem*, 8–10.

100. Gulru Necipoglu, *Architecture, Ceremonial, and Power: The Topkapi Palace in the Fifteenth and Sixteenth Centuries* (Cambridge, MA: MIT Press, 1991), xvi.

101. This was a major reason why adult males were kept out of the family quarters of the palace—any threat to the sultan's lineage was also a threat to his person.

102. D. Fairchild Ruggles, "Vision and Power: An Introduction," in D. Fairchild Ruggles, *Women, Patronage, and Self-Representation in Islamic Societies* (New York: SUNY Press, 2000), 3; Necipoglu, *Architecture, Ceremonial, and Power*, 174; Hassan Hassan, *In the House of Muhammad 'Ali: A Family Album, 1805–1952* (Cairo: American

University in Cairo Press, 2000), 60; Pierce, *Imperial Harem*. In the eighteenth and nineteenth centuries, harem women's power came from financial independence, sons, natal family, celibacy, education, and voice (which may have been connected to the previous categories). Ruggles, "Vision and Power," 8.

103. Hassan, *In the House*, 69.

104. Letter from Auguste Mariette to Camille Du Locle, 27 April 1870, rpt. Busch, ed., *Verdi's* Aida, 11.

105. Letter from Camille Du Locle to Verdi, 7 May 1870, rpt. Busch, ed., *Verdi's* Aida, 14.

106. McCants, *Verdi's* Aida, 22. Auguste Mariette, letter to Camille Du Locle, 28 April [1870], rpt. Busch, ed., *Verdi's* Aida, 12. Verdi's conditions for signing a contract appear in Giuseppe Verdi, letter to Camille Du Locle, 26 Aug. 1870, rpt. Busch, ed., *Verdi's* Aida, 57.

107. Letter from Auguste Mariette to Camille Du Locle, 29 May 1870, rpt. Busch, ed., *Verdi's* Aida, 18.

108. Said, *Culture and Imperialism*, 118, 125.

109. Edith Louisa Floyer Butcher, *Egypt As We Knew It* (London: Mills & Boon, 1911).

110. Reid, *Whose Pharaohs?*, 31.

111. This became even more pronounced upon Carter's unearthing of King Tutankhamen's tomb in November 1922. See Fayza Haikal, "Egypt's Past Regenerated by Its Own People," in *Napoleon in Egypt*, ed. Irene A. Bierman (Reading, UK: Garnet and Ithaca Press, 2003), 125–126.

112. Reid, *Whose Pharaohs?*, 65; see, for example, Georg Ebers, *An Egyptian Princess* (New York: Bigelow, Brown & Co., 1880).

113. Paul Draneht, letter to Khairi Pasha, 31 Jan. 1872, Opera House Documents (Opera House and Music Library, Cairo, Egypt). His translation of the libretto for *Les Huguenots* into Arabic earned him 1,006 francs.

114. Paul Draneht, letter to Khairi Pasha, 31 Jan. 1872, *Abdun* (DWQ, Cairo, Egypt).

115. Like many trained translators, Al-Suud was also a leader in arts and letters. He was a history master at Dar al-'Ulum, an author of history textbooks, and founder of the journals *Wadi al-Nil* (1866) and *Rawdat al-Madaris* (the first Arabic journal to publish translated European plays). The first publication of a translated European play was Muhammad Bey 'Uthman Jalal's *Al-Fakhkh al-Mansub li al-Hakim al-Maghsub* or *Al-Tabib Raghm Anfihi*. Al-Muwailihi and Jalal were also involved in the Translation Bureau's libretti translations. Sadgrove, *Egyptian Theatre*, 5; El Said Atia Abul-Naga, *Les Sources Francaises du Théâtre Égyptien (1870–1939)* (Alger: Societé Nationale d'Édition et de Diffusion, 1972), 64–65.

116. An article in *Wadi al-Nil*, for example, appealed to God to grant success to the translations of opera libretti and their use "so that the taste for them will spread amongst the native communities" (*Wadi al-Nil*, 55: 28 Feb. 1870, rpt. Sadgrove, *Egyptian Theatre*, 57–58).

117. *Al-Jawa'ib*, 513: 12 April 1871, rpt. Sadgrove, *Egyptian Theatre*, 61–62.

118. Colla, *Conflicted Antiquities*, 132.

119. William B. Heseltine and Hazel C. Wolf, *The Blue and the Gray on the Nile* (Chicago: University of Chicago Press, 1961).

120. Butler, *Court Life*, 198–199; Powell, *Different Shade*, 65–66.

121. Powell, *Different Shade*, 68.

122. Paul Robinson, "Is Aida an Orientalist Opera?" *Cambridge Opera Journal* 5:2 (1939), 135–136.

123. For more on the music of *Aida*, see Katherine Bergeron, "Verdi's Egyptian Spectacle: On the Colonial Subject of 'Aida,'" *Cambridge Opera Journal* 14:1/2 (March 2002): 149–159; Ralph P. Locke, "Beyond the Exotic: How 'Eastern' is Aida?," *Cambridge Opera Journal* 17:2 (July 2005): 105–139.

124. Robinson's discussion of Verdi's political leanings as someone sympathetic to the plight of the oppressed adds another layer to the opera. Seen through this perspective, *Aida* is about the Italian Risorgimento as much as it is about ancient Egypt.

125. See Powell, *Different Shade*, for a more detailed discussion of Egyptian perspectives on Africa in general and the ambivalent relationship between Egypt and the Sudan in particular.

126. "Representations of the Orient in 19th Century Opera," 2004 exhibition (Dahesh Museum, New York, NY).

127. Amira Sonbol, *The New Mamluks: Egyptian Society and Modern Feudalism* (Syracuse: Syracuse University Press, 2000), 87; Sadgrove, *Egyptian Theatre*, 3; Vatikiotis, *Modern History*, 103. The number of Egyptian French speakers during Isma'il's reign was about 50,000 (Abul Naga, *Les Sources Francaises*, 65).

128. "Subventions to Theatres," *Egyptian Gazette*, Sat., 27 Oct. 1906, 3.

129. Gabriel Charms, *Five Months at Cairo and in Lower Egypt* (London: Richard Bentley and Son, 1883), cited in Sadgrove, *Egyptian Theatre*, 54–55.

130. Edwin de Leon, *Egypt Under Its Khedives* (London: Sampson Low, Marston, Searle, and Revington, 1882), 182.

131. Chennelle, *Recollections*, 265.

Chapter 2

1. Su'ad Abyad, *Jurj Abyad: Ayyam lam yisbal al-sitar* (Cairo: al-Hay'a al-Misriyya al 'Amma lil Kitab, 1991), 50.

2. Alan Mikhail, "The Heart's Desire: Gender, Urban Space, and the Ottoman Coffee House," in *Ottoman Tulips, Ottoman Coffee: Leisure and Lifestyle in the Eighteenth Century*, ed. Dana Sajdi (London: I. B. Taurus, 2007); Alon Tam, "How Cairo's Cafes Made Egypt's 1919 Revolution," *Haaretz*, 14 Jan. 2017, www.haaretz.com/middle-east-news/egypt/.premium-1.763455.

3. Farah Antun, *Misr al-Jadida wa Misr al-Qadima* (Cairo: Maktabat al Ta'lif, 1913).

4. Yesim Arat, *Rethinking Islam and Liberal Democracy: Islamist Women in Turkish Politics* (Albany: SUNY Press, 2005), 1–14; Gasper, *Power of Representation*; Albert Hourani, *Arabic Thought in the Liberal Age, 1798–1939* (Cambridge, UK: Cambridge University Press, 1983), 1.

5. See, for example, Muhammad Taymur, *'Abd al-Sitar Effendi* (Cairo: Markaz al Ta'lif wa al-Targama, n.d.).

6. For more on the telling of Egyptian history, see Di-Capua, *Gatekeepers*.

7. Ilham Khuri-Makdisi rightly notes that, in theater, topics of social justice were usually tied to other issues of reform such as criticizing blind imitation of the "West"

and promoting female education. Her focus on "radical" theater led her to plays that also called for curbing the power of churches and demanding an Ottoman constitution. (Ilham Khuri-Makdisi, *The Eastern Mediterranean and the Making of Global Radicalism, 1860–1914* [Berkeley: University of California Press, 2010], 61–62).

8. "Baʿd al-Tamthil," Antun, *Misr al-Jadida*, prologue.

9. For more on the development of territoriality and legal categories of identity, see Matthew H. Ellis, *Desert Borderland: The Making of Modern Egypt and Libya* (Stanford: Stanford University Press, 2018); Will Hanley, *Identifying with Nationality: Europeans, Ottomans, and Egyptians in Alexandria* (New York: Columbia University Press, 2017).

10. Barbour, "The Arabic Theater," 173–187.

11. Sadgrove, *Egyptian Theatre*, 142.

12. See, for example, *al-Mashriq*, 2 (1899): 20–23, 71–74; and *al-Muqtataf*, 1 (Aug. 1926): 223–224.

13. Najib Effendi Hibeqa, *al-Mashriq*, 2 (1899): 20–23, 71–75.

14. Editors of *Al-Hilal* and *Al-Sufur*, respectively. Mustafa Kamil, too, wrote a play about Andalusia, which his friends performed after his death. Ramsis ʿAwad, *al-Tarikh al-Sirri li al-Masrah Qabl Thawrat 1919* (Cairo: Mutbaʿa al-Kilani, 1972), 96.

15. Jacob Landau, *Studies in the Arab Theater* (Philadelphia: University of Pennsylvania Press, 1958), 71.

16. Abul-Naga, *Les Sources Francaises*.

17. Carol Bardenstein, *Translation and Transformation in Modern Arabic Literature: The Indigenous Assertions of Muhammad ʿUthman Jalal* (Wiesbaden: Otto Harrassowitz Verlag, 2005); Mona Mikhail, "Revisiting the Theater in Egypt: An Overview," in Sherifa Zuhur, ed., *Colors of Enchantment: Theater, Dance, Music, and the Visual Arts in the Middle East* (Cairo: American University in Cairo Press, 2001), 17–26.

18. Landau, *Studies in the Arab Theater*, 74.

19. Barbour, "Arabic Theater in Egypt," 173–187. Farah's writers included Najib and Amin al-Haddad, Tanios ʿAbdu, and Ilyas Fayyad.

20. Fahmy, *Ordinary Egyptians*, 43–47.

21. M. M. Badawi, *Early Arabic Drama* (Cambridge, UK: Cambridge University Press, 1988), 74.

22. These included people like Abu Khalil al-Qabbani, Shaykh Salama Hijazi, and the ʿUkasha brothers; Barbour, "The Arabic Theater in Egypt," 173–187; Muhammad Yusuf Najm, *Al Masrahiyya fi al adab al ʿarabi al hadith 1847–1914* (Beirut: Dar Bayrut li al-Tibaʿa wa al-Nashr, 1956), 168.

23. Rawd al-Farag in Shubra, for example, offered entertainments at lower-priced and less reputable casinos, and Heliopolis hosted Luna Park, a playground for the wealthy. Baraka, *Egyptian Upper Class*, 122.

24. Most of this reconstruction comes from Alfred Farag, *Shariʿ ʿImad al-Din: Hikayat al-Fann wa al-Nijum* (Cairo: Dar al-Hilal, 2005).

25. See, for example, *The Sphinx*, 19 Feb. 1916, reporting on a Printannia fundraiser for the YMCA Solders' Club; and *The Sphinx*, 18 March 1916, presenting colors to the Jewish Boy Scout Brigade in the Printannia theater.

26. Umm Kalthum conducted her renowned Thursday performances at the Kursaal. Baraka, *Egyptian Upper Class*, 123.

27. Though the golden age for salas was in the 1930s, the few that existed earlier did especially well during World War I when foreign military troops frequented them. Baraka, *Egyptian Upper Class*, 128.

28. These were European films, as silent Egyptian films did not start until 1923. Baraka, *Egyptian Upper Class*, 124, 126.

29. Di-Capua, *Gatekeepers*, 143.

30. Di-Capua, *Gatekeepers*, 143.

31. Zachary Lockman, "Exploring the Field: Lost Voices and Emerging Practices in Egypt, 1882–1914," in *Histories of the Modern Middle East: New Directions*, ed. Israel Gershoni, Hakan Erdem, and Ursula Wokock (Boulder: Lynne Rienner Publishers, 2002), 137–153.

32. Ryzova, *Age of the Effendiyya*, 9–10.

33. Lucie Ryzova, *L'Effendiyya oû La Modernité Contestée* (Cairo: Centre d'Etudes et de Documentation Economiques, Juridiques, et Sociales, 2004), 128, 132. There would be divisions within the effendiyya over their role as arbiters of modernity. Some felt that all citizens should have rights and duties and that all should be educated to handle them. Others felt that a few "enlightened individuals" should lead "the masses." Tensions would increase after Egyptian nominal independence from Ottoman and British rule in 1923.

34. Di-Capua, *Gatekeepers*, 143.

35. Ryzova, *Age of the Effendiyya*, 9.

36. Jacob, *Working Out Egypt*, 4.

37. Jacob, *Working Out Egypt*, 63.

38. Jacob, *Working Out Egypt*, 5–6.

39. Gasper, *Power of Representation*, 72–73, 82. The Opera House was used as a fundraising site for many of these associations, such as the Coptic, Greek Catholic, and Maronite Societies. A. Rouchdy, letters to the Ministry of Public Works, 24 Feb. 1887, 10 March 1887, 12 March 1887, File 1/2, al-Ashghal, Mahafiz Majlis al-Wuzara' (DWQ, Cairo, Egypt).

40. Watenpaugh, *Being Modern in the Middle East*, 90.

41. Dina K. Hussein, "Modernity Through Café Riche (1908–): Serving Modernity, Catering to the Intellectuals and Closed to the Masses" (paper presented to the Middle East Studies Association, Washington, DC, 23 Nov. 2008).

42. Gasper, *Power of Representation*, 3.

43. Omar, "'And I Saw No Reason to Chronicle My Life,'" 298.

44. Omar, "'And I Saw No Reason,'" 305.

45. *Saturday Review* 104 (21 Sept. 1907): 350.

46. Letter from the Egyptian Liberal Party to FO Edward Grey, 4 Sept. 1907, BNA #247 1909 No. 30548. l.

47. Letter from the Egyptian Liberal Party to FO Edward Grey, 4 Sept. 1907, BNA #247 1909 No. 30548. l.

48. I draw Antun's story from Hourani, *Arabic Thought*; and Donald M. Reid, *The Odyssey of Farah Antun* (Minneapolis: Bibliotheca Islamica, 1975). At the time, Lebanon was part of greater Syria.

49. In the seventeenth and eighteenth centuries, most Greek Catholics from Syria had migrated to Lebanon or Egypt to seek economic opportunities and escape persecution by the Orthodox Christians from whom they had broken. Reid, *Odyssey*, 7.

50. Reid, *Odyssey*, 26. Western Europeans, Greeks, and Armenians also arrived in great numbers during that time, jumping from 3,000 in 1836 to 147,000 in 1907. Ministry of Finance, *Census of Egypt Taken in 1907*, 129, 148.

51. Reid, *Odyssey*, 31.

52. Moustafa El-Feki, *Copts in Egyptian Politics 1919–1952* (Cairo: General Egyptian Book Organization, 1991), 29.

53. Israel Gershoni and James P. Jankowski, *Egypt, Islam, and the Arabs: The Search for Egyptian Nationhood, 1900–1930* (New York: Oxford University Press, 1986), 15.

54. Marilyn Booth, *May Her Likes Be Multiplied: Biography and Gender Politics in Egypt* (Berkeley: University of California Press, 2001), xxxvii.

55. For details on the debate, see Hourani, *Arabic Thought*, 253–259.

56. Al-Sayyid Hassan ʿId, *Tatawwur al-Naqd al-Masrahi fi Misr* (Cairo: al-Muʾisa al-Misriyya al ʿAmma li al Taʾlif wa al-Anbaʾ wa al-Nashar, 1965), 100.

57. Reid, *Odyssey*, 107–108.

58. Reid, *Odyssey*, 131.

59. Reid, *Odyssey*, 131. For more on questions of empire, nationality, and belongingness in death, see Shana Minkin, *Imperial Bodies: Death, Governance, and Empire in Alexandria, Egypt* (Stanford: Stanford University Press, forthcoming fall 2019).

60. Some evidence of this exists in terms that crossed over between fields. The word *riwaya*, for example, meant both "story" and "play."

61. Other Syrian playwrights and actors in Egypt in the late nineteenth century included Yusuf al-Khayyat, Sulayman al-Qirdahi, and Iskandar Farah. See, for example, Landau, *Studies in the Arab Theater*; Muhammad al-Fil, *Ruʾiya wa Biyyan Hala al-Masrah al-ʿArabi al-Taʾsis* (Cairo: al-Hayʾa al-Misriyya al ʿAmma lil Kitab, 2001). For more on this, see Adam Mestyan, *Arab Patriotism: The Ideology and Culture of Power in Late Ottoman Egypt* (Princeton: Princeton University Press, 2017).

62. See various articles in *Bughyat*; they speak passionately about the benefits of theater for cultivating morals in amoral viewers. British and Egyptian elites spoke similarly of the benefits of European performances at the opera house for Egyptians, despite the fact that most Egyptians could not afford or understand them. Sulayman Hassan al-Qabbani, *Bughyat al-Mumaththilin* (Alexandria: Jurji Gharzuzi, 1914).

63. These figures come from Reid's analysis of Ministry of Finance, *Census of Egypt Taken in 1907*, and Ministry of Finance, *Census of Egypt Taken in 1917*, 2 vols. (Cairo: Cairo Government Press, 1921). The 1897 literacy figures refer to the native Egyptian population from age 0, and the 1919 figures include people from age 5. Reid, *Odyssey*, 45.

64. Yousef, *Composing Egypt*, 5.

65. This included people like Salim al-Naqqash, Adib Ishaq, and ʿUthman Jalal.

66. Antun, *Misr al-Jadida*, preface.

67. Al-Qabbani, *Bughyat*, 128–131.

68. Irene Gendzier, *The Practical Visions of Yaqub Sanuʿ* (Cambridge, MA: Harvard Middle Eastern Monographics, 1966), 31.

69. Gasper, *The Power of Representation*, 67.

70. One century before this, in 1720, a Mehmed Effendi also wrote about the Paris opera for an Ottoman audience. He described it as "a special kind of entertainment called opera, where wonders are shown. There was always a great crowd of people, for all the great lords go there. The regent goes often, and the king from time to time.... Each is seated according to his rank, and I was seated next to the king's seat, which was covered with red velvet.... The place was superb; the staircases, the columns, the ceilings and the walls were all gilded. This gilding, and the brilliance of the cloth of gold that the ladies were wearing, as well as the jewels with which they were covered, all in

the light of hundreds of candles, created the most beautiful effect" (Bernard Lewis, ed. *A Middle East Mosaic: Fragments of Life, Letters and History* [New York: The Modern Library, 2001], 364).

71. Rifa'a Rafi' al-Tahtawi, *Takhlis al-Ibriz fi Talkhis Bariz* (Cairo: 1834), rpt. and trans. in Sadgrove, *Egyptian Theatre*, 36.

72. Sadgrove, *Egyptian Theatre*, 5.

73. Sadgrove, *Egyptian Theatre*, 34–36.

74. M. Ernest Wilkinson, letter to the Ministry of Public Works, 21 Feb. 1882, File 1/2, al-Ashghal, Mahafiz Majlis al-Wuzara'(DWQ, Cairo, Egypt).

75. Sadgrove, *Egyptian Theatre*, 10.

76. *Al-Jinan* 6 (15 March 1875), rpt. Sadgrove, *Egyptian Theatre*, 56.

77. *Wadi al-Nil* 55 (28 Feb. 1870), rpt. Sadgrove, *Egyptian Theatre*, 57.

78. *Wadi al-Nil* 15 (Nov. 1870), rpt. Sadgrove, *Egyptian Theatre*, 60.

79. 'Id, *Tatawwur al-Naqd*, 100–101.

80. Individual ticket prices for a reputable theater in 1931 were as follows: baignoire—75 pastres; loge—60 piastres; fauteuil—12 piastres; special—5 piastres. Though these prices are from several years after the period of study in this chapter, they give some sense of how social stratification was spatially visible in theaters via seating arrangements. Baraka, *Egyptian Upper Class*, 126.

81. 'Ali Jihad Racy, *Making Music in the Arab World: The Culture and Artistry of Tarab* (Cambridge, UK: Cambridge University Press, 2004), 38, 83.

82. Nagwa 'Annus, *Masrah Ya'qub Sannu'* (Cairo: al-Hay'a al 'Amma lil Kitab, 1984), 11.

83. Johnson, *Listening in Paris: A Cultural History* (Berkeley: University of California Press, 1995). For more on etiquette literature and the development of moral conventions, see Norbert Elias, *The Civilizing Process: Sociogenetic and Psychogenetic Investigations* (Oxford, UK: Blackwell Publishers, 2000).

84. Al-Qabbani, *Bughyat*, 130–131.

85. Al-Qabbani, *Bughyat*, 133.

86. Al-Qabbani, *Bughyat*, 134.

87. "Reglement," 251–252.

88. "Reglement," 251–252.

89. *Al-Ahali* (7 April 1913), rpt. Muhsin Musilahi, ed., *Al-Masrah al-Misri* (Cairo: Dar al-Za'im li al-Taba' al-Haditha, 1998), 115.

90. Ibrahim Hanna al-'Atiyya, *al-Watan*, 1913, rpt. Antun, *Misr al-Jadida*, prologue.

91. Antun, *Misr al-Jadida*, 6–7.

92. Even more, hiring a nanny to raise children became a point of contention among the effendiyya, who considered it a threat to proper child-rearing. See Omnia Shakry, "Schooled Mothers and Structured Play: Child Rearing in Turn-of-the-Century Egypt," in *Remaking Women: Feminism and Modernity in the Middle East*, ed. Lila Abu-Lughod (Cairo: American University in Cairo Press, 1998), 141.

93. Huda Sha'rawi, *Harem Years: The Memoirs of an Egyptian Feminist* (Cairo: American University in Cairo Press, 1998).

94. Baraka, *Egyptian Upper Class*, 189–190, 198–199.

95. Baraka, *Egyptian Upper Class*, 198.

96. One conversation indicates that his interest rate could be 50 percent. Antun, *Misr al-Jadida*, 42.

97. Antun, *Misr al-Jadida*, 40–41.

98. Antun, *Misr al-Jadida*, 42.

99. Ministry of Finance, *Census*, 129, 148.

100. Minkin, *Imperial Bodies* (forthcoming 2019).

101. Ehud Toledano, *State and Society in Mid-Nineteenth-Century Egypt* (Cambridge, UK: Cambridge University Press, 1990), 193.

102. Margot Badran, *Feminists, Islam, and Nation: Gender and the Making of Modern Egypt* (Princeton: Princeton University Press, 1995), 199–200.

103. See Judith Tucker, *Women in 19th Century Egypt* (Cambridge, UK: Cambridge University Press, 1985).

104. Sami A. Hanna, "The Mawwal in Egyptian Folklore," *Journal of American Folklore* 80 (April–June 1967), 189.

105. Matti Moosa, *The Origins of Modern Arabic Fiction* (Boulder: Lynne Rienner Publishers, 1997), 235.

106. On more than one occasion, Almaz is told, "you could be more famous than ʿAbdu," likely a reference to the real-life al-Hamuli. Antun, *Misr al-Jadida*, 90.

107. Yaʿqub Sannuʿ and Salim al-Naqqash are some of the earliest playwrights to have employed women on stage. The women were Christian and Jewish, probably because of the greater stigma that would be associated with Muslim women mixing unveiled with men on a public stage. See, for example, Sadgrove, *The Egyptian Theatre*, 41, 94, and Bedawi, *Early Arabic Drama*, 32.

108. Van Nieuwkerk illustrates numerous examples of the competition that female entertainers encouraged between wealthy men and other strategies used to encourage patrons' spending. Some female entertainers drank too much to complete their stage performances. Karin Van Nieuwkerk, *"A Trade Like Any Other": Female Singers and Dancers in Egypt* (Austin: University of Texas Press, 1995), 44.

109. Antun, *Misr al-Jadida*, 90.

110. *Al-Ahali*, 7 April 1913, rpt. Musilahi, ed., *Al-Masrah al-Misri*, 116.

111. See Baron, *Egypt as a Woman*, 15.

112. Marun ʿAboud, "Farah Antun," *al-Kitab* 2 (Nov. 1947), 1742. In fact, Qasim Amin is referenced by name in *Misr al-Jadida*. Antun, *Misr al-Jadida*, 81.

113. Leila Ahmed, *Women and Gender in Islam* (New Haven, CT: Yale University Press, 1992), 155–165.

114. Baron, *Women's Awakening*, 4.

115. Baron, *Women's Awakening*. Such concerns neglected problems that fellahi women faced and were unrealistic for, if not irrelevant to, poorer women.

116. Baron, *Women's Awakening*, 7.

117. Reid, *Odyssey*, 19.

118. Such an array of perspectives raises questions as to the usefulness of the general term "feminist" to describe the diverse men and women seeking to improve women's status in early twentieth-century Egypt. See chapter 4 for more on this.

119. Gasper, *Power of Representation*, 71; Lisa Pollard, *Nurturing the Nation*, 153; Shakry, "Schooled Mothers," 126–170.

120. Antun, *Misr al-Jadida*, 116.

121. Antun, *Misr al-Jadida*, 115.

122. Powell, *Different Shade*, 50–51.

123. Antun, *Misr al-Jadida*, 120.

124. Powell, *Different Shade*, 214–215.

125. For more on the importance of effendi domestic life in relation to nation and citizenship, see Pollard, *Nurturing the Nation*.

126. Gasper, *Power of Representation*, 97.

127. *Egyptian Standard*, 5 Sept. 1907, 2. Attempts by Jurj Abyad to garner funding to win a concession to run the opera house's 1911–1912 season, for example, were unsuccessful; so too was his request for financial support for his troupe in 1910. Minister of Finance, letter to President of the Council of Ministers, 19 May 1910, Mahfuza 1/2, Majlis al-Wuzaraʾ, al-Magmuʿa al-Ashghal (DWQ); President of the Council of Ministers, letter to Minister, 25 Feb. 1911, Mahfuza 1/2, Majlis al-Wuzaraʾ, al-Magmuʿa al-Ashghal (DWQ).

128. Sadgrove, *The Egyptian Theatre*, 36.

129. Al-Muwaylihi was born to a conservative Muslim family in Cairo in 1858. His father was private secretary to Khedive Isma'il and also worked as a writer and journalist. He learned French as a child, attended lectures at al-Azhar, and traveled abroad, mainly in Europe. Al-Muwaylihi's writings began as a series of articles that were gathered into a book in 1907. At one time, it was used as a textbook in Egyptian schools. Moosa, *Origins*, 129–130.

130. The summary that follows is from Muhammad al-Muwaylihi, *Hadith ʿIsa ibn Hisham, A Period of Time: A Study and Translation of Hadith ʿIsa Ibn Hisham by Muhammad Al-Muwaylihi*, trans. Roger Allen (Reading, UK: Ithaca, 1992), 368–373.

131. al-Muwaylihi, *Hadith ʿIsa*, 369.

132. al-Muwaylihi, *Hadith ʿIsa*, 370.

133. al-Muwaylihi, *Hadith ʿIsa*, 371.

134. al-Muwaylihi. *Hadith ʿIsa*, 373–374.

135. The Egyptian government did, sporadically, support Arabic theater. For example, permissions were given to ʿAbd al-Hamuli and Abu Khalil to present fifteen Arabic performances in the opera house in 1885 and to Sulayman Haddad to present a series of Arabic plays in the opera house in 1895. A. Rouchdy, letter to Minister of Public Works, 24 Dec. 1884, File 1/2, al-Ashghal, Mahafiz Majlis al-Wuzaraʾ (DWQ); and Council of Ministers, letter to Comité de Finance, 8 Jan. 1895, File 1/2, al-Ashghal, Mahafiz Majlis al-Wuzaraʾ (DWQ).

136. Sayyid ʿAli Ismaʿil, *Masirat al-Masrah fi Misr* (Cairo: al-Hayʾa al-Misriyya al ʿAmma lil Kitab, 2003), 116. Together they performed in places like the Printannia theater (1916) and al-Hambra in Alexandria (1913).

137. ʿId, *Tatawwur al-Naqd*, 119.

138. Reid, *Odyssey*, 127.

139. Badawi, *Early Arabic Drama*, 10.

140. Badawi, *Early Arabic Drama*, 103.

141. Powell, *Different Shade*, 196.

142. Muhammad Taymur, "Muhakima Mu'alifi al-Riwaya al-Tamthiliya," *al-Sufur*, as reprinted in *Mu'allafat Muhammad Taymur al-Jus' al-Thani, Hayatuhu al-Tamthiliyya* (Cairo: al-Hay'a al-Misriyya al ʿAmma lil Kitab, 1963).

143. Taymur, "Muhakima," 127.

144. Taymur, "Muhakima," 129.

145. Powell, *Different Shade*, 19–48.

146. See, for example, Baron, *Egypt as a Woman*, on how women were used to rep-

resent Egypt; and Powell, *Different Shade*, on how caricatures of Sudanese people and the Sudan were central to articulations of Egyptian national identity.

147. Gershoni and Jankowski, *Egypt, Islam, and the Arabs*, 16.

Chapter 3

1. Manfred Woidich and Jacob M. Landau, *Arabisches Volkstheater in Kairo Im Jahre 1909: Ahmad ilfar Und Seine Schwanke* (Beirut and Stuttgart: Steiner, 1993), 22.

2. "Riwayat al-Saʿidi," in Woidich and Landau, *Arabisches Volkstheater*, 380. Stage directions indicate that the play was, indeed, performed in a samer.

3. Van Niuewkerk, *"A Trade Like Any Other,"* 24.

4. Sawsan El-Messiri, *Ibn al-Balad: A Concept of Egyptian Identity* (Leiden: E. J. Brill, 1978), 49.

5. Zachary Lockman, "Imagining the Working Class: Culture, Nationalism, and Class Formation in Egypt, 1899–1914," *Poetics Today* 15:2 (Summer 1994): 182.

6. Beinin and Lockman, *Workers*, 67.

7. For scholars who grapple with workers' relationships to nationalism, see, for example, Beinin and Lockman, *Workers*, and John Chalcraft, "The Cairo Cab Drivers and the Strike of 1907," in *The Empire in the City: Arab Provincial Capitals in the Late Ottoman Empire*, ed. Jens Hanssen, Thomas Philipp, and Stefan Weber (Beirut: Ergon Verlag, 2002), 173–198.

8. Hammad, *Industrial Sexuality*; and Liat Kozma, *Policing Egyptian Women: Sex, Law, and Medicine in Khedivial Egypt* (Syracuse: Syracuse University Press, 2011), and *Global Women, Colonial Ports: Prostitution in the Interwar Middle East* (Albany: SUNY Press, 2017).

9. ʿAli al-Raʾi, *al-Kumidiyya al-murtajala fi al-masrah al-misri* (Cairo: Dar al-Hilal, 1968), 36.

10. Walter Armbrust, *Mass Culture and Modernism in Egypt* (Cambridge, UK: Cambridge University Press, 1996), 27.

11. Armbrust, *Mass Culture*, 25.

12. Dina Amin, "Egyptian Theater: Reconstructing Performance Spaces," *Arab Studies Journal* 14:2 (Fall 2006): 99.

13. Di-Capua, *Gatekeepers*, 66.

14. El-Messiri, *Ibn al-Balad*, 35.

15. James R. Grippo, "The Fool Sings a Hero's Song: Shaaban Abdel Rahim, Egyptian Shaʾabi, and the Video Clip Phenomenon," Transnational Broadcasting Studies, no. 16 (2006), www.tbsjournal.com/Grippo.html.

16. Jennifer Peterson, "Sampling Folklore: The 're-popularization' of Sufi Inshad in Egyptian Dance Music," *Arab Media and Society* 4 (Winter 2008), www.arabmediasociety.com/?article=580. The scholar Katherine Zirbel adds that the term "*shaʿb*" carries cultural and class connotations, denoting, for example, traditional, patriarchal practices connected to urban working classes and peasant migrants to urban areas (Katherine Elizabeth Zirbel, "Musical Discursions: Spectacle, Experience, and Political Economy Among Egyptian Performers in Globalizing Markets" [PhD diss., University of Michigan, 1999], 184).

17. Joel Beinin and Zachary Lockman, *Workers on the Nile: Nationalism, Commu-*

nism, Islam, and the Egyptian Working Class (Princeton: Princeton University Press, 1987), 24.

18. Beinin and Lockman, *Workers*, 23.

19. Beinin and Lockman, *Workers*, 24.

20. By 1907, about 30,000 residents of Cairo came from Asyut Province. Certain jobs began to be dominated by migrants from Upper Egyptian villages. For example, many water carriers came from Dar al-Baqar in Gharbiyya, porters often came from Musha village in Asyut, and large numbers of construction workers came from Tirsa in Giza. For more on the decline of guilds and other economic shifts in nineteenth-century Egypt, see Gabriel Baer, *Fellah and Townsman in the Middle East* (London: Frank Cass, 1982).

21. Baer, *Fellah and Townsman*, 67, 74. As Robert Tignor points out, however, in a few cases small-scale manufactures, such as those in textiles, metallurgy, and leather making, managed to thrive into the early twentieth century (Robert L. Tignor, *State, Private Enterprise, and Economic Change in Egypt, 1918–1952* [Princeton: Princeton University Press, 1984]).

22. Beinin and Lockman, *Workers*, 37.

23. Lockman, "Imagining," 182.

24. Lockman, "Imagining," 182.

25. Beinin and Lockman, *Workers*, 67.

26. Ilham Khouri-Makdisi, *Theater and Radical Politics in Beirut, Cairo, and Alexandria: 1860–1914* (Washington, DC: Center for Contemporary Arab Studies, 2006), 1.

27. Sadgrove, *Egyptian Theatre*, 146.

28. Khouri-Makdisi, *Theater and Radical Politics*, 3–4.

29. Khouri-Makdisi, *Theater and Radical Politics*, 88.

30. Jason Thompson, "Edward William Lane's 'Description of Egypt'," *International Journal of Middle East Studies* 28 (1996): 567.

31. Al-Ra'i, *al-Kumidiya*, 26–27; Badawi, *Early Arabic*, 12.

32. Edward Lane, *The Manners and Customs of the Modern Egyptians* (London: J. M. Dent & Co., 1908), 395–397. This translation is Lane's.

33. Dina Amin, "Egyptian Theater: Reconstructing Performance Spaces," *Arab Studies Journal* (Fall 2006): 78–106.

34. Sadgrove, *Egyptian Theatre*, 23.

35. Amin, "Egyptian Theater," 78–106.

36. Amin, "Egyptian Theater," 78–106.

37. Amin, "Egyptian Theater," 78–106.

38. Carsten Niebuhr, *Travels Through Arabia*, vol. 1 (Beirut: Librarie du Liban, n.d.), 143–144.

39. Al-Ra'i, *al-Kumidiya*, 161.

40. Al-Ra'i, *al-Kumidiya*, 162.

41. See Laila Nessim Abou Seif, "Theatre of Najib al-Rihani: The Development of Comedy in Modern Egypt" (PhD diss., University of Illinois, 1969), 17. Dakhul influenced the writing of both *sha'bi* and more formal comedies. He influenced Rihani, al-Kassar, Ibrahim Ramzi, Muhammad Taymur, and Tewfiq al-Hakim. See al-Ra'i, *al-Kumidiya*, 8. George Dakhul's performances point to a different circuit of culture. His skits became so popular among the sha'b that they inspired several muqallidin of their own, many of whom modified his plays to be even more ribald and licentious.

They forced Dakhul to refer to his Syrian stage character, Kamil, as Kamil the Original, or Kamil al-Asil, so as not to be mistaken for a copy.

42. Sannuʿ's first experiments with stage theater were performed in colloquial Arabic and included the "quick-witted" native, the hypocritical religious man, and the silly foreigner—stock characters drawn from *karagoz*, *khayal al-zill*, and *muhabbizun*. As a child, the comedic playwright Badiʿ Khayri used to attend fasl mudhik at cafés in Sayyidna al-Husayn. Cynthia Metcalf, "From Morality Play to Celebrity: Women, Gender, and Performing Modernity in Egypt, 1850–1939" (PhD diss., University of Virginia, 2008), 206.

43. Joseph T. Zeidan, "Modern Arab Theater: The Journey Back," in *Tradition and Modernity in Arabic Literature*, ed. Issa J. Boullata and Terri DeYoung (Fayetteville: University of Arkansas Press, 1997), 173–191.

44. Al-Rihani most likely witnessed muhabbizun performing fasl mudhik, especially as an unemployed actor hanging out in Cairo's coffeehouses. See Abou Seif, "Theatre of Najib al-Rihani," 17.

45. Al-Kassar, *ʿAli al-Kassar*, 7.

46. Farouk ʿAbdel Wahab, *Modern Egyptian Drama: An Anthology* (Minneapolis: Bibliotheca Islamica, 1974), 22. Al-Raʾi defines improvisational theater as involving a written text that is changeable based on circumstances; actors who perform on stage but are able to perform in other settings; and vigilant, intelligent spectators who critique and judge the performance. See Al-Raʾi, *al-Kumidiya*, 29–30.

47. Abul Naga, *Les Sources Francaises*, 38.

48. Badawi, *Early Arabic*, 14; ʿAbdel Wahab, *Modern Egyptian*, 14–15.

49. Abul Naga, *Les Sources Francaises*, 59–60; Shmuel Moreh, *Live Theatre and Dramatic Literature in the Medieval Arab World* (New York: New York University Press, 1992), 157–160.

50. ʿAli al-Kassar was one of many who started his career performing farcical one-act plays called fasl mudhik in shaʿbi theater-cafés like Dar al-Tamthil al-Zaynabi, Dar al-Salam, and the Egypt Club.

51. Amira Mitchell, comp., *Women of Egypt* (Topic Records, 2006).

52. *Misr*, 26 Dec. 1905, rpt. Fathi al-ʿAshri, ed., *Al-Masrah al-Misri* (Cairo: Dar al-Zaʾim li al-Tabaʾa al-Haditha, 1998), 241; and *Misr*, 30 Jan. 1906; *Misr*, 10 Sept. 1908, rpt. Sakhsukh, ed., *Al-Masrah al-Misri*, 20, 181.

53. See, for example, *Misr*, 19 Dec. 1905, rpt. Fathi al-ʿAshri, ed., *Al-Masrah al-Misri* (Cairo: Dar al-Zaʾim li al-Tabaʾa al-Haditha, 1998), 240; *al-Watan*, 23 Jan. 1906; *al-Muʾayyid*, 6 Aug. 1908; *al-Muqattam*, 22 April 1909; *Misr*, 27 Jan. 1910, rpt. Sakhsukh, ed., *Al-Masrah al-Misri*, 18, 178, 215, 228.

54. Zeidan, "Modern Arab Theater," 173–191.

55. Mieke Kolk, "The Performance of Comedy in East and West: Cultured Boundaries and the Art of Cunning," in *The Performance of the Comic in Arabic Theatre: Cultural Heritage Western Models and Postcolonial Hybridity*, ed. Mieke Kolk and Freddy Decreus (The Hague: Prince Claus Foundation, 2005), 151–165.

56. Zeidan, "Modern Arab Theater," 173–191. Margaret Litvin points out that ʿAbdu's version hewed closely to Alexander Dumas's French version of *Hamlet*, which also had a happy ending. [Margaret Litvin, *Hamlet's Arab Journey: Shakespeare's Prince and Nasser's Ghost* (Princeton: Princeton University Press, 2011), 64–66].

57. Al-Raʾi, *al-Kumidiya*, 33.

58. Khouri-Makdisi, *Theater and Radical Politics*, 29.

59. Stuart Hall, "Notes on Deconstructing the Popular," in *People's History and Socialist Theory*, ed. Raphael Sauel (London and Boston and Henley: Routledge and Kegan Paul, 2016), 228.

60. al-Ra'i, *al-Kumidiya*, 38.

61. Woidich and Landau, *Arabisches*, 18–19.

62. *Al-Mu'ayyid*, 8 Aug. 1907, rpt. Sakhsukh, ed., *Al-Masrah al-Misri*, 124.

63. *Al-Muqattam*, 13 Aug. 1907, rpt. Sakhsukh, ed., *Al-Masrah al-Misri*, 125.

64. *Misr*, 7 Aug. 1908, rpt. Sakhsukh, ed., *Al-Masrah al-Misri*, 178.

65. *Al-Mu'ayyid*, 16 July 1910, rpt. Sakhsukh, ed., *Al-Masrah al-Misri*, 240.

66. Manfred Woidich now owns the M manuscript. The scholars Jacob Landau and Woidich's painstaking analysis of the scripts concluded that they documented performances of the non-effendi al-Far.

67. It is also possible that the vagueness of the text may have meant that it was written as an open script to offer a general storyline without impinging on the actors' improvisation.

68. "*Riwayat al-Shaykh al-Turqi wa al-Mar'a wa Zawjaha*," 391.

69. James Scott, *Domination and the Arts of Resistance: Hidden Transcripts* (New Haven, CT: Yale University Press, 1990), 161.

70. "Riwayat al-Sa'idi," 178.

71. The seven-languages comment appears in the L version but not the M. "Riwayat al-Sa'idi," 180.

72. "Riwayat al-Sa'idi," 234.

73. "Riwayat al-Sa'idi," 234.

74. Tawfiq al-Hakim, *Ya Tali' al-Shajara* (Cairo: Multazim li al-Tab' wal-Nashr, 1962), 24.

75. al-Hakim, *Ya Tali'*, 24.

76. Even though elements of what would later be termed "absurdism" had been central to sha'bi performance for as long as can be traced, it was not labeled as such until the mid-twentieth century.

77. Barak, *On Time*, 5, 7–8, 236–250.

78. "Riwayat al-Sa'idi," 382. At another point, the Sa'idi says *magluba* (upside-down) for *ma'luba* ("Riwayat al-Sa'idi," 188).

79. Fahmy, *Ordinary Egyptians*, 171.

80. Fahmy, *Ordinary Egyptians*, 8.

81. Fahmy, *Ordinary Egyptians*, 9.

82. "Riwayat al-Sa'idi," 196.

83. The Trickster-Fool is a prevalent type in Arabic theater and storytelling. Popular folk characters such as Juha, and stage characters like Najib al-Rihani's Kishkish Bey, exemplify the dual Trickster-Fool character. See, for example, Salma Khadra Jayyusi, ed., *Tales of Juha: Classic Arab Folk Humor* (Northhampton, MA: Interlink Publishing Group, 2007).

84. "Riwayat al-Sa'idi," 192, 394. The Sa'idi acts as if he doesn't know math but talks the numbers down.

85. Scott, *Domination and the Arts*, 162–163.

86. "Riwayat al-Sa'idi," 386.

87. "Riwayat al-Sa'idi," 174–176, 381.

88. See Lila Abu-Lughod, *Veiled Sentiments* (Berkeley: University of Chicago Press, 1986), 46–47, 72, 115–116.

89. "Riwayat al-Saʿidi," 382.

90. "Riwayat al-Saʿidi," 184.

91. "Riwayat al-Saʿidi," 184.

92. Gasper, *Power of Representation*, 3.

93. "Riwayat al-Saʿidi," 196–198. He considers the zaʿbut to be precious because it carries a considerable amount of lice. The notion of the zaʿbut being lice-ridden was common in Egypt at the time; it is unclear whether it was based in fact or fiction.

94. "Riwayat al-Saʿidi," in Woidich and Landau, *Arabisches Volkstheater*, 200.

95. Seizer, *Stigmas*, 197.

96. Seizer's study of special drama on the Tamil stage led to the same conclusion: a "Buffoon's comedy deftly reenacts the very conventions . . . that the public telling of such jokes would seem to transgress." Seizer, *Stigmas*, 177.

97. Fahmy, *Ordinary Egyptians*, 130.

98. "Riwayat al-Saʿidi," 386, 388.

99. "Riwayat al-Saʿidi," 182.

100. Woidich and Landau, *Arabisches Volkstheater*, 28–30.

101. Woidich and Landau, *Arabisches Volkstheater*, 33.

102. M. M. Bakhtin, *The Dialogic Imagination: Four Essays*, ed. Michael Holquist and trans. Caryl Emerson and Michael Holquist, University of Texas Press Slavic Series (Book 1), rpt. ed. (Austin: University of Texas Press, 1983).

103. Al-Kassar, *ʿAli al-Kassar*, 7; Abou Seif, "Theatre of Najib al-Rihani," 17.

104. Titles of his monologues include: *Pampering the Fellahins' Children*, *Pampering the Dhawats' Children*, and *The Telephone*. Frédéric Lagrange, "Male Homosexuality in Modern Arabic Literature," in *Imagined Masculinities: Male Identity and Culture in the Modern Middle East*, ed. Mai Ghoussoub and Emma Sinclair-Webb (London: Saqi Books, 2000), 169–198. Lagrange notes that a few of the recordings are about queer characters, which Lagrange attributes to a previous openness to discussing homosexuality in *karagoz* and early vaudeville.

105. Fahmy, "Media-Capitalism," 83–103.

Chapter 4

1. Abyad, *Jurj Abyad*, 152–153.

2. Harun al-Rashid was the fifth Abbasid caliph who governed at the height of the dynasty's power and prosperity. His life and court were the subject of many stories, most notably *One Thousand and One Nights*. *Othello* was one of many popular Arabicized Shakespearean plays in Egypt at the turn of the century. The Jurj Abyad, Salama Hijazi, Sulayman al-Qirdahi, and Ramsis acting troupes all performed the play many times. For more on Shakespeare in Egypt, see Ramsis ʿAwad, *Shayksbir fi Misr* (Cairo: Dar al-Hilal, 1992); and Margaret Litvin, *Hamlet's Arab Journey: Shakespeare's Prince and Nasser's Ghost* (Princeton: Princeton University Press, 2011).

3. Al-Kassar, *ʿAli al-Kassar*, 27–28.

4. These political concepts, along with "rights," were repeated demands in the period of study. See, for example, Letter from Saʿd Zaghlul to the Minister of the In-

terior and President of the Council of Ministers, 23 Nov. 1918, FO 141/810/1 (BNA, London, England); Circular, "Free in our Country—Generous to Our Guests," 28 Nov. 1918, FO 141/810/1 (BNA, London, England); Report, T. W. Russell to Ministry of the Interior, "Demonstration on the occasion of the celebration of the day of Mustafa Kamil's death," 13 Feb. 1919, FO 141/810/1 (BNA, London, England).

5. Male performers also joined the protests of 1919. The actor Jurj Abyad, for example, led a large demonstration of male actors, playwrights, and composers. Abyad, *George Abyad*, 152–153.

6. Ahmed, *Women and Gender*, 173–174.

7. I avoid use of the terms "feminism" and "feminist" in this chapter for a few reasons. First, in most of the period under study, female reformers referred to themselves as participants in a "women's/*nisa'iyya*" rather than a "feminist" movement. It was not until the 1920s that the word *nisa'iyya* would take on the additional meaning of "feminist," though its historical connection to Western activists made Egyptian reformers wary of taking on the additional meaning. Furthermore, the range of Egyptian female perspectives on how best to advocate for women makes it difficult to categorize all female reformers under the same rubric of "feminist." For thoughtful discussions on this in the Egyptian context, see Beth Baron, *The Women's Awakening in Egypt* (New Haven, CT: Yale University Press, 1994), 6–7. For a global perspective, see Bonnie G. Smith, "Introduction," in *Global Feminisms Since 1945*, ed. Bonnie G. Smith (London: Routledge, 2000), 1–10.

8. Russell, *Creating the New Egyptian Woman*.

9. Laura Bier, *Revolutionary Womanhood: Feminisms, Modernity, and the State in Nasser's Egypt* (Stanford: Stanford University Press, 2011), 28.

10. Bier, *Revolutionary Womanhood*, 28.

11. Afsanah Najmabadi, "The Gender of Modernity: Reflections from Iranian Historiography," in *Histories of the Modern Middle East, New Directions*, ed. Israel Gershoni, Hakan Erdem, and Ursula Wokock (Boulder: Lynne Rienner Publishers, 200), 77.

12. See, for example, Badran, *Feminists, Islam, and Nation*; Selma Botman, *Engendering Citizenship* (New York: Columbia University Press, 1999).

13. This was also true of effendis who saw their controlled sexuality as making them superior to both a "licentious and frivolous" elite and the "riff-raff" at the bottom of social hierarchy. Ernest K. Bramsted, *Aristocracy and the Middle Classes in German: Social Types in German Literature, 1830–1900* (Chicago and London: Phoenix Books, 1964), 34–35. The category of respectability loomed large, especially in the regulation of women's sexuality, an expansion of the policing of female sexuality that was institutionalized in the preceding khedivial era (Kozma, *Policing Egyptian Women*).

14. Robert Tignor, "The Egyptian Revolution of 1919: New Directions in the Egyptian Economy," in *The Middle Eastern Economy*, ed. Elie Kedourie (London: Frank Cass & Co., 1976), 47–51.

15. Ramsis 'Awad, *Ittijahat Siyasiya fi al-Masrah Qabla Thawrat 1919* (Cairo: al-Hay'a al-Misriyya al 'Amma lil Kitab, 1979), 235.

16. Pollard, *Nurturing the Nation*, 170–171; Mahmud Y. Zayid, *Egypt's Struggle for Independence* (Beirut: Khayats, 1965), 76.

17. Letter from 'Imad al-Din theater directors to Husayn Pasha Rushdi, Prime Minister and Minister of the Interior, 10 Aug. 1917; Letter from P. M. Tothenham,

Acting Under Secretary of State for the Fuel Committee to the Prime Minister, 19 Aug. 1917, Mahfuza 1/2, al-Magmuʿa al-Ashghal, Majlis al-Wuzaraʾ (DWQ, Cairo, Egypt).

18. ʿAwad, *al-Tarikh al-Sirri*, 117.

19. Tignor, *State, Private Enterprise*, 43.

20. On one particular occasion, he remembered when "three of the men who worked our land were detained while ploughing a field." Musa managed to bribe the officers who detained the men in order to secure their release. (Salama Musa, *The Education of Salama Musa* [Leiden: E. J. Brill, 1961], 92).

21. Percival George Elgood, *Egypt and the Army* (London: Oxford University Press, Humphrey Milford, 1924), 318; Pollard, *Nurturing the Nation*, 170; M. Rifaat, *The Awakening of Modern Egypt* (Cairo: Palm Press, 2005), 209.

22. Peter Mansfield, *The British in Egypt* (New York: Holt, Rinehart and Winston, 1972), 205; Rifaat, *Awakening*, 209.

23. Letter from the Egyptian Association in Britain, 14 May 1919, FO 608/214/1 (BNA, London, England). By the end of the war, serious shortfalls in food supplies resulted in war-related malnutrition across the Egyptian countryside and an increase in the death rate. (Mario Ruiz, "Imperial Policing in Wartime Egypt" [paper presented to the Rutgers Center for Historical Analysis, New Brunswick, NJ, 16 Oct. 2007], 16).

24. On more than one occasion, Wilson's name was chanted in anti-British protests in Egypt. Audience members who attended a speech by Zaghlul on January 15, 1919, chanted "Long live America, long live President Wilson, long live Egypt, long live independence" in response to the speech. Report, "Hamad Pasha El Bassel's Tea Party," 16 Jan. 1919, FO 141/810/1 (BNA, London, England).

25. See, for example, Marius Deeb, *Party Politics in Egypt: The Wafd and Its Rivals, 1919–1939* (London: Ithaca Press, 1979).

26. Fatma al-Yusuf, *Dhikrayat* (Cairo: Kitab Ruz al-Yusuf, 1953), 53–55. She is better known as Ruz al-Yusuf.

27. al-Yusuf, *Dhikrayat*, 54.

28. The first issue of her journal, *Ruz al-Yusuf*, was put out in October 1925.

29. For more on Egyptian social relations in 1919, see "Social Relations in Egypt," *Al-Fusul* 10 (April 1933): 36–37.

30. Beinin and Lockman, *Workers*, 23; Baron, *Women's Awakening*, 16.

31. Husayn Fawzi, *Sindbad fi rihal al-haya'* (Cairo: Dar al-Maʿarif Iqraʾ series, 1968), 27.

32. Ahmad, *Women and Gender*, 172.

33. Badran, *Feminists, Islam, and Nation*, 51, 56; Baron, *Women's Awakening*, 121, 142.

34. Ahmad, *Women and Gender*, 173.

35. Ahmad, *Women and Gender*, 172; Baron, *Women's Awakening*, 121.

36. Badran, *Feminists, Islam, and Nation*, 81.

37. Ahmad, *Women and Gender*, 173; Badran, *Feminists, Islam, and Nation*, 81; Shaʿrawi, *Harem Years*, 112–115, 118. Their work continued after independence as well. Between 1923 and 1931 legislation addressed child marriages, polygamy, and abuses by husbands in matters of divorce. Women's degree of involvement in political life was limited, however, for several reasons. For one, women failed to secure voting rights in the newly independent Egypt, as the constitution only allowed for male suffrage. For

another, the emphasis of most female reformers' work lay in the elevation of women's status within the family rather than outside it, along with addressing social problems like poverty and prostitution. [See, for example, Badran, *Feminists, Islam, and Nation*; Botman, *Engendering Citizenship*, 25, 28.]

38. Mary Louise Roberts, *Disruptive Acts: The New Woman in Fin-de-Siècle France* (Chicago: University of Chicago Press, 2002).

39. Badran, *Feminists, Islam, and Nation*, 63; Baron, *Egypt as a Woman*; Beth Baron, *The Women's Awakening in Egypt: Culture, Society, and the Press* (New Haven, CT: Yale University Press, 1994), 159; Booth, *May Her Likes Be Multiplied*, 109–170; Russell, *Creating the New Egyptian Woman*, 3.

40. Western reformers and nationalists made women into symbols of the moral nation, just as Egyptians did. For more on Western women in relation to empire and nation, see, for example, Anna Davin, "Imperialism and Motherhood," *History Workshop* 5 (1978): 9–65; Ann Stoler, "Carnal Knowledge and Imperial Power: Gender, Race, and Morality in Colonial Asia," in *Gender at the Crossroads of Knowledge: Feminist Anthropology in the Postmodern Era*, ed. Micaela di Lenoardo (Berkeley and Los Angeles: University of California Press, 1991), 51–101.

41. Nabawiyya Musa, *Tarikhi Biqalmi* (Cairo: Multaqa al-Mar'a wa al-Dhakira, 1999), 93–98. In the 1940s and 1950s, women like Durriya Shafiq and Inji Aflatun would focus on an even broader range of issues that moved well beyond motherhood. These included addressing questions of human rights and antiauthoritarianism to embracing a Marxist progressive nationalist feminism. See Cynthia Nelson, *Doria Shafik Egyptian Feminist: A Woman Apart* (Gainesville: University Press of Florida, 1996); and Menna Taher, "The Life of Inji Aflatoun, an Artist and a Rebel," *ahramonline*, 18 Sept. 2011, english.ahram.org.eg/NewsContent/5/25/21577/Arts—Culture/Visual-Art/The-life-of-Inji-Aflatoun,-an-artist-and-a-rebel-.aspx.

42. Shakry, "Schooled Mothers," 137. Kenneth Cuno addresses the shift from the polygamous to the nuclear family in Egypt at this time in *Modernizing Marriage: Family, Ideology, and Law in Nineteenth and Early Twentieth Century Egypt* (Syracuse: Syracuse University Press, 2015), 19–44.

43. Bier, *Revolutionary Womanhood*, 33.

44. Shakry, "Schooled Mothers," 143–148.

45. Mervat Hatem, "The Pitfalls of Nationalist Discourse on Citizenship in Egypt," in *Gender and Citizenship in the Middle East*, ed. Suad Joseph (Syracuse: Syracuse University Press, 2000), 33–57.

46. Skakry, "Schooled Mothers," 128.

47. Shakry, "Schooled Mothers," 137–138, 141.

48. Baron, *Women's Awakening*, 166. In 1919, the New Woman Society (Jam'iyat al-Mar'a al-Jadida) opened in the Munira section of Cairo to provide training in handcrafts for poor girls. In addition to being taught work skills, the girls learned how to read and write and guidelines for proper hygiene. Badran, *Feminists, Islam, and Nation*, 51. Huda Sha'arawi was a donor and honorary president of the organization.

49. Hanan Kholoussy, *For Better, For Worse: The Marriage Crisis That Made Modern Egypt* (Stanford: Stanford University Press, 2010), 100.

50. Huda Shaʿrawi, *Mudhakkirat Ra'idat al-ʿArabiya al-Haditha* (Cairo: Dar al-Hilal, 1981), 322.

51. Mervat Hatem, "The 1919 Revolution and Nationalist Constructions of the

Lives and Works of Pioneering Women Writers," in *Re-Envisioning Egypt: 1919–1952*, ed. Arthur Goldschmidt, Amy J. Johnson, and Barak A. Salmoni (Cairo: American University in Cairo Press, 1998), 398–423.

52. Saiza Nabrawi, "Une Nouvelle Etoile du Firmament Egyptien," *L'Egyptienne*, Sept. 1928, 7, rpt. Badran, *Feminists, Islam, and Nation*, 191.

53. "Ihtijab al-Khatiba," *al-Hilal*, 1898, 418, cited in Kholoussy, *For Better, For Worse*, 58.

54. Ibrahim ʿAli Salim, "Mushkilat al-Zawaj," *al-Ahram* 57, no. 16730 (7 July 1931): 10, cited in Kholoussy, *For Better, For Worse*, 58–59. For more on the "marriage crisis" to which this article refers, see Kholoussy, *For Better, For Worse*.

55. Van Nieuwkerk, *"A Trade Like Any Other,"* 293.

56. *Duniyat al-Fan*, 9 March 1948, 19.

57. Virginia Danielson, "Artists and Entrepreneurs: Female Singers in Cairo During the 1920s," in *Women in Middle Eastern History Shifting Boundaries in Sex and Gender*, ed. Nikki R. Keddie and Beth Baron (New Haven, CT: Yale University Press, 1991), 292–309.

58. Danielson, "Artists and Entrepreneurs," 294.

59. Danielson, "Artists and Entrepreneurs," 295.

60. ʿAli Jihad Racy, "Musical Change and Commercial Recording in Egypt, 1904–1932" (PhD diss., University of Illinois, Urbana-Champaign, 1977).

61. Danielson, "Artists and Entrepreneurs," 295.

62. Baraka, *Egyptian Upper Class*, 122–124.

63. Mitchell, *Women of Egypt*, 3.

64. Van Nieuwkerk, *"A Trade Like Any Other,"* 44–45.

65. Mitchell, *Women of Egypt*, 4–5.

66. Mitchell, *Women of Egypt*, 4–5.

67. Ismaʿil, *Masirat al-Masrah*, 330.

68. Shakry, "Schooled Mothers," 127.

69. Pollard, *Nurturing the Nation*.

70. Accounts of Mahdiyya's year of birth vary.

71. *Al-Masrah*, 30 May 1927, rpt. Sayyid ʿAli Ismaʿil, *Masirat al-Masrah fi Misr 1900–1935* (Cairo: al-Hayʾa al-Misriyya al ʿAmma lil Kitab, 2003), 307; Danielson, "Artists and Entrepreneurs," 296.

72. *al-Masrah*, 27 May 1927, 308.

73. *Al-Masrah*, 27 May 1927, rpt. Ismaʿil, *Masirat al-Masrah*, 308.

74. "Munira al-Mahdiyya bi Hadith Idhaʿi Qadim—Sultanat al-Tarab," YouTube, uploaded 5 March 2011, www.youtube.com/watch?v=aIMyIaL2NuM&p=EE9C7630F40A2404.

75. Shows for 9 P.M. sold out by 7 P.M. at the box office. Ratiba al-Hafni, *al-Sultana Munira al-Mahdiyya wa al-Ghinaʾ fi Misr Qablaha wa fi Zamaniha* (Cairo: Dar al-Sharuk, 1968), 90–91.

76. *Al-Afkar*, 11 Nov. 1915, reproduced in Ismaʿil, *Masirat al-Masrah*, 310.

77. Danielson, "Artists and Entrepreneurs," 297.

78. *Al-Afkar*, 16 June 1918, 2; 2 Aug. 1918; 3 Oct. 1918, 2, rpt. *al-Masrah al-Misri*: 1917–1918, 247, 255, 285. Apart from the opera house, it was unusual for women in the early twentieth century to attend performances outside the home. Badiʿa al-Masabni changed this by initiating the women's-only matinee.

79. *Al-Afkar*, 11 Nov. 1915, rpt. Isma'il, *Masirat al-Masrah*, 310.

80. *al-Zuhur*, July 1911, cited in Fahmy, "Popularizing Egyptian Nationalism," 211.

81. *Al-Masrah*, 27 May 1927, rpt. Isma'il, *Masirat al-Masrah*, 307. In an interview, Mahdiyya stated that her troupe might earn between 600 and 1,000 pounds per evening for a performance at Dar al-Tamthil al-'Arabi ("Munira al-Mahdiyya"). An ad in *al-Muqattam* on August 20, 1918, listed ticket prices for a Mahdiyya show as follows: baignoire, 60 piastres; loge, 40 piastres; special, 10 piastres; fauteil, 5 piastres. Other ads in the same year indicated that general admission for her shows cost 5 piastres. *Al-Afkar*, 2 Aug. 1918; 3 Oct. 1918, reproduced in Isma'il, *Masirat al-Masrah*, 255, 264, 285.

82. See, for example, *al-Akhbar*, 25 Nov. 1916; *al-Akhbar*, 17 Dec. 1916; *Misr*, 20 Jan. 1917; *Masirat al-Masrah*, 317–318; *al-Muqattam*, 12 Sept. 1919, rpt. Isma'il, *Masirat al-Masrah*, 317, 318, 331.

83. See *al-Basir*, 13 Jan. 1916; *al-Basir*, 14 Jan. 1916; *al-Basir*, 15 Jan. 1916; *al-Akhbar*, 18 Jan. 1917, rpt. *Al-Masrah al-Misri: 1916* (Cairo: 3B Studio, 2000), 24, 26, 32.

84. Adapted plays included: *Shatirtun*, by Alfred Duquenes, *Arabicized* by 'Abbas Hafiz; *Hamlet*; *'Aida*, adapted by Selim al-Naqqash; *Carmen*, by Bizet, adapted by Farah Antun; *Thais*, by Massanet, adapted by Farah Antun; *Edna*, an Italian opera; and *Telemak*. Original plays included: *Salah al-Din al-Ayubi*, by Farah Antun; *'Ali Nur al-Din*; *Kalam fi Sirk*, by Shaykh Muhammad Yunis al-Qadi; *Kulaha Yumayn*, by Yusuf al-Qadi; *al-Talta Tabita*, by Yusuf al-Qadi; and *Antony and Cleopatra*.

85. *Al-Minbar*, 5 Jan. 1916 and 13 Jan. 1916, rpt. Isma'il, *Masirat al-Masrah*, 310.

86. The ad for the play *Rosina*, for example, boasted that it had more songs than the operas *Carmen* and *Thais*. *Al-Muqattam*, 31 July 1918, rpt. *Al-Masrah al-Misri: 1917–1918* (Cairo: 3B Studio, 2001), 253–254; *Al-Afkar*, 19 Dec. 1918, rpt. *Al-Masrah al-Misri: 1917–1918*, 305.

87. See, for example, *al-Akhbar*, 14 Nov. 1917; *al-Afkar* 18 Dec. 1917, 16 June 1917, 12, 13 Sept. 1917; *al-Ahram*, 1 June 1918; *al-Basir*, 22 Sept. 1917; *Misr*, 18 April 1918, 1, 7, 9, May 1918; 13 June 1918; *al-Muqattam*, 25 July 1918, rpt. Isma'il, *Masirat al-Masrah*, 328.

88. *Al-Minbar*, 1 Feb. 1916; *al-Muqattam*, 21 Nov. 1917; *al-Ahram*, 1 June 1918; *Misr*, 30 July 1918; *al-Muqattam*, 12 Sept. 1919; *Misr*, 11 Sept. 1919, rpt. Isma'il, *Masirat al-Masrah*, 311, 327–328, 331.

89. The ability of a singer to create a feeling of *tarab*, or ecstatic engagement, in audience members was indicative of the performer's authenticity and talent. al-Hafni, *al-Sultana*, 83. A movie about Mahdiyya, directed by Hassan El Imam in 1979, was titled *Sultanat al-Tarab*. For more on tarab, see 'Ali Jihad Racy, *Making Music in the Arab World: The Culture and Artistry of Tarab* (Cambridge, UK: Cambridge University Press, 2004).

90. Danielson, "Artists and Entrepreneurs," 296.

91. Isma'il, *Masirat al-Masrah*, 324. Gabr was considered the financial manager of the troupe and rented the theater, Dar al-Tamthil al-'Arabi, under his name for Mahdiyya's troupe. This was not unusual, as most female artists up to that point had spouses or male benefactors who supported their endeavors. The dancer and singer Tawhida, for example, performed in the club Alf Layla wa Layla, which her husband, an Egyptian Greek, opened for her. When he died, she managed it on her own. The popular singer Badi'a Masabni initially depended on wealthy lovers in order to support her career. This changed in the mid-1920s when she used the money she had accumulated to open what

would become a landmark music hall, Sala Badiʿa. See Danielson, "Artists and Entrepreneurs," 295; Van Nieuwkerk, *"A Trade Like Any Other,"* 46.

92. *al-Akhbar*, 8 Aug. 1915, 10 Aug. 1915; an article in *al-Basir* noted that any charity interested in communicating with Mahdiyya should do so "via the home of her husband, Mahmoud Gabr, villa number 108 in Heliopolis." 15 Jan. 1916, rpt. Ismaʿil, *Masirat al-Masrah*, 311.

93. In the following years, Mahdiyya would go on to marry and divorce at least four other men. Danielson, "Artists and Entrepreneurs," 301.

94. As Virginia Danielson illustrates, some of the more important male mentor/female performer relations included: ʿAziz ʿId to Munira al-Mahdiyya, Ruz al-Yusuf, and Fatma Rushdi; Salama Hijazi to Mahdiyya; composer Dawud Hosni to the singers Fatma Sirri and Asmahan. Danielson, "Artists and Entrpreneurs," 307–308.

95. See, for example, Fatma Rushdi, *Al-Hub wa al-Fan* (Cairo: Sa'adi wa Shandi, 1961), 26–29.

96. Armbrust, *Mass Culture*, 199–200.

97. A *sala*, or "hall," was a place of entertainment that often served food and drink and where musicians, singers, dancers, and variety acts performed. They were also called "clubs" or "casinos." *al-Radiu*, no. 31, 23 Oct. 1931.

98. Danielson, "Artists and Entrepreneurs," 296.

99. *al-Musawwar*, no. 233 (1929), 29.

100. ʿAli Jihad Racy, "Arabian Music and the Effects of Commercial Recording," *World of Music* 20:1 (1978): 47–55.

101. Frederic Lagrange, "Women in the Singing Business, Women in Songs," *History Compass* 7:1 (2009), 247.

102. Lagrange, "Women in the Singing Business," 235.

103. Lagrange, "Women in the Singing Business," 235.

104. Lagrange, "Women in the Singing Business," 233–246.

105. *Qabadan, Qabadan* (Baidaphon B 085467/68).

106. Lagrange, "Women in the Singing Business," 12.

107. *al-Afkar*, 1 April 1917. In 1927, she earned forty pounds per record filled. (*Ruz al-Yusuf*, 12 May 1927, 12.)

108. Danielson, "Artists and Entrepreneurs," 297; *Ruz al-Yusuf*, 15 Feb. 1926, 9; *Ruz al-Yusuf*, 29 Sept. 1926, 11.

109. *Ruz al-Yusuf*, 24 Nov. 1926, 9.

110. An article in *Ruz al-Yusuf* indicated that she had set a record for having had eighteen marriages and divorces. *Ruz al-Yusuf*, no. 185, 30 Aug. 1930.

111. See, for example, *al-Masrah*, 4 July 1927, 10.

112. These included *Ruz al-Yusuf*, *al-Sitar*, *al-Masrah*, and *al-Fanun*.

113. Mitchell, *Women of Egypt*, 9.

114. *Ruz al-Yusuf*, 19 May 1926, 7; 2 June 1926, 14.

115. *Ruz al-Yusuf*, 9 June 1926, 11; 16 June 1926, 13.

116. See, for example, "ʿAlat Rihani," *Ruz al-Yusuf*, 15 Feb. 1926, 9; "Gok al-kawakib fi biyut al-nijum," *al-Kawakib*, 13 June 1932, 8; "Muhammad Shaʿrawi wa Fatma Sirri," *Ruz al-Yusuf*, 24 Nov. 1926, 9.

117. George Mosse, "Nationalism and Respectability," *Journal of Contemporary History* 17:2 (April 1982): 227.

118. Pollard, *Nurturing the Nation*, 87–94; Julia Clancy-Smith, "La Femme Arabe:

Women and Sexuality in France's North African Empire," in *Women, the Family, and Divorce Laws in Islamic History*, ed. Amira El-Azhary Sonbol (New York: Syracuse University Press, 1996), 52–63.

119. Isma'il, *Masirat al-Masrah*, 333–335.

120. Pollard, *Nurturing the Nation*, 2.

121. *al-Muqattam*, 27 April 1916; *Misr*, 20 Dec. 1916; *al-Akhbar*, 5 Jan. 1917, 13 Aug. 1917; *al-Afkar*, 16, 18 April 1918, rpt. Isma'il, *Masirat al-Masrah*, 315, 321, 327.

122. *al-Basir*, 15 Jan. 1916, rpt. Isma'il, *Masirat al-Masrah*, 311.

123. *al-Basir*, 15 Jan. 1916, rpt. Isma'il, *Masirat al-Masrah*, 311.

124. Danielson, "Artists and Entrepreneurs," 303.

125. al-Hafni, *al-Sultana*, 90; Isma'il, *Masirat al-Masrah*, 335; *Ruz al-Yusuf*, no. 498, 30–31. In an interview, Mahdiyya pointed out that Sa'd Zaghlul was in frequent attendance at her theater, "to see these plays in which I struggled with the English." Isma'il, *Masirat al-Masrah*, 335.

126. *al-Masrah*, no. 27, 24 March 1927, 23; *Ruz al-Yusuf*, no. 83, 9 June 1927, 1; *Ruz al-Yusuf*, no. 48, 29 Sept. 1926, 15; *Ruz al-Yusuf*, no. 176, 10 June 1930, 24.

127. For more on this, see Baron, *Women's Awakening*; Ellen L. Fleischman, *The Nation and Its "New" Women: The Palestinian Women's Movement, 1920–1948* (Berkeley: University of California Press, 2003); Russell, *Creating the New Egyptian Woman*; Elizabeth Thompson, *Colonial Citizens: Republican Rights, Paternal Privilege, and Gender in French Syria and Lebanon* (New York: Columbia University Press, 1999).

128. Ouissal Mejri, "Women in Egyptian Silent Cinema: The 1920s Pioneers," unpublished paper given at Women and the Silent Screen VI, University of Bologna, 2010.

129. Mejri, "Women in Egyptian Silent Cinema."

130. Negar Azimi, "A Life Reconstructed: A Lost Musical Legacy Finds Its Voice In Cairo," *Bidoun* no. 2 (Fall 2002), bidoun.org/articles/a-life-reconstructed.

131. *Ruz al-Yusuf*, 2 May 1926, 12.

132. For more on Umm Kalthum, see Virginia Danielson, *The Voice of Egypt: Umm Kulthum, Arabic Song, and Egyptian Society in the Twentieth Century* (Chicago: University of Chicago Press, 1997); and Laura Lohman, *Umm Kulthum: Artistic Agency and the Shaping of an Arab Legend, 1967–2007* (Middletown, CT: Wesleyan University Press, 2010).

133. Lohman, *Umm Kalthum*, 132.

Conclusion

1. Gasper, *Power of Representation*, 30, 38.

2. 'Afaf Lutfi al-Sayyid Marsot, *Egypt's Liberal Experiment, 1922–1936* (Cambridge, UK: Cambridge University Press, 1984).

3. See, for example, Armbrust, *Mass Culture*.

4. Sam Bardaouil, *Surrealism in Egypt: Modernism and the Art and Liberty Group* (London: I. B. Taurus, 2017), 39.

5. Bardaouil, *Surrealism*, 47.

6. Charles Shafiah, "Art et Liberté: Egypt's Surrealists," *The New York Review of Books* (3 Feb. 2018), www.nybooks.com/daily/2018/02/03/art-et-liberte-egypts

-surrealists/?utm_medium=email&utm_campaign=NYR%20Cairo%20Tina%20 Brown%20Israel%20and%20Palestine&utm_content=NYR%20Cairo%20Tina%20 Brown%20Israel%20and%20Palestine+CID_aeb3da0d3c5c21a419f97337795969e5& utm_source=Newsletter.

7. The group was short-lived, but the curators Sam Bardaoiul and Till Fellrath gathered 130 artworks and 200 archival documents to create the first comprehensive exhibition of the Art and Liberty Group. It toured Paris, Madrid, Düsseldorf, Liverpool, and Stockholm between October 2016 and March 2018. See *Exhibition Fact Sheet* at www.artreoriented.com/content/2-exhibitions/18-art-et-liberte/art_et _liberte_fact_sheet.pdf.

Bibliography

Archival and Unpublished Sources

Egypt, Dar al-Watha'iq (Egyptian National Archive), Cairo 'Asr Isma'il
Majlis al-Wuzara'
Abdun
Egypt, Opera House and Music Library, Cairo
Opera House Documents
Great Britain, British National Archives, Kew Gardens
FO 5/331
FO 141/810/1
FO 464/141
FO 608/214/1

Periodicals

Al-Afkar
Al-Ahram
Al-Akhbar
Egyptian Gazette
Egyptian Standard
Al-Fanun
Al-Fusul
Al-Hilal
Al-Masrah
Al-Minbar
Misr
Al-Muqattam
Al-Musawwar
Al-Mu'ayyid
Revue du Monde Musulman
Ruz al-Yusuf
Al-Sitar
The Sphinx
Al-Watan

Online Sources

Azimi, Negar. "A Life Reconstructed: A Lost Musical Legacy Finds Its Voice in Cairo." *Bidoun* 2 (Fall 2002). bidoun.org/articles/a-life-reconstructed.

Grippo, James R. "The Fool Sings a Hero's Song: Shaaban Abdel Rahim, Egyptian Sha'abi, and the Video Clip Phenomenon." *Transnational Broadcasting Studies* 16 (2006). www.tbsjournal.com/Grippo.html.

"Munira al-Mahdiyya bi Hadith Idha'i Qadim—Sultanat al-Tarab." YouTube. Uploaded March 5, 2011. www.youtube.com/watch?v=aIMyIaL2NuM&p=EE9C7630F40A2404.

Peterson, Jennifer. "Sampling Folklore: The 'Re-popularization' of Sufi Inshad in Egyptian Dance Music." *Arab Media and Society* 4 (Winter 2008). www.arabmediasociety.com/?article=580.

Shafiah, Charles. "Art et Liberté: Egypt's Surrealists." *The New York Review of Books*. February 3, 2018. www.nybooks.com/daily/2018/02/03/art-et-liberte-egypts-surrealists.

Taher, Mena. "The Life of Inji Aflatoun, an Artist and a Rebel." *ahramonline*. September 18, 2011. english.ahram.org.eg/NewsContent/5/25/21577/Arts—Culture/Visual-Art/The-life-of-Inji-Aflatoun,-an-artist-and-a-rebel-.aspx.

Recorded Sources

Qabadan, Qabadan (Baidaphon B 085467/68)

Printed Sources

'Abdu 'Ali, 'Arafa. *Al-Qahira fi 'Asr Isma'il*. Cairo: Dar al-Misriyya al-Lubnaniyya, 1998.

'Aboud, Marun. "Farah Antun." *al-Kitab* 2 (November 1947): 1742.

Abrahamson, Rita. "African Studies and the Postcolonial Challenge." *African Affairs* 102 (2003): 189–210.

Abu-Lughod, Janet. *Cairo: 1001 Years of the City Victorious*. Princeton: Princeton University Press, 1971.

Abu-Lughod, Lila. *Veiled Sentiments*. Berkeley: University of California Press, 1986.

Abul-Naga, El Said Atia. *Les Sources Francaises du Theatre Egyptien, 1870–1939*. Alger: Société Nationale d'Edition et de Diffusion, 1972.

Abyad, Su'ad. *Jurj Abyad: Ayyam lam yisbal al-sitar*. Cairo: al-Hay'a al-Misriyya al 'Amma lil Kitab, 1991.

Adas, Michael. *Machines as the Measure of Men: Science, Technology, and Ideologies of Western Dominance*. Ithaca: Cornell University Press, 1989.

Ahmed, Leila. *Women and Gender in Islam*. New Haven, CT: Yale University Press, 1992.

Al-Hilal, 1897–1997. Volume 1. Cairo: Dar al-Hilal, 1992.

Allah, Isis Fath. *Salama Hijazi*. Cairo: Dar al-Shurouk, 2002.

AlSayyad, Nezar, Irene A. Bierman, and Nasser Rabbat, eds. *Making Cairo Medieval*. Oxford, UK: Lexington Books, 2005.

Amin, Dina A. *Alfred Farag and Egyptian Theater: The Poetics of Disguise, with Four Short Plays and a Monologue*. Syracuse: Syracuse University Press, 2008.

———. "Egyptian Theater: Reconstructing Performance Spaces." *Arab Studies Journal* 14:2 (Fall 2006): 78–106.

ʿAnnus, Nagwa. *Masrah Ya'qub Sannu'*. Cairo: al-Hay'a al ʿAmma lil-Kitab, 1984.

Antun, Farah. *Misr al-Jadida wa Misr al-Qadima*. Cairo: Maktabat al-Ta'lif, 1913.

Arat, Yesim. *Rethinking Islam and Liberal Democracy: Islamist Women in Turkish Politics*. Albany: SUNY Press, 2005.

Armbrust, Walter. *Mass Culture and Modernism in Egypt*. Cambridge, UK: Cambridge University Press, 1996.

Asfour, Khaled. "The Domestication of Knowledge: Cairo at the Turn of the Century." *Muqarnas X: An Annual on Islamic Art and Architecture*. Volume 10, *Essays in Honor of Oleg Grabar*. Leiden: E. J. Brill (1993): 125–137.

ʿAshri, Fathi al-, ed. *Al-Masrah al-Misri*. Cairo: Dar al-Za'im li al-Taba'a al-Haditha, 1998.

Askew, Kelly M. *Performing the Nation: Swahili Music and Cultural Politics in Tanzania*. Chicago: University of Chicago Press, 2002.

ʿAwad, Ramsis. *al-Tarikh al-Sirri li al-Masrah Qabl Thawrat 1919*. Cairo: Mutbaʿa al-Kilani, 1972.

———. *Ittijahat Siyasiya fi al-Masrah Qabla Thawrat 1919*. Cairo: al-Hay'a al-Misriyya al ʿAmma lil Kitab, 1979.

———. *Shayksbir fi Misr*. Cairo: Dar al-Hilal, 1992.

Badawi, M. M. *Early Arabic Drama*. Cambridge, UK: Cambridge University Press, 1988.

Badran, Margot. *Feminists, Islam, and Nation: Gender and the Making of Modern Egypt*. Princeton: Princeton University Press, 1995.

Baedeker, Karl, ed. *Egypt: Handbook for Travellers, Part 1. Lower Egypt with the Fayum and the Peninsula of Sinai* [Baedeker's Lower Egypt]. 2nd ed. Leipsic: Karl Baedeker, 1885.

Baer, Gabriel. *Fellah and Townsman in the Middle East*. London: Frank Cass, 1982.

Bakhtin, Mikhail. *The Dialogic Imagination: Four Essays*. Edited by Michael Holquist and translated by Caryl Emerson and Michael Holquist. University of Texas Press Slavic Series (Book 1), rpt. ed. Austin: University of Texas Press, 1983.

———. *Rabelais and His World*. Translated by Helen Iswolsky. Cambridge, MA: MIT Press, 1965.

Baraka, Magda. *The Egyptian Upper Class between Revolutions, 1919–1952*. Reading, UK: Ithaca Press, 1998.

Barbour, Nevill. "The Arabic Theater in Egypt." *Bulletin of the School of Oriental Studies, University of London* 8:1 (1935): 173–187.

Bardenstein, Carol. *Translation and Transformation in Modern Arabic Literature: The Indigenous Assertions of Muhammad ʿUthman Jalal*. Wiesbaden: Otto Harrassowitz Verlag, 2005.

Baron, Beth. *Egypt as a Woman: Nationalism, Gender, and Politics*. Berkeley: University of California Press, 2005.

———. "Mothers, Morality, and Nationalism in Pre-1919 Egypt." In *The Origins of Arab Nationalism*, ed. Rashid Khalidi et al., 271–288. New York: Columbia University Press, 1991.

———. *The Women's Awakening in Egypt: Culture, Society, and the Press*. New Haven, CT: Yale University Press, 1994.

Bayly, C. A. *The Birth of the Modern World, 1780–1914: Global Connections and Comparisons*. Malden, MA: Blackwell Publishing, 2004.

Beinin, Joel, and Zackary Lockman. *Workers on the Nile: Nationalism, Communism, Islam, and the Egyptian Working Class.* Princeton: Princeton University Press, 1987.
Berman, Marshall. *All That Is Solid Melts into Air: The Experience of Modernity.* New York: Simon and Schuster, 1982.
Bhabha, Homi K. *The Location of Culture.* London: Routledge, 1994.
Bhatia, Nandi. *Acts of Authority, Acts of Resistance: Theater and Politics in Colonial and Postcolonial India.* Ann Arbor: University of Michigan Press, 2004.
Bier, Laura. *Revolutionary Womanhood: Feminisms, Modernity, and the State in Nasser's Egypt.* Stanford: Stanford University Press, 2011.
Blanchard, Jerrold. *Egypt under Isma'il Pasha.* London: Samuel Tinsley and Co., 1879.
Boctor, Michel. *Aida, 1871–1971.* Alexandria: Les Cahiers d'Alexandrie, 1972.
Booth, Marilyn. *May Her Likes Be Multiplied: Biography and Gender Politics in Egypt.* Berkeley: University of California Press, 2001.
Botman, Selma. *Engendering Citizenship.* New York: Columbia University Press, 1999.
Bramsted, Ernest. K. *Aristocracy and the Middle Classes in German: Social Types in German Literature, 1830–1900.* Chicago and London: Phoenix Books, 1964.
Brecht, Bertolt. *Brecht on Theatre: The Development of an Aesthetic.* Edited and translated by John Willet. London: Methuen, 1964.
Brown, Kathleen. *Good Wives, Nasty Wenches, Anxious Patriarchs: Gender, Race, and Power in Colonial Virginia.* Chapel Hill: University of North Carolina Press, 1996.
Busch, Hans, ed. *Verdi's "Aida": The History of an Opera in Letters and Documents.* Minneapolis: University of Minnesota Press, 1978.
Butcher, Edith Louisa Floyer. *Egypt as We Knew It.* London: Mills & Boon, 1911.
Butler, Alfred. *Court Life in Egypt.* London: Chapman & Hall, Scribner & Welford, 1887.
Butler, Judith. *Gender Trouble: Feminism and the Subversion of Identity.* London: Routledge, 1990.
Caillard, Mabel. *A Lifetime in Egypt, 1876–1935.* London: G. Richards, 1935.
Caillos, Roger. *Man, Play, and Games.* Translated by Helen Iswolsky. Cambridge, MA: MIT Press, 1965.
Cannadine, David. *Ornamentalism: How the British Saw Their Empire.* Oxford: Oxford University Press, 2001.
Carlson, Marvin. *Performance: A Critical Introduction.* London: Routledge, 2003.
———. *Places of Performance: The Semiotics of Theatre Architecture.* Ithaca and London: Cornell University Press, 1989.
Carmona, Michel. *Haussmann: His Life and Times, and the Making of Modern Paris.* Chicago: Ivan R. Dee, 2002.
Celik, Zeynep. *Empire, Architecture, and the City: French-Ottoman Encounters, 1830–1914.* Seattle: University of Washington Press, 2008.
———. *The Remaking of Istanbul: Portrait of an Ottoman City in the Nineteenth Century.* Berkeley: University of California Press, 1986.
Chalcraft, John. "The Cairo Cab Drivers and the Strike of 1907." In *The Empire in the City: Arab Provincial Capitals in the Late Ottoman Empire*, edited by Jens Hanssen, Thomas Philipp, and Stefan Weber, 173–198. Beirut: Ergon Verlag, 2002.
Charms, Gabriel. *Five Months at Cairo and in Lower Egypt.* London: Richard Bentley and Son, 1883.
Chennelle, Ellen. *Recollections of an Egyptian Princess by Her English Governess.* London: William Blackwood and Sons, 1893.

Cixoux, Helene, and Catherine Clement. *The Newly Born Woman.* Translated by Betsy Wing. London: I. B. Taurus, 1996.
Clendinnen, Inga. *Ambivalent Conquests: Maya and Spaniard in Yucatan, 1517–1570.* Cambridge, UK: Cambridge University Press, 1987.
Clancy-Smith, Julia. "La Femme Arabe: Women and Sexuality in France's North African Empire." In *Women, the Family, and Divorce Laws in Islamic History,* edited by Amira El-Azhary Sonbol, 52–63. New York: Syracuse University Press, 1996.
Cleveland, William L. *A History of the Modern Middle East.* Boulder: Westview Press, 1994.
Cole, Juan R. I. *Colonialism and Revolution in the Middle East: Social and Cultural Origins of Egypt's 'Urabi Movement.* Cairo: American University in Cairo Press, 1999.
———. "Feminism, Class, and Islam in Turn-of-the-Century Egypt." *International Journal of Middle East Studies* 13 (1981): 387–407.
———. *Napoleon's Egypt: Invading the Middle East.* New York: Palgrave Macmillan, 2007.
Colla, Elliot. *Conflicted Antiquities: Egyptology, Egyptomania, Egyptian Modernity.* Durham, NC: Duke University Press, 2007.
Cook, Thomas. *Cook's Tourists' Handbook for Egypt, the Nile, and the Desert.* London: Thomas Cook and Son, 1876.
Cooke, Miriam. *Dissident Syria: Making Oppositional Arts Official.* Durham, NC: Duke University Press, 2007.
Cuno, Kenneth. *Modernizing Marriage: Family, Ideology, and Law in Nineteenth and Early Twentieth Century Egypt.* Syracuse: Syracuse University Press, 2015.
Danielson, Virginia. "Artists and Entrepreneurs: Female Singers in Cairo During the 1920s." In *Women in Middle Eastern History Shifting Boundaries in Sex and Gender,* edited by Nikki R. Keddie and Beth Baron, 292–309. New Haven: Yale University Press, 1991.
———. *The Voice of Egypt: Umm Kalthum, Arabic Song, and Egyptian Society in the Twentieth Century.* Chicago: University of Chicago Press, 2007.
Davin, Anna. "Imperialism and Motherhood." *History Workshop* 5 (1978): 9–65.
De Certeau, Michel. *The Practice of Everyday Life.* Translated by Steven F. Rendall. Berkeley: University of California Press: 1984.
Deeb, Marius. *Party Politics in Egypt: The Wafd and Its Rivals, 1919–1939.* London: Ithaca Press, 1979.
De Kusel, Samuel Selig. *An Englishman's Recollections of Egypt, 1863–1888.* London: John Lane, 1915.
De Leon, Edwin. *Egypt under Its Khedives.* London: Sampson Low, Marston, Searle, and Revington, 1882.
Di-Capua, Yoav. *Gatekeepers of the Arab Past: History and History Writing in Twentieth-Century Egypt.* Berkeley: University of California Press, 2009.
Earl of Cromer. *Modern Egypt.* New York: MacMillan, 1908.
Ebers, Georg. *An Egyptian Princess.* New York: Bigelow, Brown and Co., 1880.
Egypt, Ministry of Finance. *The Census of Egypt Taken in 1907.* Volume 1. Cairo: National Printing Department, 1909.
———. *The Census of Egypt Taken in 1917.* Cairo: Cairo Government Press, 1920.
El-Feki, Moustafa. *Copts in Egyptian Politics 1919–1952.* Cairo: General Egyptian Book Organization, 1991.

El-Messiri, Sawsan. *Ibn al-Balad: A Concept of Egyptian Identity*. Leiden: E. J. Brill, 1978.

Ellis, Matthew H. *Desert Borderland: The Making of Modern Egypt and Libya*. Stanford: Stanford University Press, 2018.

Elgood, Percival George. *Egypt and the Army*. London: Oxford University Press, Humphrey Milford, 1924.

Fahmy, Khaled. *All the Pasha's Men: Mehmed Ali, His Army, and the Making of Modern Egypt*. Cambridge, UK: Cambridge University Press, 1997.

———. "An Olfactory Tale of Two Cities." In *Historians in Cairo: Essays in Honor of George Scanlon*, edited by Jill Edwards, 155–187. Cairo: American University in Cairo Press, 2002.

Fahmy, Ziad. "Media-Capitalism: Colloquial Mass Culture and Nationalism in Egypt, 1908–18." *International Journal of Middle Eastern Studies* 42:1 (February 2010): 83–103.

———. *Ordinary Egyptians: Creating the Modern Nation through Popular Culture*. Stanford: Stanford University Press, 2011.

Farag, Alfred. *Shari' 'Imad al-Din: Hikayat al-Fann wa al-Nijum*. Cairo: Dar al-Hilal, 2005.

Fawzi, Husayn. *Sindbad fi rihal al-hayah*. Cairo: Dar al-Ma'arif Iqra' series, 1968.

Fil, Muhammad al-. *Ru'iya wa Biyyan Hala al-Masrah al-'Arabi al-Ta'sis*. Cairo: al-Hay'a al-Misriyya al 'Amma lil Kitab, 2001.

Fischer-Lichte, Erika. "Culture as Performance." *Modern Austrian Literature* 423 (2009): 1–10.

Fleischmann, Ellen L. *The Nation and Its "New" Women: The Palestinian Women's Movement, 1920–1948*. Berkeley: University of California Press, 2003.

Freud, Sigmund. *Civilization and Its Discontents*. New York: W. W. Norton & Co., 1989.

Gasper, Michael Ezekiel. *The Power of Representation: Publics, Peasants, and Islam in Egypt*. Stanford: Stanford University Press, 2008.

Gendzier, Irene. *The Practical Visions of Ya'qub Sanu'*. Cambridge, MA: Harvard Middle Eastern Monographs, 1966.

Gershoni, Israel, and James P. Jankowski. *Egypt, Islam, and the Arabs: The Search for Egyptian Nationhood, 1900–1930*. New York: Oxford University Press, 1986.

Goffman, Erving. *Frame Analysis*. Garden City, NY: Doubleday, 1974.

Goldschmidt, Arthur. *Biographical Dictionary of Modern Egypt*. Cairo: American University in Cairo Press, 2000.

Goldstein, Joshua. *Drama Kings: Players and Publics in the Re-creation of Peking Opera, 1870–1937*. Berkeley: University of California Press, 2007.

Habermas, Jurgen. *The Structural Transformation of the Public Sphere: An Inquiry into a Category of Bourgeois Society*. Translated by Thomas Burger. Cambridge, MA: MIT Press, 1962.

Hafni, Ratiba al-. *al-Sultana Munira al-Mahdiyya wa al-Ghina' fi Misr Qablaha wa fi Zamaniha*. Cairo: Dar al-Sharuk, 1968.

Haghani, Fakhri. "The 'New Woman' on the Stage: The Making of a Gendered Public Sphere in Interwar Iran and Egypt." PhD diss. Georgia State University, November 14, 2008.

Haghani, Fakhrolmolouk. "The 'New Woman' of the Interwar Period: Gender, Identity, and Performance in Egypt and Iran." *Al-Raida*, no. 122–123 (Summer/Fall 2008): 32–41.

Haikal, Fayza. "Egypt's Past Regenerated by Its Own People." In *Napoleon in Egypt*, edited by Irene A. Bierman, 161–180. Reading, UK: Garnet and Ithaca Press, 2003.

Haim, Sylvia G. "Salama Musa, An Appreciation of His Autobiography." *Die Welt des Islams* 2, no. 1 (1952): 1–24.

Hakim, Tawfiq al-. *Ya Tali' al-Shajara*. Cairo: Multazim li al-Tab' wal-Nashr, 1962.

Hall, Stuart. "Notes on Deconstructing the Popular." In *People's History and Socialist Theory*, rpt. (Routledge Revivals series), edited by Raphael Samuel, 227–241. Oxford and New York: Routledge and Kegan Paul, [1981] 2016.

———. "The Question of Cultural Identity." In *Modernity: An Introduction to Modern Societies*, edited by Stuart Hall et al. Oxford, UK: Blackwell, 1996.

———. "Who Needs Identity?" In *Questions of Cultural Identity*, edited by Stuart Hall and Paul du Gay. London: Sage Press, 1996.

Hamdan, Mas'ud. *Poetics, Politics, and Protest in Arab Theatre: The Bitter Cup and the Holy Rain*. Portland, OR, and Brighton, UK: Sussex Academic Press, 2006.

Hanley, Will. *Identifying with Nationality: Europeans, Ottomans, and Egyptians in Alexandria*. New York: Columbia University Press, 2017.

Hanna, Nelly. *In Praise of Books: A Cultural History of Cairo's Middle Class*. Syracuse: Syracuse University Press, 2003.

———. "The Urban History of Cairo Around 1900." In *Historians in Cairo: Essays in Honor of George Scanlon*, edited by Jill Edwards, 189–202. Cairo: American University in Cairo Press, 2002.

Hanna, Sami A. "The Mawwal in Egyptian Folklore." *Journal of American Folklore* 80 (April–June 1967): 182–190.

Harrison, Thomas Skelton. *The Homely Diary of a Diplomat in the East: 1897–1899*. Boston: Houghton Mifflin Co., 1917.

Harvey, David. *The Condition of Postmodernity*. Oxford, UK: Blackwell Publishing, 1990.

Hassan, Hassan. *In the House of Muhammad Ali: A Family Album, 1805–1952*. Cairo: American University in Cairo Press, 2000.

Hatem, Mervat. "The 1919 Revolution and Nationalist Constructions of the Lives and Works of Pioneering Women Writers." In *Re-Envisioning Egypt: 1919–1952*, edited by Arthur Goldschmidt, Amy J. Johnson, and Barak A. Salmoni, 398–423. Cairo: American University in Cairo Press, 1998.

———. "The Pitfalls of Nationalist Discourse on Citizenship in Egypt." In *Gender and Citizenship in the Middle East*, edited by Suad Joseph. Syracuse: Syracuse University Press, 2000.

Heseltine, William B., and Hazel C. Wolf. *The Blue and the Gray on the Nile*. Chicago: University of Chicago Press, 1961.

Hifni, Mahmud Ahmad al-. *Sayyid Darwish: Hayatuh wa 'athar 'abqariatuh*. Cairo: Dar Misr Lil-Tiba'a, 1962.

Hourani, Albert. *Arabic Thought in the Liberal Age, 1789–1939*. London: Oxford University Press, 1962.

Humbert, Jean-Marcel. "Les Expositions Universelles de 1867 et 1878 et La Création d'Aida." In *La France et L'Égypte à l'Époque des Vice-Rois 1805–1882*, edited by Daniel Panzac and André Raymond, 289–309. Cairo: Institut Francais d'Archéologie Orientale, 2002.

Hunter, F. Robert. *Egypt under the Khedives, 1805–1879: From Household Government to Modern Bureaucracy*. Cairo: American University in Cairo Press, 1999.

Hussein, Dina K. "Modernity Through Café Riche: Serving Modernity, Catering to the Intellectuals and Closed to the Masses." Paper presented to the Middle East Studies Association, Washington, DC, November 23, 2008.

ʿId, Al-Sayyid Hassan. *Tatawwur al-Naqd al-Masrahi fi Misr*. Cairo: al-Muʾisa al-Misriyya al ʿAmma li al Taʾlif wa al-Anbaʾ wa al-Nashar, 1965.

Iolita, Otello. "Training and Stylistic Background of Italian Architects and Planners in Modern Egypt." In *Le Caire-Alexandrie*, edited by Mercedes Volait, 179–191. Cairo: Institut Francais d'Archéologie Orientale, 2004.

Ismaʿil, Sayyid ʿAli. *Masirat al-Masrah fi Misr: 1900–1935*. Cairo: Al-Hay'a al-misriyya al ʿAmma lil Kitab, 2003.

Jabarti, ʿAbd al-Rahman al-. *ʿAja'ib al-Athar fi al-Tarajim wa 'l-Akhbar*. Cairo: Bulaq Press, 1879.

Jacob, Wilson Chacko. *Working Out Egypt: Effendi Masculinity and Subject Formation in Colonial Modernity, 1870–1940*. Durham, NC: Duke University Press, 2011.

James, William. *The Philosophy of William James*. New York: Random House, 1925.

Jayyusi, Salma Khadra, ed. *Tales of Juha: Classic Arab Folk Humor*. Northampton, MA: Interlink Publishing Group, 2007.

Johnson, James H. *Listening in Paris: A Cultural History*. Berkeley: University of California Press, 1995.

Jones, Toby Craig. *Desert Kingdom: How Oil and Water Forged Modern Saudi Arabia*. Cambridge, MA: Harvard University Press, 2010.

Karabell, Zachary. *Parting the Desert: the Creation of the Suez Canal*. New York: Knopf, 2003.

Kassar, Majid al-. *ʿAli al-Kassar: Berberi Misr al-wahid*. Cairo: Akhbar al-Yom, 1991.

Kholoussy, Hanan. *For Better, For Worse: The Marriage Crisis That Made Modern Egypt*. Stanford: Stanford University Press, 2010.

Khouri-Makdisi, Ilham. *The Eastern Mediterranean and the Making of Global Radicalism*. Berkeley: University of California Press, 2010.

———. *Theater and Radical Politics in Beirut, Cairo, and Alexandria: 1860–1914*. Washington, DC: Center for Contemporary Arab Studies, 2006.

Khozai, Mohamed Ali al-. *The Development of Early Arabic Drama, 1847–1900*. London and New York: Longman, 1984.

Kolk, Mieke. "The Performance of Comedy in 'East' and 'West': Cultured Boundaries and the Art of Cunning." Translated by Samira Tarjisti. In *The Performance of the Comic in Arabic Theatre: Cultural Heritage, Western Models and Postcolonial Hybridity*, edited by Mieke Kolk and Freddy Decreus, 151–165. The Hague: Prince Claus Foundation, 2005.

Kozma, Liat. *Global Women, Colonial Ports: Prostitution in the Interwar Middle East*. Albany: State University of New York, 2017.

———. *Policing Women: Sex, Law, and Medicine in Khedivial Egypt*. Syracuse: Syracuse University Press, 2011.

Lagrange, Frederic. "Male Homosexuality in Modern Arabic Literature." In *Imagined Masculinities: Male Identity and Culture in the Modern Middle East*, edited by Mai Ghoussoub and Emma Sinclair-Webb, 169–198. London: Saqi Books, 2000.

———. "Women in the Singing Business, Women in Songs." *History Compass* 7:1 (2009): 226–250.

Landau, Jacob M. "Abu Naddara: An Egyptian Jewish Nationalist." *Journal of Jewish Studies* 3:1 (1952): 30–44.

———. "Popular Arabic Plays, 1909." *Journal of Arabic Literature* 17 (1986): 120–125.

———. *Studies in the Arab Theater and Cinema*. Philadelphia: University of Pennsylvania Press, 1958.

Landes, David S. *Bankers and Pashas: International Finance and Economic Imperialism in Egypt*. New York: Harper & Row, 1958.

Lane, Edward. *The Manners and Customs of the Modern Egyptians*. London: J. M. Dent & Co., 1908.

Lears, T. J. Jackson. *No Place of Grace: Antimodernism and the Transformation of American Culture*. Chicago: University of Chicago Press, 1981.

Lesseps, Ferdinand de. *The Suez Canal: Letters and Documents Descriptive of Its Rise and Progress in 1854–56*. London: Henry S. King and Co., 1876.

Lewis, Bernard, ed. *A Middle East Mosaic: Fragments of Life, Letters, and History*. New York: The Modern Library, 2001.

———. *What Went Wrong? Western Impact and Middle Eastern Response*. Oxford, UK: Oxford University Press, 2002.

Lewis, David Levering. *Race to Fashoda: Colonialism and African Resistance*. New York: Henry Holt and Co., 1987.

Litvin, Margaret. *Hamlet's Arab Journey: Shakespeare's Prince and Nasser's Ghost*. Princeton: Princeton University Press, 2011.

Lockman, Zachary. "Exploring the Field: Lost Voices and Emerging Practices in Egypt, 1882-1914." In *Histories of the Modern Middle East: New Directions*, edited by Israel Gershoni, Hakan Erdem, and Ursula Wokoeck, 137–153. Boulder: Lynne Rienner Publishers, 2002.

———. "Imagining the Working Class: Culture, Nationalism, and Class Formation in Egypt, 1899–1914." *Poetics Today* 15:2 (Summer 1994): 157–190.

Lohman, Laura. *Umm Kalthum: Artistic Agency and the Shaping of an Arab Legend, 1967–2007*. Middletown, CT: Wesleyan University Press, 2010.

Macfie, A. L. *Orientalism: A Reader*. Cairo: American University in Cairo Press, 2000.

Mansfield, Peter. *The British in Egypt*. New York: Holt, Rinehart and Winston, 1972.

Marsot, Afaf Lutfi al-Sayyid. *Egypt in the Reign of Muhammad Ali*. Cambridge, UK: Cambridge University Press, 1984.

———. *Egypt's Liberal Experiment, 1922–1936*. Berkeley: University of California Press, 1977.

McCants, Clyde T. *Verdi's* Aida*: A Record of the Life of the Opera On and Off the Stage*. Jefferson, NC: McFarland and Co., 2006.

McCoan, J. C. *Egypt As It Is: 1829–1904*. New York: H. Holt, 1877.

McDougall, James. *History and the Culture of Nationalism in Algeria*. Cambridge, UK: Cambridge University Press, 2006.

Mejri, Ouissal. "Women in Egyptian Silent Cinema: The 1920s Pioneers." Unpublished paper given at Women and the Silent Screen VI, University of Bologna, 2010.

Mestyan, Adam. *Arab Patriotism: The Ideology and Culture of Power in Late Ottoman Egypt*. Princeton: Princeton University Press, 2017.

———. "Arabic Theater in Early Khedivial Culture, 1868–72: James Sanua Revisited." *International Journal of Middle East Studies* 46 (2014): 117–137.

Metcalf, Cynthia. "From Morality Play to Celebrity: Women, Gender, and Performing Modernity in Egypt, 1850–1939." PhD diss., University of Virginia, 2008.

Mikhail, Alan. "The Heart's Desire: Gender, Urban Space, and the Ottoman Coffee House." In *Ottoman Tulips, Ottoman Coffee: Leisure and Lifestyle in the Eighteenth Century*, edited by Dana Sajdi. London: I. B. Taurus, 2007.

Mikhail, Mona. "Revisiting the Theater in Egypt: An Overview." In *Colors of Enchantment: Theater, Dance, Music, and the Visual Arts in the Middle East*, edited by Sherifa Zuhur, 17–26. Cairo: American University in Cairo Press, 2001.

Minkin, Shane. *Imperial Bodies: Death, Governance, and Empire in Alexandria, Egypt.* Stanford: Stanford University Press, forthcoming fall 2019.

Mitchell, Amira, comp. *Women of Egypt, 1924–1931* (Pioneers of Stardom and Fame series). UK: Topic Records, 2006.

Mitchell, Timothy. *Colonising Egypt.* Berkeley: University of California Press, 1988.

———. *Rule of Experts: Egypt, Techno-Politics, Modernity.* Berkeley: University of California Press, 2002.

———. "The Stage of Modernity." In *Questions of Modernity*, edited by Timothy Mitchell, 1–34. Minneapolis: University of Minnesota Press, 2000.

Moosa, Matti. *The Origins of Modern Arabic Fiction.* Boulder: Lynne Rienner Publishers, 1997.

Moreh, Schmuel. *Live Theatre and Dramatic Literature in the Medieval Arab World.* New York: New York University Press, 1992.

Mosse, George. "Nationalism and Respectability." *Journal of Contemporary History* 17:2 (April 1982): 221–246.

Mostyn, Trevor. *Egypt's Belle Epoque: Cairo, 1869–1952.* London: Quartet, 1989.

Musa, Nabawiyya. *Tarikhi Biqalmi.* Cairo: Multaqal Mar'a wa al-Dhakira, 1999.

Musa, Salama. *The Education of Salama Musa.* Leiden: E. J. Brill, 1961.

Musilahi, Muhsin, ed. *Al-Masrah al-Misri.* Cairo: Dar al-Za'im li al-Taba' al-Haditha, 1998.

Muwaylihi, Muhammad al-. *Hadith 'Isa ibn Hisham, A Period of Time: A Study and Translation of Hadith 'Isa Ibn Hisham by Muhammad Al-Muwaylihi*, translated by Roger Allen. Reading, UK: Ithaca Press, 1992.

Naga, El Said Atia Abul. *Les Sources Francaises du Théâtre Égyptien (1870–1939).* Algeria: Société Nationale d'Edition et de Diffusion, 1972.

Najm, Muhammad Yusuf. *Al Masrahiyya fi al adab al 'arabi al hadith 1847–1914.* Beirut: Dar Bayrut li al-Tiba'a wa al-Nashr, 1956.

Najmabadi, Afsanah. "Crafting an Educated Housewife in Iran." In *Remaking Women: Feminism and Modernity in the Middle East*, edited by Lila Abu-Lughod, 91–125. Cairo: American University in Cairo Press, 1998.

———. "The Gender of Modernity: Reflections from Iranian Historiography." In *Histories of the Modern Middle East: New Directions*, edited by Israel Gershoni, Hakan Erdem, and Ursula Wokock, 75–91. Boulder: Lynne Rienner, 2002.

Necipoglu, Gulru. *Architecture, Ceremonial, and Power: The Topkapi Palace in the Fifteenth and Sixteenth Centuries.* Cambridge, MA: MIT Press, 1991.

Nelson, Cynthia. *Doria Shafik, Egyptian Feminist: A Woman Apart.* Gainesville: University Press of Florida, 1996.

Nelson, Nina. *Shepheard's Hotel.* London: Barrie and Rockliff, 1960.

Niebuhr, Carsten. *Travels through Arabia.* Volume 1. Beirut: Librarie du Liban, no date.

Nietzsche, Friedrich. *Human, All Too Human.* Translated by Marion Faber. Lincoln: University of Nebraska Press, 1984.

Omar, Hussein. "'And I Saw No Reason to Chronicle My Life': Tensions of Nationalist Modernity in the Memoirs of Fathallah Pasha Barakat." In *The Long 1890s in Egypt: Colonial Quiescence, Subterranean Resistance*, edited by Marilyn Booth and Anthony Gorman, 287–314. Edinburgh, UK: Edinburgh University Press, 2014.

Omar, Hussein A. H. "'Snatched by Destiny's Hand': Obituaries and the Making of Class in Modern Egypt." *History Compass* 15:6 (2017): 1–12.

Pappe, Ilan. *The Modern Middle East*. London: Routledge, 2005.

Philipp, Thomas, Moshe Permann, and Guido Schwald, eds. *'Abd al-Rahman al-Jabarti's History of Egypt*. 4 volumes and guide. Stuttgart: Franz Steiner Verlag, 1994.

Pierce, Leslie P. *The Imperial Harem: Women and Sovereignty in the Ottoman Empire*. New York: Oxford University Press, 1993.

Pollard, Lisa. *Nurturing the Nation: The Family Politics of Modernizing, Colonizing, and Liberating Egypt, 1805–1923*. Berkeley: University of California Press, 2005.

Powell, Eve M. Troutt. *A Different Shade of Colonialism: Egypt, Great Britain, and the Mastery of the Sudan*. Berkeley: University of California Press, 2003.

———. "Burnt-Cork Nationalism: Race and Identity in the Theater of 'Ali al-Kassar." In *Colors of Enchantment: Theater, Dance, Music, and the Visual Arts in the Middle East*, edited by Sherifa Zuhur, 27–38. Cairo: American University in Cairo Press, 2001.

Qabbani, Sulayman Hassan al-. *Bughyat al-Mumaththilin*. Alexandria: Gharzuzi, 1914.

Racy, Ali Jihad. "Arabian Music and the Effects of Commercial Recording." *World of Music* 20:1 (1978): 47–55.

———. *Making Music in the Arab World: The Culture and Artistry of Tarab*. Cambridge, UK: Cambridge University Press, 2004.

———. "Musical Change and Commercial Recording in Egypt, 1904–1932." PhD diss., University of Illinois, Urbana-Champaign, 1977.

Ra'i, 'Ali al-. *al-Kumidiya al-murtajalah fi al-masrah al-misri*. Cairo: Dar al-Hilal, 1968.

Ramzy, Carolyn. "Untold Coptic Music Narratives: Taratil and a History of Oral Resistance." Paper presented to the Middle East Studies Association, Boston, MA, November 2009.

Raymond, André, ed. *Arab Cities in the Ottoman Period: Cairo, Syria, and the Maghreb*. Burlington, VT: Ashgate, 2002.

"Reglement sur les theatres promulgué par arrête du Ministère de l'Intérieur." *Recueil des Documents Officiels du Gouvernement Egyptien*. July 12, 1911.

Reid, Donald M. *The Odyssey of Farah Antun*. Minneapolis: Bibliotheca Islamica, 1975.

———. *Whose Pharaohs? Archaeology, Museums, and Egyptian National Identity from Napoleon to World War I*. Berkeley: University of California Press, 2002.

Reinhard, C. "Colonization and Resistance: The Egyptian Peasant Rebellion, 1919." In *Peasants and Politics in the Modern Middle East*, edited by Farhad Kazemi and John Waterbury. Miami: Florida International University Press, 1991.

"Representations of the Orient in 19th Century Opera," 2004, exhibition. Dahesh Museum, New York, NY.

Reynolds, Nancy. *A City Consumed: Urban Commerce, the Cairo Fire, and the Politics of Decolonization in Egypt*. Stanford: Stanford University Press, 2012.

Rifaat, M. *The Awakening of Modern Egypt*. Cairo: Palm Press, 2005.

Rihani, Najib al-. *Mudhakkirat Najib al-Rihani: Za'im al-Masrah al-Fukahi*. Cairo: Al-Mutahida li al-Tabi'a wa al-Nashr, 2000.

Roberts, Mary Louise. *Disruptive Acts: The New Woman in Fin-de-Siècle France*. Chicago: University of Chicago Press, 2002.

Robinson, Paul. "Is *Aida* an Orientalist Opera?" *Cambridge Opera Journal* 5:2 (1993): 133–140.

Rodenbeck, Max. *Cairo: The City Victorious*. New York: Alfred A. Knopf, 1999.

Ruggles, D. Fairchild. "Vision and Power: An Introduction." In *Women, Patronage, and Self-Representation in Islamic Societies*, edited by D. Fairchild Ruggles, 1–16. New York: State University of New York Press, 2000.

Ruiz, Mario. "Imperial Policing in Wartime Egypt." Paper presented to the Rutgers Center for Historical Analysis, New Brunswick, NJ, October 16, 2007.

Rushdi, Fatma. *Al-Hub wa al-Fan*. Cairo: Sa'adi wa Shandi, 1961.

Russell, Mona. *Creating the New Egyptian Woman: Consumerism, Education, and National Identity, 1863–1922*. New York: Palgrave Macmillan, 2004.

Ryzova, Lucie. *The Age of the Effendiyya: Passages to Modernity in National-Colonial Egypt*. Oxford, UK: Oxford University Press, 2014.

———. *L'Effendiyya où La Modernité Contestée*. Cairo: Centre d'Etudes et de Documentation Economiques, Juridiques, et Sociales, 2004.

Sadgrove, P. C. *The Egyptian Theatre in the Nineteenth Century, 1799–1882*. Reading, UK: Ithaca Press, 2007.

Said, Edward W. *Culture and Imperialism*. New York: Vintage Books, 1994.

Sakhsoukh, Ahmad, ed. *Al-Masrah al-Misri*. Cairo: Dar al-Za'im li al-Taba'a al-Haditha, 1998.

Salim, Sameh. *The Novel and the Rural Imaginary, 1880–1985*. New York: Routledge Curzon, 2004.

Sanders, Paula. *Creating Medieval Cairo: Empire, Religion, and Architectural Preservation in Nineteenth-Century Egypt*. Cairo: American University in Cairo Press, 2008.

Scholch, Alexander. *Egypt for the Egyptians: The Socio-political Crisis in Egypt, 1878–1882*. London: Ithaca Press, 1981.

Scott, James. *Domination and the Arts of Resistance: Hidden Transcripts*. New Haven, CT: Yale University Press, 1990.

———. *Seeing Like a State: How Certain Schemes to Improve the Human Condition Have Failed*. New Haven, CT: Yale University Press, 1998.

Seif, Laila Nessim Abou. "Theatre of Najib al-Rihani: The Development of Comedy in Modern Egypt." PhD diss., University of Illinois, 1969.

Seizer, Susan. *Stigmas of the Tamil Stage: An Ethnography of Special Drama Artists in South India*. Durham, NC: Duke University Press, 2005.

Sha'rawi, Huda. *Harem Years: The Memoirs of an Egyptian Feminist*. Cairo: American University in Cairo Press, 1998.

———. *Mudhakkirat Ra'idat al-Mar'a al-'Arabiyya*. Cairo: Dar al-Hilal 1981.

Shakry, Omnia S. El. *The Great Social Laboratory: Subjects of Knowledge in Colonial and Postcolonial Egypt*. Stanford: Stanford University Press, 2007.

———. "Schooled Mothers and Structured Play: Child Rearing in Turn-of-the-Century Egypt." In *Remaking Women: Feminism and Modernity in the Middle East*, edited by Lila Abu-Lughod, 126–170. Cairo: American University in Cairo Press, 1998.

Sharabi, Hisham. *Nationalism and Revolution in the Arab World (the Middle East and North Africa)*. New York: Van Nostrand, 1966.

Silvera, Alain. "The First Egyptian Student Mission to France Under Muhammad Ali." In *Modern Egypt: Studies in Politics and Society*, edited by Ellie Kedourie and Sylvia G. Him, 1–22. London: Frank Cass, 1980.

Smith, Bonnie G. "Introduction." In *Global Feminisms Since 1945*, edited by Bonnie G. Smith, 1–10. London: Routledge, 2000.

Snir, Reuven. "The Palestinian Hakawati Theater: A Brief History." In *Colors of Enchantment: Theater, Dance, Music, and the Visual Arts in the Middle East*, edited by Sherifa Zuhur, 107–124. Cairo: American University in Cairo Press, 2001.

Sonbol, Amira, ed. *The Last Khedive of Egypt: Memoirs of Abbas Hilmi II*. Reading, UK: Ithaca Press, 1998.

———. *The New Mamluks: Egyptian Society and Modern Feudalism*. Syracuse: Syracuse University Press, 2000.

Spivak, Gayatri Chakravorty. "Can the Subaltern Speak?" In *Marxism and Interpretation of Culture*, edited by C. Nelson and L. Grossberg, 271–313. Basingstoke, UK: Macmillan, 1988.

Stoler, Ann. "Carnal Knowledge and Imperial Power: Gender, Race, and Morality in Colonial Asia." In *Gender at the Crossroads of Knowledge: Feminist Anthropology in the Postmodern Era*, edited by Micaela di Leonardo, 51–101. Berkeley and Los Angeles: University of California Press, 1991.

Storrs, Ronald. *Orientations*. London: Ivor Nicholson & Watson, 1937.

Tahtawi, Rifaʿa Rafiʾ al-. *Takhlis al-Ibriz fi Talkhis Bariz*. Bulaq: Dar al-Tabiʿaʾ al-Khidiwiya, 1834/5.

Tamraz, Nihal S. *Nineteenth-Century Cairene Houses and Palaces*. Cairo: American University in Cairo Press, 1994.

Tarek, Mohamad Refaat. *Early Twentieth-Century Islamic Architecture in Cairo*. Cairo: American University in Cairo Press, 1993.

Taymur, Muhammad. *ʿAbd al-Sitar Effendi*. Cairo: Markaz al-Taʾlif wa al-Targama, no date.

———. *Mu'allafat Muhammad Taymur al-Jusʾ al-Thani, Hayatuhu al-Tamthiliyya*. Cairo: al-Hay'a al-Misriyya al ʿAmma lil Kitab, 1963.

Thompson, Elizabeth. *Colonial Citizens: Republican Rights, Paternal Privilege, and Gender in French Syria and Lebanon*. New York: Columbia University Press, 1999.

Thompson, Jason. "Edward William Lane's 'Description of Egypt.'" *International Journal of Middle East Studies* 28 (1996): 565–583.

Tignor, Robert L. *State, Private Enterprise, and Economic Change in Egypt, 1918–1952*. Princeton: Princeton University Press, 1984.

———. "The Egyptian Revolution of 1919: New Directions in the Egyptian Economy." In *The Middle Eastern Economy*, edited by Elie Kedourie, 47–51. London: Frank Cass and Co., 1976.

Toledano, Ehud R. "Social and Economic Change in the 'Long Nineteenth Century.'" In *The Cambridge History of Egypt, Volume Two: Modern Egypt from 1517 to the End of the Twentieth Century*, edited by M. W. Daly, 252–284. Cambridge, UK: Cambridge University Press, 1998.

———. *State and Society in Mid-Nineteenth-Century Egypt*. Cambridge, UK: Cambridge University Press, 1990.

Tucker, Judith. *Women in 19th Century Egypt*. Cambridge, UK: Cambridge University Press, 1985.

Turner, Victor. *From Ritual to Theatre*. New York: Performing Arts Journal Publications, 1982.

Van Dyke, John C. *In Egypt*. New York: C. Scribner's Sons, 1931.

Van Nieuwkerk, Karin. *"A Trade Like Any Other": Female Singers and Dancers in Egypt*. Austin: University of Texas Press, 1995.

Vatikiotis, P. J. *The Modern History of Egypt*. New York: Frederick A. Praeger, 1969.

Volait, Mercedes. *Architectes et Architectures de l'Egypte Moderne 1830–1950*. Paris: Maisonneuve et Larose, 2005.

———, ed. *Le Caire-Alexandrie: Architectures europeennes, 1850–1950*. Cairo: Institut Francais d'Archeologie Orientale, 2004.

Wahab, Farouk 'Abdel. *Modern Egyptian Drama: An Anthology*. Minneapolis: Bibliotheca Islamica, 1974.

Watenpaugh, Keith David. *Being Modern in the Middle East: Revolution, Nationalism, Colonialism, and the Arab Middle Class*. Princeton: Princeton University Press, 2006.

Weber, Max. *The Protestant Ethic and the Spirit of Capitalism*. New York: Charles Scribner's Sons, 1958.

Wendell, Charles. *The Evolution of the Egyptian National Image: From Its Origins to Ahmad Lutfi al-Sayyid*. Berkeley: University of California Press, 1972.

Woidich, Manfred, and Jacob M. Landau. *Arabisches Volkstheater in Kairo Im Jahre 1909: Ahmad ilfar Und Seine Schwanke*. Beirut and Stuttgart: Steiner, 1993.

Yousef, Hoda A. *Composing Egypt: Reading, Writing, and the Emergence of a Modern Nation, 1870–1930*. Stanford: Stanford University Press, 2016.

Yusuf, Fatma al-. *Dhikrayat*. Cairo: Kitab Ruz al-Yusuf, 1953.

Zayid, Mahmud Y. *Egypt's Struggle for Independence*. Beirut: Khayats, 1965.

Zeidan, Joseph T. "Modern Arab Theater: The Journey Back." In *Tradition and Modernity in Arabic Literature*, edited by Issa J. Boullata and Terri DeYoung, 173–191. Fayetteville: University of Arkansas Press, 1997.

Zirbel, Katherine Elizabeth. "Musical Discursions: Spectacle, Experience, and Political Economy Among Egyptian Performers in Globalizing Markets." PhD diss., University of Michigan, 1999.

Ziter, Edward. *The Orient on the Victorian Stage*. Cambridge, UK: Cambridge University Press, 2003.

Index

Note: Page numbers in *italics* refer to figures.

www.ingramcontent.com/pod-product-compliance
Lightning Source LLC
LaVergne TN
LVHW100024310826
846742LV00012B/33

9781477333600